HEAVENLY
MINDED
for EARTHLY
GOOD

AN 8-WEEK STUDY OF LIFE IN HEAVEN THAT WILL
FOREVER CHANGE YOUR LIFE ON EARTH

HEAVENLY
MINDED
for EARTHLY
GOOD

KAREN CHAFFIN

TATE PUBLISHING *& Enterprises*

TATE PUBLISHING
& Enterprises

Tate Publishing is committed to excellence in the publishing industry. Our staff of highly trained professionals, including editors, graphic designers, and marketing personnel, work together to produce the very finest books available. The company reflects the philosophy established by the founders, based on Psalm 68:11,

"THE LORD GAVE THE WORD AND GREAT WAS THE COMPANY OF THOSE WHO PUBLISHED IT."

If you would like further information, please contact us:
1.888.361.9473 | www.tatepublishing.com
TATE PUBLISHING & Enterprises, LLC | 127 E. Trade Center Terrace
Mustang, Oklahoma 73064 USA

Book design copyright © 2007 by Tate Publishing, LLC. All rights reserved.
Cover design and Interior design by Taylor Chaffin Rauschkolb

Published in the United States of America

ISBN: 1-6024705-5-3
07.10.03

a special thank you

To Taylor, for the artwork and layout, and constant encouragement and help. Sharing this project with you is a mom's dream come true.

To Ross, for wonderful theological discussions and much needed technical help!

To Andy, for giving me great material for Week Eight.

To Barbara, for the first Bible study that led to this one.

To my mom and all others who prayed for me, encouraged me, and believed with me.

You have blessed my life so deeply.

TABLE *of* CONTENTS

INTRODUCTION

*A*ll of Scripture points to one grand promise: Heaven. So glorious are its rewards, all the treasure of this world pales in comparison. Yet most of our lives are driven by what our eyes can see and our hands can hold. That needn't be! God knows what we need to live our lives with hope and purpose. We need Heaven in our sights.

You may have heard the expression: "He (or she) is too heavenly-minded to be of any earthly good!" I used to believe that statement was correct—until I began to study what the Bible has to say about Heaven. I was surprised to discover a multitude of scriptures about Heaven set in the context of encouragement for earthly living. I realized that if I took the message of Heaven to heart, I would live my life very differently. And it was the kind of "different" I longed for—a life filled with hope, joy, peace, contentment, freedom, purpose, and courage.

We need to know what awaits us after death. Perhaps you've picked up this Bible study with the hope of finding answers to specific questions you have about Heaven. Perhaps a loved one has died and you need to know what he or she is experiencing in Heaven. Maybe life has been difficult lately and you need a reason to hope there is something more, something beyond this life. Maybe you don't even know if you believe there *is* a life after this one. You may simply wish it were so. This study will guide you to God's answers as recorded in the Bible.

Solomon, a man blessed with great wisdom, writes of God:

> "He has made everything beautiful in its time. He has also set eternity in the hearts of men; yet they cannot fathom what God has done from beginning to end."
>
> (Eccl. 3:11)

Solomon expresses both the hope and the mystery of life. God has pressed His eternal image on our souls and placed us in a world which testifies of our infinite heritage—the vastness of the sky and the expanse of the stars causes our hearts to long for more than this world can provide. Deep down inside we believe we are eternal beings created for an eternal purpose. Yet life on Earth is so fragile and so fleeting that we rarely *feel* immortal. Why would God create finite beings to long for the infinite? As Solomon testifies, our finite brains cannot fathom what our Eternal God is up to! We understand little of His overall plan for mankind. We only wish we lived in a better world, with less poverty, war, and disease. We only wish people (ourselves included) would love more and hate less, laugh more and cry less. We long for a life where all our needs are met, all our dreams fulfilled, and we live happily ever after.

C. S. Lewis addresses this dilemma:

> If I find in myself a desire which no experience in this world can satisfy, the most probable explanation is that I was made for another world. If none of my earthly pleasures satisfy it, that does not prove that the universe is a fraud. Probably earthly pleasures were never meant to satisfy it, but only to arouse it, to suggest the real thing. If that is so… I must keep alive in myself the desire for my true country, which I shall not find till after death; I must never let it get snowed under or turned aside; I must make it the main object of life to press on to that other country and to help others to do the same.[1]

- Do you long for more than this world can offer?
- Is the desire for Heaven alive in your heart?
- Are you able to help others prepare for eternity?

My need to explore the subject of Heaven began on September 11, 2001. The horror of that day will never be forgotten. Unfathomable scenes of planes crashing into buildings, towers falling, and people running for their lives played over and over on television. Turning off the TV only resulted in my replaying the scenes in my mind.

I took my questions and despair to God. Could there be true comfort in the light of such tragedy? I felt God calling me to exchange the images of the victims' last moments on Earth for their first moments in Heaven. But I found that visualizing Heaven was difficult. I knew God's plan as to *how* one enters into Heaven, but I had only a vague understanding of what I would find when I arrived there. I needed clearer pictures of Heaven's joy and peace to counter the very vivid pictures of the world's pain and suffering. So began my search for Heaven. What I discovered surprised me, delighted me, comforted me, and made me want to tell the world:

God plans to make everything beautiful in His time!

In the process of writing this study, I realized the Lord had "ulterior" motives in assigning me this subject. A long-standing prayer of mine—really my deepest desire from the moment of my salvation—was to fulfill the purpose for which God created me. I longed to know God intimately and live as His Word instructs. But wholeheartedly following Jesus is not an easy trek. The way is narrow, risky, and opposed to the pull of the world. All too often I found my love for God wasn't strong enough to "forsake all" and follow Him. What was I lacking? Why was I holding back?

Do you long for more than this world can offer?

While immersed in the scriptures on Heaven, the revelation came: This was my missing piece of truth! This was God's answer to my deepest prayer! The secret of "letting go" of the things of this world lay in fully embracing the promises of the world to come. Such an embrace would free me to forge ahead in radical obedience to Jesus Christ, leading to incalculable earthly good and purpose.

Many books have been written on life in Heaven; many have been written on victorious living on Earth. The two are inseparable. As we unlock the gates of Heaven, we will discover abundant life on Earth.

God is shining His flashlight down the pathway to eternity. Care to come along and see what lies ahead? I'd be thrilled to have you join me on a journey to the True Country. There is much to learn and, best yet, much to *gain* from what we learn.

WEEK 1
A Happy Ending

*H*ave you ever been tempted to read the end of a novel first? I confess I have peeked on occasion, especially if the novel has started out a bit slow. To me, a story is only as good as its ending. I've witnessed my husband toss a book across the room when the ending fell short of his expectations. On the other hand, a good ending can save even a tragic story.

If you were to read the end of a novel first, would it change your experience of the book? When I know a book ends well, I'm not tempted to rush through it. I'll persevere through the difficult and laborious chapters. Knowing the ending gives me courage through the nail-biting episodes and hope in the heart-wrenching ones. I'm secure through the twists and turns of the unfolding drama—unafraid of any temporary setbacks. I'm free to enjoy the journey!

If you were to read the end of a novel first, would it change your experience of the book?

My children used to love reading mystery books that allowed the reader to choose the ending. After each chapter, two options were given in solving a mystery. Your choice determined which chapter you read next. The ending changed according to the choices you made while reading.

Isn't that how life is? We make decisions that affect the next chapter of our life. We even make decisions that determine the "ending" to our life's story. That is an enormous responsibility! But God has good news for us. His Word reveals the "mystery." God allows us to know our options and where they ultimately lead us. He has written a *fabulous* ending to the human story, which really isn't an ending at all! The *last* page of our earthly story will be the *first* page of a heavenly story—"the Great Story which no one on earth has read: which goes on for ever: in which every chapter is better than the one before."[2] Knowing the "ending" to our life's story will give us strength in difficult times, courage in fearful times, hope in painful times, and security in uncertain times. *It will free us to fully enjoy our lives.*

Let's begin this first week of our study by discovering *why* we need to know about Heaven. We'll discover that how we live now not only matters for eternity, but how we view eternity affects *how we live now.*

DAY 1 *better by far*

I AM SO HAPPY that you have joined me for this journey into eternity! The Eternal God has given us powerful binoculars that we might peer into the unseen world to come. I need a good, long-lasting look, don't you? What we will see will fill our hearts with hope and joy, positively impacting the way we think and live. The apostle Paul had a life-changing glimpse into the beauty of Heaven, described in *2 Corinthians 12:2–7*. Let's start by reading his vision.

How did he describe Paradise? (vs. 4, 7)

Even if you are new to Bible study, you probably have heard of the Apostle Paul. Once fervent to *persecute* all those who proclaimed Jesus to be the Son of God, he had an encounter with the Risen Christ that made him equally fervent to *persuade* all of that very truth! Scripture claims Paul "turned the world upside down" (Acts 17:6, KJV) as he traveled from place to place with the message of eternal life. History proves it to be true. His letters in the New Testament have extended his influence throughout the ages and have led countless numbers to faith in Christ. Paul loved God with all his heart, mind, soul, and strength.

(?) Think about his visit to Heaven described in this passage. **What impact might it have had upon his life?**

(?) **If you were to have a similar experience, how would it impact your life?**

Undoubtedly, the vision that Paul had of Paradise had much to do with his unwavering dedication to spread the gospel of Jesus Christ. He caught a glimpse of a future life that compelled him to spend every ounce of his energy telling the world how to enter the Kingdom of Heaven. I imagine he replayed the heavenly vision over and over in his mind, most especially while he was imprisoned. Read his words written from a jail cell in *Philippians 1:21–25.*

(?) **How did he describe departing to be with Christ in Heaven versus remaining on Earth?**

You may be doubtful that you could ever make such a statement and mean it! But if you will commit your heart and mind to this study of God's Word, you may come to agree with Paul—to depart and be with Christ is better by far! The goal of our study is to replace any fear of death and doubt of Heaven's existence with a faith and confidence like Paul's. We will learn what Heaven is like, what we will do there, what our new bodies will be like, and how we will interact with others. We will study the Judgment Seat of Christ, what rewards are promised, and how to earn them. We will determine how we live our lives on Earth will affect how we enjoy Heaven. So often we hear "I don't care if I am in the lowliest part of Heaven or not, just as long as I'm there." Well…is that really the way we will feel when we get there?

Like Paul, the more we know about Heaven, the more passionately we will live on Earth. Jesus repeatedly told His disciples that He had come forth from God and was going back to God. That knowledge permeated every decision, every action, and every reaction of His journey on Earth. Scripture testifies to the many benefits in knowing God's truths concerning Heaven—precious commodities such as peace, joy, and freedom from the demands of the world. So fasten your seatbelt! The next eight weeks will be an adventure into the future that has the power to radically change your present!

Scripture encourages us to know all we can about life after death. Read *1 Thessalonians 4:13–18*. We will study this passage in more detail later.

For now, note how Paul begins this passage. (v. 13)

How does he conclude? (v. 18)

Paul is answering the Thessalonians' questions regarding their loved ones who have died and gone to be with the Lord. Our point for now is this: God does not want us to be ignorant or uninformed about our eternal destinies! Paul's words concerning Heaven were given to bring encouragement and comfort. God knows our questions, our concerns, and our fears concerning life and death. He knows that for us to live well, we need hope for the future.

Look back at verse 13. Paul did not want the Thessalonians to grieve

like the rest of men, who have no_____ .

The Thessalonians had come to false conclusions concerning the return of Christ and how it affected their loved ones who had died (those Paul referred to as "asleep" in Christ). Their ignorance resulted in unnecessary grief. They needed to know God's truth concerning life after death. *And so do we!* If we are ignorant of what the Bible teaches about life after death, we too may live without the hope God intends for us to possess.

Heaven should be the focus of our hope on Earth. Biblical hope differs in meaning from our typical use of the word. We often use the word "hope" for something that may or may not happen. In contrast, the Greek word for hope (*elpis*) is defined as "a sure expectation or confidence; to anticipate with pleasure." Biblical hope is a sure thing! Its focus is not on what *might* happen but rather what *must* happen. It's a future happening, but a *sure* happening.

Read *Titus 3:4–7*.

According to verse 7, what have we become heirs to?

Look back to verses 5–6. How is our hope of eternal life possible?

I love verses that mention each member of the Trinity! The Father, the Son, and the Holy Spirit all desire our company in Heaven and play a role in making it possible. God's kindness, love, mercy, generosity, and grace enable us to become heirs of eternal life.

Read the scripture below and circle why our "hope" of Heaven is a sure thing:

"Because God wanted to make the unchanging nature of his purpose very clear to the heirs of what was promised, he confirmed it with an oath. God did this so that, by two unchangeable things in which it is impossible for God to lie, we who have fled to take hold of the hope offered to us may be greatly encouraged. We have this hope as an anchor for the soul, firm and secure."

(HEBREWS 6:17–19)

Heaven is real, you have God's *word* on it! He has confirmed it with an oath. Unlike people, God does not go back on His word and He cannot lie. We don't "hope" for Heaven because it *might* be so or because we *wish* it were so—it *is* so! Its promise can be our anchor, holding us steady in a tumultuous world.

But exactly what are we hoping for? Streets of gold? Pearly gates? Harps and clouds? Eternal life is a *long* time! What will it be like?

Sometimes our understanding of Heaven is so distorted we couldn't possibly look forward to spending eternity there. There is a story about a young boy who hated the idea of Heaven. He would puzzle his Sunday school teachers by stating quite boldly that he didn't want to go to Heaven. Finally someone asked him why. He answered, "I don't like peas." He had heard the Christmas carol "Silent Night" and thought the refrain "sleep in heavenly peace" was actually "sleep in heavenly peas." No wonder Heaven was unappealing! Who would want to sleep in peas?

Our images aren't much better. People have very different concepts of Heaven. Some are valid differences based on how one interprets Scripture. But some of our ideas aren't based on what the Bible says, or even on the character of God. Opinions are often formed from movies, television, comments made at funerals, and personal wish lists.

(☺) **What are some popular images of Heaven?**

(☺) **Are there any that disturb you?**

We've all seen the pictures of Heaven with seemingly bored saints lying around on clouds, strumming a harp every now and then. I confess I used to fear I'd be singing 5000 rounds of *Amazing Grace* every day in Heaven. I grimaced at the thought of an endless worship service. How could anything keep my attention *forever*, after all?

Peter Kreeft writes:

> Our pictures of Heaven simply do not move us; they are not moving pictures. Our pictures of heaven are dull, platitudinous and syrupy; therefore, so is our faith, our hope, and our love of Heaven. Dullness, not doubt, is the strongest enemy of faith, just as indifference, not hate, is the strongest enemy of love.[3]

Kreeft tells a story of an English vicar who was asked what to expect after death. He answered, "Well, if it comes to that, I suppose I shall enter into eternal bliss, but I really wish you wouldn't bring up such depressing subjects."[4] When turning forty or fifty years old, people often tease saying "It's better than the alternative!" All joking aside, do you hear the implication? Do we really think life on Earth surpasses life in Heaven? Even in jest, we are a far cry from Paul's statement "to depart and be with Christ is better by far."

If we have incorrect images of Heaven, we may only desire Heaven because the alternative seems worse. We need a vision, like Paul. Scripture gives us one!

Read *Matthew 13:44–46.*

What does Jesus communicate in these parables about the Kingdom of Heaven?

The Kingdom of Heaven is a treasure beyond measure. Surely if it were an earthly place we would all want to live there. We would most certainly seek to know about it and save our money to go there. Yet, most of us spend more time researching our vacation destinations than we do our eternal one. Are you willing to search the Scriptures for glimpses of your future home?

Some have claimed it is impossible to envision Heaven. After all, Paul did write, "No eye has seen, no ear has heard, no mind has conceived what God has prepared for those who love him" (1 Cor. 2:9). Yet the verse that follows it is often overlooked.

Read *1 Corinthians 2:9–10.*

Can we understand the deep things of God? If so, how?

Grasping the wondrous joys of Heaven may be beyond *human* understanding, but we have access to *divine* understanding! God wants us to desire His Heaven, so He gives us revelation knowledge through His Spirit. This is vital to the mission before us. We need the Holy Spirit to open our minds and expand our imaginations. The Bible contains ample information for us to envision Heaven. True, it does not explain everything or give us an exhaustive understanding, but what God *has* revealed is more than enough to set our hearts on fire.

The goal of this study is to paint a picture of Heaven that will energize our faith, relieve our fears, and enliven the way we live and love. Let's ask God's Spirit to be our Tour Guide each and every day of our journey. Surely a mystery will remain; we will undoubtedly be surprised in a multitude of ways when we arrive in Heaven. But we will live this life in greater victory, knowing as Paul, that to depart and be with Christ is *better by far!*

DAY 2 *"do you believe this?"*

A FEW YEARS AGO, I was leading a weekly Bible study at a retirement village. God had just begun to prick my interest in the subject of Heaven and I thought it would interest this group of senior citizens. Much to my surprise, I discovered the prevalent attitude to be "I just trust Heaven will be good." This otherwise knowledgeable group only knew isolated scriptures concerning Heaven. One very sweet and godly lady insisted we would not know one another in Heaven. When I asked her why she believed this way, she explained: "Because if we knew one another, then we would know who was *not* in Heaven. Scripture says there will be no more tears in Heaven. How could there not be tears if a loved one is missing?" Her reasoning was understandable, but not entirely accurate. Leading her to Bible passages that indicated we would recognize one another in Heaven did not help. It only upset her, which unsettled me and caused me to question my choice of topics for our Bible study. What I thought would bring comfort was causing discomfort! Being a coward, I planned to change topics the next week.

But God had a purpose in our study. That very week, this precious woman's grown son died unexpectedly. At the funeral, she pulled me aside and praised God for our study on Heaven. She believed with all her heart that the Lord placed her in the study because He knew this day was before her. Truths she previously fought were now her greatest source of comfort and hope. She couldn't get over God's goodness to her.

Our question this week is "Why should we study Heaven?" As we learned yesterday, one reason is to get a clear, accurate, and scriptural picture of Heaven. Like the Thessalonians, our misunderstandings can lead to confusion, sorrow, and despair. Our vague and sometimes boring images of Heaven robs us of the joy and hope Jesus came to Earth to give.

Read *1 Peter 1:3–9.*

(?) **What is our hope, according to verses 3–5?** (Remember that biblical "hope" is a "sure expectation.")

(?) **How does this hope become ours, according to verse 3?**

(?) **Many Bible translations describe this hope as "living" or "lively." What does such a description reveal about the effect of hope?**

Can't you sense Peter's jubilation? His heart is full of praise and thanksgiving to God for giving us such hope. The Greek word *zao,* translated "living," means "causing to live, quickening."[5] The hope that is born into the believer's heart generates *life.* We literally become *alive* with hope! Through the power of the promise of eternal life, we receive a new and invigorating outlook on life. It causes us to live in a way we never could otherwise, bringing support and encouragement into life's toughest trials.

(?) **What words does Peter use to describe our inheritance?** (v. 4)

(?) **What does such an inheritance cause us to do according to verses 6 and 8?**

I love the language used to describe our inheritance. Incorruptible! Imperishable! Undefiled! Kept! Reserved! There is nothing wishy-washy about *this* hope! It is a *durable* hope based on the surety of Jesus' resurrection from the dead. Earthly inheritances are rarely a sure thing. Stock markets crash. Relationships change. Unexpected needs arise. But God's children never need worry about *their* inheritance. Our reservation is sure and protected by God's very own power. Peter is telling us to go ahead and consider it ours! We can bet our lives on *this* inheritance. Remember our treasure hunter and pearl merchant from *Day One?* So great is the value of the Kingdom of Heaven, they joyfully sold all they had to purchase it.

Peter claims we don't simply rejoice at such news; we *greatly* rejoice. He claims that faith in future grace will cause our hearts to soar with love for Jesus. Loving and believing in Jesus produces a joy that is so overwhelming it is inexpressible. It's a joy that defies circumstances, under-girding life's sorrows. It brings honor to God, for it is "full of glory." Even when times are hard, we can find comfort in Heaven's unwavering promise: "joy cometh!" (Ps. 30:5, KJV). For our inheritance cannot perish or fade away.

🤔 **What is the goal of trials?** (v. 7)

Have you ever considered your trials as having a goal? When they do, we possess hope in an otherwise dismal reality. Although our trials may well distress us now, if we allow them to refine our faith they will one-day result in praise, glory, and honor. Therefore, they have purpose and will bear fruit. Which is much better than being for naught, agreed?

🤔 Peter tells us our faith has a goal as well. **What is it, according to verse 9?**

We could go one step more and ask, "What is the goal of the salvation of our souls?" Is it not Heaven; eternal life with God? Peter is encouraging us to get our heads *in* the clouds! Doing so brings purpose and perspective to even the most desperate circumstances.

Before we move on to what Peter tells us to do in the light of such a grand hope, let's nail down the *reason* for our hope given in verse 3: "In his great mercy he has given us new birth into a living hope through the resurrection of Jesus Christ from the dead."

Read *Romans 8:11.*

How was Jesus raised from the dead?

How will we be raised from the dead?

Now read *1 Corinthians 15:12–19.*

How is our faith described if Christ has not been raised? (vs. 14, 17, 19)

Why is the resurrection of Jesus crucial to the promise of our resurrection?

The resurrection of Jesus Christ is the means by which we gain eternal life. Without it, we would have no hope. Jesus said, "Because I live, you also will live" (John 14:19). Jesus *is* our Living Hope. He Himself is our inheritance. He is incorruptible, undefiled, always and forever in Heaven, kept for a reunion with you.

Read *Acts 1:1–3.*

To whom did Jesus appear after His resurrection and for how long?

(?) **What did He give them?**

The Greek word translated "convincing proofs" or "infallible proofs" is *tekmerion*. Vine's Expository Dictionary defines it as "a sure sign, a positive proof." Although the KJV translates it as "infallible proofs," Vine's states: "a 'proof' does not require to be described as infallible, the adjective is superfluous."[6] It's as though the proof Jesus gave His followers over those forty days was beyond what was necessary, beyond what was convincing, beyond any possible doubt—it was *undeniable* proof.

It wasn't just the apostles who were eyewitnesses. According to 1 Corinthians 15:6, Jesus appeared to more than five hundred brethren at one time. Paul, Peter, James, and other eyewitnesses went on to both live and die for Jesus Christ.

(?) **Why do you think they were willing to do so?**

(?) **In the following scriptures, circle what has happened to death's power as a result of the death and resurrection of Jesus Christ. Underline the result for you and me.**

2 Tim. 1:10 …but it has now been revealed through the appearing of our Savior, Christ Jesus, who has destroyed death and has brought life and immortality to light through the gospel.

1 Cor. 15:54–57 When the perishable has been clothed with the imperishable, and the mortal with immortality, then the saying that is written will come true: "Death has been swallowed up in victory." Where, O death, is your victory? Where, O death, is your sting?

Hebrews 2:14–15 Since the children have flesh and blood, he too shared in their humanity so that by his death he might destroy him who holds the power of death—that is, the devil—and free those who all their lives were held in slavery by their fear of death.

Life for death, imperishable for perishable, immortality for mortality, victory for defeat, and freedom for slavery—quite an exchange, don't you agree? The power of death held by the devil—destroyed! All made possible by the appearing of our Savior, Jesus Christ.

As Hebrews 2:15 states, many people live in fear of death—whether their own death or the death of a loved one—and it is a fear that enslaves them. The fear of death can be so intense that it paralyzes our willingness to love, stealing joy from life. We may fear the physical pain of death, or what happens after death. We may fear separation from loved ones. We may fear Heaven won't compare to this life... or that no one will know us... or that we will be in some disembodied form in some far away place in the air. Deep down inside, we fear *life as we know it* will end. Therefore, we mistakenly place our hope in *this* life rather than in the one to come. When we do, we become slaves—slaves to the pursuit of money, happiness, and fame.

Matthew Henry explains the good news of this passage in Hebrews 2:

> Christ became man, and died, to deliver them from those perplexities of soul, by letting them know that death is not only a conquered enemy, but a reconciled friend, not sent to hurt the soul, or separate it from the love of God, but to put an end to all their grievances and complaints, and to give them a passage to eternal life and blessedness.[7]

Death... described as a reconciled friend; a passage to eternal life with God! Wouldn't it be wonderful to view death that way? Jesus declared, "You shall know the truth, and the truth shall make you free" (John 8:32, NAS). As we discover the truth of Heaven, we will be set free from the fear of death.

(?) **Record the words of *John 11:25–26:***

"Do you believe this?" Jesus asks each of us the same question today. No question ever asked is more important than this one. *"Those who do shall live*

even if he dies." There is no greater claim, no greater promise, and no greater hope than this.

Do you believe that faith in Jesus Christ results in everlasting life?

If you have never said "yes" to God's gift of eternal life, why not do so now? Remember our mystery books? *Right this moment* you have the opportunity to change the ending of your novel (which is just the beginning!) and every subsequent chapter of your life. There is a prayer of salvation at the conclusion of *Day Two/Week Eight* of this study. If it would be helpful to you, turn to it now. It would be God's greatest joy to give you Himself and His Heaven!

> *"Fear not... for it is your Father's good pleasure to*
> *give you the kingdom."*
> (Luke 12:32, kjv)

DAY 3 *ready...set...hope!*

I HOPE YOU WERE SWEPT up yesterday in Peter's impassioned praise of the marvelous, living hope God has granted us. What wonders are ours when we put our trust in Jesus Christ as our Lord and Savior! Like Peter, I'm tempted to put an exclamation point after each sentence I write! There is simply *no way* to express on paper what the heart cries out in response to the love of God. We may have to wait on God's timing to enter into Heaven, but Heaven in the form of the Holy Spirit enters into us the moment we say "YES" to God's love and forgiveness.

The focus of this study is Heaven. Yet the focus of Heaven is God and His Son Jesus Christ. The greatest declaration to human ears comes from an unidentified voice at the throne of God:

> Now the dwelling of God is with men, and he will live with them. They
> will be his people, and God himself will be with them and be their God.
>
> (Rev. 21:3)

God has a moving date on His calendar! One day soon, He will make His home with us! The created will meet their Creator! May we never lose sight as to *why* Heaven will be so heavenly. Peter's exuberance over the inheritance that awaits us in Heaven flows from a man who had years of one-on-one time with the Son of God. When he was thinking about Heaven, *he was thinking about Jesus.* He had stars in his eyes—and it got the lead out of his feet!

You'll see what I mean when you read *1 Peter 1:13–25.*

In several Bible versions, this section begins with the word "therefore." What is the "therefore" there for? (Glance back at verses 3–9.)

The *therefores* of Scripture are important. Often they lead us from truth to application of truth. Peter has just expounded upon how very GOOD the GOOD NEWS of our salvation is. We are to believe it and celebrate it! Such "inexpressible and glorious joy" has an effect on the way we think and live.

List each way Peter exhorts us to live in the light of our great salvation. (Three are found in verse 13 alone.)

1. v. 13

2. v. 13

3. v. 13

4. v. 14

5. vs. 15–16

6. v. 17

7. v. 22

For today, let's take a look at the first three instructions. They deal directly with God's call to be heavenly-minded people.

1. Prepare your minds for action.

Have you ever "prepared your mind for action"? What did you do?

Mental preparation is key to victorious living. In the swim meets I competed in as a child, the starting official would begin each race with "Swimmers ready?... On your mark... Get set . . ." Then the gun would fire and we'd be off! In those few seconds before the race, I had to set my mind for action! My mental readiness had as much to do with my performance as my physical readiness. I recall one race when I actually thought up excuses for swimming poorly while I was in the water! Needless to say, I didn't win! I also remember times when I was physically depleted, yet I was able to mentally "toughen up" and race well. Once I swam a personal best in the backstroke even though I gashed my head on a turn. I kept on going, bleeding and crying until the end! (Sometimes it's a good thing to have a hard head!)

The King James Version of this phrase reads, "gird up the loins of your mind." Such an expression makes little sense to us today, but Peter's readers knew just what he meant. The men wore long robes, which could keep them from getting anywhere quickly. To "gird the loins" meant to gather up your robe and tuck it into your belt. The prophet Elijah "girded up his loins and outran Ahab to Jezreel" (1 Kings 18:46, NAS). Scripture records Elijah ran seventeen miles in the rain as a mad king chased him in a chariot! Can you imagine? That certainly beats my swimming story! And he must have had a better tucking technique than any child of mine!

With this visual in mind, to "gird up the loins of your mind" means to gather in all your mental resources and let nothing distract you from the goal before you. The world will constantly present diversions and, like the men's robes, they can tangle us up and slow us down along the path of life. We must employ the energy of our minds and be disciplined in our thinking in order to stay on a heavenly course. *Therefore,* Peter writes, since you have such an amazing destination, don't be slack! Gird up and buckle down! When our minds are pre-set for victory, we can overcome obstacles that would otherwise defeat us.

2. Be self-controlled.

What thoughts come to mind when you are told to be "sober" or "self-controlled"?

Read the following scriptures and record your insights, noting *why* we are to be self-controlled.

1 Peter 4:7

1 Peter 5:8

2 Timothy 4:3–5

The Greek word translated "self-controlled" means "to abstain from wine, to be discrete, sober, watch." I like how the NIV uses the phrase "keep your head" in lieu of "self-controlled" (2 Timothy 4:5). Heavenly-minded people have their heads on straight! They are aware of a very real, very powerful, and very active enemy with a game plan to cast doubt upon the goodness of God's heart and the authenticity of His Word. Sober-minded people are alert to how insidious worldly philosophy can be, influencing our thinking in both overt and covert ways—from jingles to billboards to the media. The human tendency is to ignore truth and believe whatever makes us feel good about ourselves. To be self-controlled means to watch over our behavior and opinions, acutely aware of our weaknesses. Hebrews 2:1 warns: "We must pay more careful attention, therefore, to what we have heard, so that we do not drift away."

Which situation(s) is likely to cause you to drift away from seeking God?

- ❑ In the midst of hardship or suffering
- ❑ When life is going great
- ❑ When work is demanding
- ❑ When I'm on vacation
- ❑ When I'm tempted to sin
- ❑ When I want to "fit in"
- ❑ When money is tight
- ❑ When money is abundant

Recognizing when we are most apt to shift our focus from eternal goals to earthly ones is vital to our victory in becoming heavenly-minded. Sometimes the hardships we view as "curses" actually cause us to draw near to God for comfort and strength. Many songs about Heaven were written by slaves in the harshest of times. On the other hand, what we call "blessings" may cause us to take our eyes *off* of Heaven. Affluence or popularity may lull us into a false sense of security. Peter warns us: Don't be intoxicated with worldliness!

3. *Set your hope fully on the grace to be given to you when Jesus Christ is revealed.*

This third exhortation from 1 Peter 1:13 underscores how badly we need to know all we can about Heaven. Let's read other biblical translations of this instruction to help us grasp what Peter is telling us to do.

... hope to the end for the grace that is to be brought unto you at the revelation of Jesus Christ (kjv).

... rest your hope fully upon the grace that is to be brought to you at the revelation of Jesus Christ (nkj).

... fix your hope completely on the grace to be brought to you at the revelation of Jesus Christ (nas).

☺ What would it mean for you to fix, rest, or set your hope completely upon something?

It's easy to see only what is available to us on Earth, but to focus on things *unseen* requires discipline and determination. The Greek word *teleios,* translated "fully" in the NIV, means "perfectly, entirely, to the end."[8] Peter is telling us to let our hope be fully developed and to not let go of that hope until Christ appears!

Our hope has an aim: the grace brought to us when Jesus returns. Did you know that Jesus is coming a second time? We will explore this subject much more thoroughly later. But for now, let's look at a few scriptures that speak of Jesus' future return to Earth.

☺ Circle what will be given to you when Jesus returns:

Colossians 3:4 (NAS) When Christ, who is our life, is revealed, then you also will be revealed with Him in glory.

Hebrews 9:27–28 Just as man is destined to die once, and after that to face judgment, so Christ was sacrificed once to take away the sins of many people; and he will appear a second time, not to bear sin, but to bring salvation to those who are waiting for him.

Revelation 22:12 Behold, I am coming soon! My reward is with me, and I will give to everyone according to what he has done.

Residence in glory… salvation… reward… that's plenty to capture our attention! Even the knowledge of the coming judgment gives us hope when we are living for Jesus Christ. We have so much to look forward to when we belong to Him! And as we dig in His Word to see the magnitude of what is promised, our hearts will overflow with expectancy. Tomorrow we will learn what Paul has to say on the matter. Until then… Ready?… Set?… HOPE!

Day 4 *incredible!*

YESTERDAY PETER ENCOURAGED US TO fix our hope upon the future—the time when Jesus will return to Earth and bring His Heaven with Him.

(☺) **Are you eager for the return of Jesus? Why or why not?**

Different situations in life can influence whether we are anxious for the return of Jesus. A friend whose adolescent son died suddenly can hardly bear the wait. Another friend who doesn't have all her "ducks in a row" spiritually would prefer Jesus wait until she does. Yet another friend wants to have children before Jesus comes. Many people lack an eagerness for the return of Jesus because they have a misconception about what life will be like from that point forward. Even if we love Jesus and know that His coming will be a good thing, it's difficult to fix our hope upon something that we know little about. Just trusting that eternal life with Jesus will be *good* rarely produces the victorious living Peter described. *We need details!*

Most of us have at one time or another eagerly awaited a vacation. I had the opportunity to travel to Israel several years ago. My mom booked the trip for the two of us nearly a year prior to the event. Isn't life good when you have something amazing to look forward to? During this waiting period, I led a Bible study on the Gospel of John. I tried to envision every place Jesus visited. When the itinerary for the trip arrived, I studied maps, history, architecture—anything that would help me better understand what I would be seeing when I arrived. The anticipation was nearly as wonderful as the actual visit!

Interestingly, I discovered my mental pictures were not too different from the actual terrain. The Sea of Galilee was my favorite sight because I knew it had changed little since the time Jesus walked around it and upon it. Our tour group spent one night in Tiberias. From my hotel room you could see a bit of the lake below. The next morning I awoke before dawn. (I was still on Oklahoma time!) Peeking through the window, I longed to take in the entire scene. Then it occurred to me—I could climb out of the window onto the flat roof below! I bundled up, grabbed my camera, and excitedly scrambled out of the window. And oh…what glory! I watched in reverent awe as the sun rose over the hills surrounding the lake. The city was quiet; the lake was still. One lone fishing boat idled across the shimmering water. I was back in time, in Jesus' day. The time when God came to Earth… *as a Person!* A Person one could talk with, laugh with, sail with, hold hands with, and share the sunrise with. Upon that rooftop, I felt a nearness to Jesus I have never gotten over. Upon that rooftop, an eagerness for His return was birthed in my heart.

The entire trip was *incredible.* I have no doubt that what my eyes took in was enhanced by what my heart had taken in during my pre-trip preparation. I had my video camera with me at all times, and it not only captured the scenery, it captured my excitement and loss of words. To listen to my commentary, you would think "incredible" was the only word in my vocabulary. I must have exclaimed it hundreds of times in ten short days!

We who believe on the Lord Jesus have one "incredible" vacation coming! Our reservation is firm. Our itinerary is in hand. The only thing we don't know is our departure date. Let's use our time to prepare! Envision the scenery and pour over the details of Scripture. Anticipate His return! Daydream about it! Life is good when you have something amazing to look forward to!

It's even encouraged in *Colossians 3:1–2.*

(☺) **What are we to set our hearts upon?**

(☺) **According to verse 2, what are we *not* to set our minds upon?**

In verse one, Paul uses the Greek word *zeteo,* which means "to seek; to inquire; to earnestly covet." It implies a search for something hidden, an activity that requires dedication and single-minded devotion. The verb tense indicates a command to do something in the future involving *continuous* or *repeated* action.

Verse two repeats the exhortation, underscoring its importance. It, too, indicates continual action and could read, "set your minds and *keep* them set." In this verse, the Greek word *phroneo* is used, which means "to exercise the mind, to entertain, or have a sentiment or opinion; to interest oneself with concern or obedience; to savor."

Do you get the message? You are to have an opinion; you are to concern yourself with Heaven. It is something to be *consumed* with, to seek after, to *investigate,* and eagerly long for!

🤔 **Why would God command us to set our hearts and minds** *continually* **upon Heaven? Is that even possible?**

It is so easy to get sidetracked in this busy world! By nature, our hearts are self-absorbed and our minds are occupied with what we can see and touch. Therefore, the only way we can win the battle over our shortsighted natures is to *radically* train our thoughts to think upon the things of Heaven.

Notice Paul mentions the presence of the Son and the Father when he instructs us to set our minds on the things above. Setting our hearts on Heaven is inseparable from setting our hearts on God. If we are focused on Heaven, we'll be focused on God. Across the pages of Scripture, God entreats us to seek Him. He wants to be the object of our hearts and minds!

Likewise, setting our hearts on the Lord transports us to Heaven. Whenever someone I love moves into a new place, I hate not being able to visualize their surroundings! I'm anxious to go visit so that later, when I'm talking to them on the phone or just thinking about them, I am able to picture their physical surroundings. Somehow it makes me feel closer to them. As we paint in the backdrop of the home of God, we will feel closer to Him as well.

Is it possible to set our hearts *continually* upon things above? Our answer is found in the fact that this scripture is written as a command. God does not command us to do something without giving us the supernatural ability to obey. His commands do not cause a burden for us to fulfill (1 John 5:3). So, *we* set our minds... and *God* fills our hearts.

Paul gives us an example to follow. Read *Philippians 3:4–21*.

How would you describe Paul's personality from this passage?

What did Paul consider worth forsaking all earthly things to gain?
- ❑ Knowing Christ
- ❑ Being right with God through faith in Christ
- ❑ Being a powerful preacher of the gospel
- ❑ Attaining the resurrection from the dead
- ❑ A reputation as a philanthropist
- ❑ The prize of Heaven
- ❑ Resurrection power in his life
- ❑ The fellowship of Christ's sufferings

Do you think he attained his goals? Why or why not?

Keeping your place in Philippians, flip over to *2 Timothy 4:6–8*. You might enjoy reading what scholars believe to be Paul's last recorded words.

How did Paul view his life?

Can you think of any greater peace than knowing you had fully accomplished God's purpose for your life? What a marvelous "end to this story" and beginning to the next! I love how Paul refers to his imminent death as a "departure." Here is a man who had traveled the world to tell the Story. He was looking forward to one last trip… a trip that would take him *home* to the Savior he so passionately loved and served. Single-minded, dedicated, and purposeful, Paul determined nothing past or present would deter his pursuit of his future with Christ in Heaven.

Look again at *Phil. 3:20.*

(?) **Where was Paul's citizenship?**

Perhaps we've stumbled onto *how* to set our minds continually upon the things of Heaven! Paul was homesick! He considered Heaven his Homeland, his Country, the place of his allegiance.

Paul wasn't the only one. Glance at *Hebrews 11:8–10, 13–16.*

(?) **What were Abraham and the others looking for and longing for?** (vs. 10, 16)

(?) **How did they describe themselves?** (v. 13)

Abraham was so "looking forward to" God's City that he felt like an alien and stranger on Earth. In verse 14, the Greek word translated "looking" is *epizeteo,* which means "to search for; to demand, to crave." Abraham and the other commended faithful of Hebrews 11 were not half-hearted about their desire for Heaven! Their longings pleased God. He has prepared an *incredible* city for all who believe in Him and therefore wants us to live in *anticipation* of this marvelous destination. Our stay on Earth is so short; it makes little sense to spend all our time and thought on what will soon be left behind.

Scripture is clear: We are to actively seek to know the things of Heaven and set our hearts upon what we discover. We are to do this continually, completely, until the end—not allowing our affections to be set on earthly things. The more we learn about Heaven and about the Savior who awaits us there, the easier that will be. Often our churches teach us *how* to get into Heaven, but not *why* we would want to! By the time you turn the last page of this study, you will know why you want Heaven!

Our diligent attention towards Heaven will not only result in eager anticipation now, I believe it will also enhance our experience when we arrive. While I was in Israel, I imagined Jesus on the sea, on the hillside, on the Emmaus road. But in Heaven, we won't have to imagine! We will *see* Jesus—face-to-face. We will walk with Jesus—hand-in-hand. Maybe we will even sail with Him across the Sea of Galilee. And I'm afraid all I'll be able to say is, "Incredible… incredible… oh my, how *incredible!*"

DAY 5 *eyes for the prize*

ARE YOU BEGINNING TO ANTICIPATE our journey to Heaven? I hope so! We don't need a rocket ship to get there, but we do need a spirit of adventure! We must travel all over the Bible for an accurate view of Heaven. Some passages will require several visits. So limber up your fingers each day and use your Bible's table of contents when needed. We are on the hunt for the True Country! As John Wesley declared, "In God's presence I open, I read this book, for this end: to find the way to heaven."[9]

Before we blast off, we've got more pre-trip work to do. Let's revisit *Philippians 3:7–17.*

What is Paul asking us to do in verses 15–17?

As mature believers, we are to share Paul's earthly goals. His example is there for us to follow. Let's look once again at his goals in order to judge our own state of heavenly-mindedness.

Check which one(s) you desire:

- ❑ To personally and intimately know Christ
- ❑ To be right with God through faith in Christ
- ❑ To possess resurrection power in my life
- ❑ To experience the fellowship of Christ's sufferings
- ❑ To attain the resurrection from the dead
- ❑ To take hold of Christ's full purpose for my life
- ❑ To obtain the prize of Heaven

(⟐) **Now go back through the list and circle which one(s) you are currently pursuing.**

If you couldn't circle any, don't be discouraged—Paul is a hard act to follow! Hopefully, by the end of this study you will circle them all! In the meantime, let's mull over three of Paul's goals. Take a few moments with each of the questions below. You don't need to write down answers; just give the Spirit of God a chance to speak to you. If anything comes to mind, give God permission to deal with it as we work through this study.

- **Do I value knowing Christ over any earthly thing?** Over any person? Over my reputation? Over any habit or sin?

- **Do I desire to attain the resurrection from the dead?** (This seems a ridiculous question, but let it sink in.) Do I have any doubts of Heaven's existence? Do I have any fears that this life is better than Heaven?

- **Is the goal of my life to win the prize of Heaven?** If not, what is?

I have found that the Holy Spirit doesn't bring conviction to shame me; He brings it to empower me! If I will confess where I'm lacking, God will fill in the gaps. His desire for our success is even greater than our own. With that in mind, let's end our week by praying for a heavenly mindset. We have tackled the question of *why* we should study Heaven. Now let's pray it into our hearts!

Although there are many wonderful books written on prayer, I learned one trade secret years ago that revolutionized my prayer life. I've forgotten the source and the author, but I've never forgotten the principle written in capital letters: PRAY THE SCRIPTURES. This method of praying has given me the ability to pray with great faith because I know what I am asking for is God's will. It focuses my faith upon God and His faithfulness to perform His Word. Conveniently, we have a prayer already written in Scripture for our heavenly-minded success.

Please read Paul's prayer found in *Ephesians 1:15–21.*

(⟐) **What is Paul's first prayer request for the Ephesians?** (v. 17)
#1

Remember *Day One* of our study? We learned we must depend upon the Holy Spirit to reveal the mysteries of Heaven. Always invite the Holy Spirit

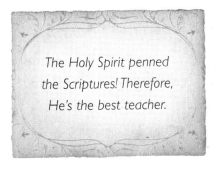

The Holy Spirit penned the Scriptures! Therefore, He's the best teacher.

to join you each time you open God's Word. He penned the Scriptures! Therefore, He's the *best* teacher.

Paul's first prayer request is for the Ephesians (and you and I) to *know God* better. That always should be #1 on our prayer list! We can pray with absolute assurance that God will grant our request. God intends for us to know Him:

> "You are my witnesses," declares the LORD, "and my servant whom I have chosen, so that you may know and believe me . . ."
>
> (ISAIAH 43:10)

Paul prays that the eyes of our hearts will be enlightened so that we can possess knowledge in three additional areas. In becoming heavenly-minded, we are going to have to depend upon the eyes of our heart to see what our physical eyes cannot. We need eyes to see the prize!

What do our eyes need to be opened to? (vs. 18–19)

#2

#3

#4

Paul's prayer requests for the Ephesians have a familiar ring, don't they? They are similar to his desires for his own walk with the Lord, as noted in the passage in Philippians that we began with today.

Paul's second request is that we *know the hope to which God has called us.* The word "hope" keeps popping up in our study! As we learned in *Day Two*, God "has given us new birth into a *living hope* through the resurrection of Jesus Christ from the dead, and into an inheritance that can never perish, spoil or fade" (1 Peter 1:3–4, emphasis mine). The hope of our calling is to know God on Earth and enjoy Him for all eternity. And nothing will make us long for Heaven more than a longing for God.

Inseparable from the hope of our calling is Paul's third request for us: We are to *know the riches of our glorious inheritance in the saints.* This is the quest of this study! God's "riches" indicates not only wealth, but also *abundance.* Our inheritance begins the moment we are saved and continues to increase and expand throughout all of eternity. Heaven is so vast that we will spend all of eternity exploring and enjoying it. And let's not overlook the mention of the saints in Paul's prayer. The word "saints" is used to describe *all* believers—those in Heaven and those on Earth. One of the greatest joys of the Christian experience is that it is a *shared* experience. We become family—blood relatives, in fact.

Keeping a mark in Ephesians, turn to *Matt. 12:49–50.*

What does Jesus call those who do the will of His Father?

Now read *Mark 10:28–30.*

In addition to eternal life, what does Jesus promise to those who leave loved ones to follow Him?

I will never forget the wonderful surprise of new relationships after joining God's family. I knew when I surrendered my life to God it would result in the undoing of some of my friendships (at least temporarily). I did not expect the immediate and deep love I would feel for the community of believers. I had new moms and dads in the Lord, granddads and grandmas, not to mention a passel of brothers and sisters. I later became a spiritual mom to children in the church and to precious younger women. As Jesus promised in the passage in Mark 10, I received and continue to receive a hundred times what I lost. That number will explode in Heaven! What an inheritance! Just thinking about the relationships we will have in Heaven makes me want to love people better now. We are family forever! How rich we will be.

Next Paul prays we will *know the unlimited power of God.* This is the very power that raised Jesus from the dead and seated Him upon His throne in Heaven! *Think about that!* Does that sound like enough power to meet the needs you have? When we believe the promises of Heaven, *resurrection* power becomes ours. Jesus claimed that we can do the works *He* did (John 14:12). Hmm... I think I'm not living up to my potential in Christ! I can be a real coward when it comes to living by faith. I most readily trust what I can see and touch and follow paths that are safe. How about you? Unfortunately, none of us will ever utilize God's power if we are content to live within our own limitations and accomplish what our hard work and some good luck can afford. *What great things we will miss!* Let's not settle for *little* when we've been promised *much!* Can you imagine arriving in Heaven, seeing God face-to-face, and thinking, "I wish I hadn't believed in God so much on Earth"? Oh heavens! We will wonder why we lived in such weakness when God's might was ours for the asking. Heavenly-mindedness leads to bold and powerful living. God is *unlimited* in what He can do and what He can empower us to do!

We will learn how to utilize this incomparably great power as we move through our study. It begins with *hope*—this life is not all there is! Then, as the eyes of our hearts take in the majesty of our God and His Heaven, our *faith* will grow. Great faith accesses great *power.* The greater the power of God in our lives, the more *fruitful* our lives and the more praise and glory to God.

Heavenly-minded people reach for the stars! And by the working of God's Spirit, they reach them. Are your eyes on the prize? Are you ready to press on to the goal? Let's start off by engaging the help of the Trinity. As you pray Paul's prayer, remember: *pray in great faith!* This is *God's will* for your life! I've reoriented Paul's prayer so that you can easily pray it for yourself. It would be a great beginning to each day of study. Write it out and use it as a bookmark! After eight weeks of praying it day after day, there is no telling what God may reveal to you! You will become a hopelessly hopeful, heavenly-minded believer armed with His power to accomplish much earthly good!

God of my Lord Jesus Christ, the glorious Father, I ask You to give me the Spirit of wisdom and revelation, so that I may know You better. I pray also that the eyes of my heart may be enlightened in order that I may know the hope to which You have called me, the riches of Your glorious inheritance in the saints, and Your incomparably great power for us who believe. To the praise of Your glory! Amen.

WEEK 2
Things Worth Bothering About

C. S. Lewis wrote:

> Christianity asserts that every individual human being is going to live forever, and this must be either true or false. Now there are a good many things which would not be worth bothering about if I were going to live only seventy years, but which I had better bother about very seriously if I am going to live for ever.[10]

*L*ewis' comment raises the question of this week's study: Knowing we will live forever, what are the things we need to be bothering about? The most important issue, of course, is the matter of where we will spend eternity. As we will study later, Jesus taught that there are two eternal destinations: Heaven and Hell. We choose *where* we reside forever, but not *whether* we reside forever. Every soul is eternal. Unfortunately, we often forget this all-important reality.

Does the truth that you will live forever impact your daily living and decisions? I'm just the personality type that would like to thoroughly investigate every scripture that addresses the things "worth bothering about." But since we need to complete this study on Heaven before we find ourselves there, we're going to take one more week to examine *why* we need a thorough knowledge of Heaven.

> Does the truth that you will live forever impact your daily living and decisions?

We want our trip to Heaven to produce *heart* knowledge, not just head knowledge. We want our lives to be changed *today* because of what is promised for tomorrow. Let's allow God to use this time to build expectation in our hearts and put a longing in our souls.

Scripture is clear as to what to "bother about." Let's look and see what those things might be.

D AY 1 *wholly holy*

LAST WEEK WE JOINED THE Apostle Peter in his joyful declaration of God's amazing grace. The benefits of being claimed by God caused Peter's heart to burst in thankfulness, even in the midst of great persecution and hardship. When we truly believe the message of redemption and allow its reality to "get to us," it changes everything about us. The Good News Jesus brought into the world has both the *purpose* and the *power* to make us into the person we long to be. Peter is able to speak from experience of the miraculous effect Jesus could have upon one's life! So let's learn from him how to respond to so great a salvation. We left Peter in the middle of a very powerful *therefore...*

Please read *1 Peter 1:13–16.*

(⟡) Last week we learned from verse 13 to be mentally prepared, self-controlled, and expectant. **What are Peter's next instructions, found in verses 14–16?**

(⟡) **What "evil desires" are ours when we are ignorant of the promises of God?**

How do you respond to the instruction to change your former behavior and to "be holy in all you do"?

We actually have two instructions in these verses: 1) we are to forsake our former way of living and 2) we are to live holy lives. The two work together. It's impossible to successfully forsake old desires if we don't have superior desires with which to replace them. But when we understand the amazing gift of salvation that *has* come and *will* come, we are liberated from the fears and needs that once dominated our lives.

We begin with our thinking. We fix our hope on grace—on the glorious promise of a happy immortality! We take our eyes off of earthly things and gaze upon the things above. In other words, we *think* on a higher plane. As we do, we start *living* on a higher plane.

At first Peter's call to "be holy" seems burdensome and a bit unrealistic; don't you agree? Just the thought of obedience and holiness used to make me grimace! As a young girl, I imagined "holy" people as strict, joyless nay-say-ers, who seldom smiled and never caused me to! Such a false notion was probably why I told God I'd follow Him when I was old and life was no longer fun anyway. (Can you believe such teen-aged ego? Not to mention ignorance...)

Glance down to *1 Peter 1:18*.

How is life apart from God described?

Life without God is "empty"—void of meaning, vain or futile. The greatest human love and the greatest human accomplishment cannot fix what is broken in the human soul. When I finally acknowledged that truth, I handed my life to God with no strings attached. Desperate for a "new me," I was willing to become whatever He could make of me—no matter what. Imagine my surprise when Christ filled me with the greatest joy I'd ever known!

I grew up attending church. As a child, I loved hearing the stories of Jesus. I understood and respected the commandments I was supposed to obey. But somehow I missed the part about how the Holy Spirit would help me keep the rules. I missed the part about how God's commandments were tailor-made to fit the desires of my heart. I missed the part about the joy in knowing and belonging to God. How had I missed such a crucial attraction to Christianity?

In all fairness, I'm sure I wasn't "all ears." But it's also probable that the church whispered this truth instead of shouting it. So if you haven't heard, listen up—*holiness* does not result in *joylessness*. This is mighty Good News, and it deserves top billing:

> The precepts of the LORD are right, giving joy to the heart. The commands of the LORD are radiant, giving light to the eyes.
>
> (Ps. 19:8)

Do God's precepts give joy to your heart and light to your eyes? It was a "light bulb" moment for me to realize God's commandments are *not* burdensome! They are, in fact, the *secret* to abundant, joyful, and yes, *holy* living, made possible by the Holy Spirit of God. He is called the *Holy* Spirit for a reason, after all. Part of His job description is to turn us away from evil desires and to turn us toward godly ones, producing in us a penchant for holiness! Imagine that!

As a much wiser (and older) child of His, I now *long* to be wholly holy! My need for fun hasn't changed, but I've discovered the secret of where true happiness and satisfaction is found. It's found in a God who Himself is quite fun *and* quite holy.

He's also quite giving. Read *2 Peter 1:3–4*.

(?) **What things has God given us?**

(?) **How do we participate in His nature and escape the corruption of the world?**

(?) **Think for a moment...what promises could liberate us from evil desires?**

Heavenly-mindedness produces *holy*-mindedness. Peter tells us how:

1. Through His very own power, God has *given* us everything we need for life and godliness. He has *given* us His nature. The more we hang out with Him and grow in our knowledge of Him, the more we become like Him. Holy kids are the product of a Holy Parent.

2. We have been *given* magnificent, precious promises of an inheritance that can never perish, spoil, or fade—promises of a pardon from sin, comfort in trials, strength in weakness, and resurrection in death. There is power in these promises, if we will take them into our heart, believe them, and live in the light of them.

3. Did you notice the word "given" or "granted" in this passage? It doesn't say "earned." When God *gives* us something, it's called *grace*. And because of grace, the call to obedience and holiness need not cause us to grimace! Here's why: The grace that saves us is the same grace that has the power to change us.

God doesn't save us by faith, forgive our sins, and then expect us to carry on from there. He continues to "save" us as we continue to "believe" Him. The grace that has *cancelled* our sin will also *conquer* our sin.[11] In other words, those of us who are on our way to see the Lord are getting a Holy Spirit workout in obedience and holiness! If it seems to you that the workout never ends—be glad! It is a sure sign that you are a child of God, filled with the Holy One and being fitted for the Holy Place. The only time to be alarmed is when we are *not* being corrected by God's truth! Because of the constant transforming work of God, we often don't see our own progress or "feel" holy. It's rather like peeling an onion; one layer comes off only to reveal another. God keeps peeling off the sin that enslaves us in order to free us to the core!

> The grace that saves us is the same grace that has the power to change us.

Remember, Peter told us to set our hope upon the *grace* that is to be revealed when Jesus comes again. "Our faith and hope are in God," not in ourselves; *not in our ability to make ourselves holy.* We depend on God's power and grace, allowing His *magnificent promises* to turn our heads and win our hearts.

Aren't you glad God goes to the trouble of making you holy? Truly, nothing feels quite like being set free from your own "self." It just feels *good* to get rid of the *yuck* that grows inside an empty and self-centered soul. God *created* you to be holy.

Continue reading *2 Peter 1:5–11.*

(?) **According to verse 8, what will godliness keep our lives from being?**

(?) **Why would that be true?**

(?) **Don't miss verse 11! What does it promise?**

Now please read *1 John 3:2–3.*

(?) **What will happen to us when Jesus appears?** (v. 2)

(?) **What happens to us now when we are heavenly-minded?** (v. 3)

Lastly, read *Titus 2:11–14.*

(❓) **How does God's grace teach us to live?** (vs. 12–13)

(❓) **What did Jesus' death accomplish in us and what does the hope of His appearing make us eager to do?** (v. 14)

More evidence for our "heavenly-minded for earthly good" credo! The more we contemplate seeing Jesus face-to-face, the less appealing sin becomes. Our efforts aren't primarily directed toward trying to sin *less*, but towards loving God *more*. Do you remember Paul's hope of reward?

> Now there is in store for me the crown of righteousness, which the Lord, the righteous Judge, will award to me on that day—and not only to me, but also to all who have longed for his appearing.
>
> (2 TIM. 4:8)

(❓) **In light of all we've learned today, why would a crown of *righteousness* be given to those who have longed for Jesus' appearing?**

I believe only those who are living *righteously* truly long for Jesus' appearing. Why would we be eager for Him to return if we are ashamed of how we are living? A crown of *righteousness* is therefore a fitting reward.

One day we will receive a *rich welcome* into the eternal Kingdom by Jesus Himself! *Just the sight of Him* will make us wholly holy. We will never again have to deal with our sin (or anybody else's)! Until then, let's allow

His holiness to rub off on us. His purity, joy, and pleasure come with the package. That's something worth bothering about… and even worth smiling about!

DAY 2 *motivational material*

THIS WEEK WE ARE EXPLORING the "things worth bothering about" in light of our eternal status. The truth that we will live *forever* should impact our daily decisions and attitudes. Peter has been teaching us about the affects of a heavenly mindset since we began studying his epistle last week. Below is a list of what Peter claims is ours when we focus upon our inheritance in Heaven. Take a few minutes to assess how you are faring.

Which one(s) do you need the most?

- ❑ Irrepressible joy over my salvation
- ❑ Lively hope for what is to come
- ❑ Purpose and faith through trials
- ❑ Mental resolve to live for God
- ❑ Self-control over worldly excesses
- ❑ Expectancy of Jesus' return
- ❑ Power to forsake former sins
- ❑ Desire for holy living
- ❑ Reverent fear of God
- ❑ Sincere love for others

Heavenly-mindedness will *revolutionize* our earthly lives. Jesus came that we might have *life*, and have it more abundantly (John 10:10). He's done His part; let's do ours!

Are you ready for Peter's sixth exhortation? Read *1 Peter 1:17–21*.

What does verse 17 call us to do?

The big question that comes to my mind is what this scripture means by "fear." The thought of living in fear is a little terrifying...so let's see what we can learn.

- The NIV of verse 17 reads, "live your lives as strangers here in reverent fear."
- The KJV, "pass the time of your sojourning here in fear."
- The NAS, "conduct yourselves in fear during the time of your stay upon earth."

The Greek word translated "fear" is *phobos,* which means "flight, that which is caused by being scared."[12] *Phobos* is what the crowd around Jesus felt when a crippled man began to walk and a dead man began to talk. *Phobos* is what the disciples felt when Jesus appeared on the water and disappeared from the tomb. It is what the church felt when Ananias dropped dead when he lied to the Holy Spirit. Wouldn't such experiences cause your heart to take flight?

Vine's Dictionary defines *phobos* as "not a mere 'fear' of His power and righteous retribution, but a wholesome dread of displeasing Him, a 'fear' which banishes the terror that shrinks from His presence."[13] The Hebrew word for "fear" (*yir'ah*) means "to reverence or respect." Reverential fear of God is an awe of who He is and what He can do. So, how can we *fear* God but not be *afraid* of Him? Good question!

Marking your place in 1 Peter, turn to *Exodus 20:18–21.* The Israelites gathered at Mt. Sinai at God's request. God declared His Ten Commandments in a manner that got their undivided attention. Read what followed.

How did the Israelites respond to God's display of power? (vs. 18–19)

Why does God desire for us to fear Him? (v. 20)

What are we *not* to be afraid of? (v. 21)

The Israelites were fearful of drawing near to God. And who could blame them? Such a display of God's power would make most of our knees knock! And don't be fooled, Moses' teeth were chattering along with them—"The sight was so terrifying that Moses said, 'I am trembling with fear'" (Hebrews 12:21). God was not just showing off that day. He was making a statement concerning the seriousness of His Holy Law. Breaking His commandments would result in unpleasant consequences for His children. And like any good father, God was using fear to protect His loved ones.

Sin separates us from God. Therefore, a healthy fear of disobeying God actually results in greater intimacy with Him. We are *not* to be afraid of a relationship with God! After all, we were created for that very purpose!

Matthew 10:28–31 tells us what to *fear* so that we won't be *afraid*.

Who are we not to fear? (v. 28)

Why are we to fear God? (v. 28)

Yet, why shouldn't we be afraid of God? (vs. 29–31)

Now read *Acts 18:9–10*.

How can we overcome our fears?

Read the following scriptures and underline what you learn about the proper fear of God. Make other helpful insights below.

Ps. 33:8–9 Let all the earth fear the LORD; let all the people of the world revere him. For he spoke, and it came to be; he commanded, and it stood firm.

Ps. 25:12, 14 Who, then, is the man that fears the LORD? He will instruct him in the way chosen for him. The LORD confides in those who fear him; he makes his covenant known to them.

Jer. 32:40 I will make an everlasting covenant with them: I will never stop doing good to them, and I will inspire them to fear me, so that they will never turn away from me.

Proverbs 8:13–14 To fear the LORD is to hate evil; I hate pride and arrogance, evil behavior and perverse speech. Counsel and sound judgment are mine; I have understanding and power.

Life can be scary when our eyes are on our mortality and ourselves. We can have courage in this life only because of the *presence* of our Lord. Proper fear of God doesn't result in distance from God; it draws us closer to His side! We become quick to obey and slow to rebel. We shun evil ways and embrace God's ways. We cease to fear men and even death. Fear of God frees us from all other fears.

Therefore… live your lives as strangers here in reverent fear.

(?) **Have you ever felt like a "stranger"? What caused you to feel that way?**

If you have ever visited a foreign country, moved to a new town, changed jobs, or attended your spouse's class reunion, you know what it's like to feel like a stranger. The surroundings, the people, and the lingo are all unfamiliar. You don't quite fit in. You're not even sure you want to.

When Jesus captivates our hearts, we cease to fit in a world that denies His Lordship. We think differently and act differently and even grieve differently. The greater our dependence upon God, the greater our independence from the world. Yet the need to fit in and be like everyone else can often override our need to please God. Well aware of this, Peter provides some "motivational material."

Let's return to *1 Peter 1:17–21*. **What three things should motivate us to "live our lives as strangers here in reverent fear"?**
1. (v. 17)

2. (vs. 18–19)

3. (v. 21)

Let's examine each motivation:

1. God is going to judge each one's works.

There is coming a Day when everyone who has ever lived will be judged for the works of his or her life. To some this news may come like a bombshell, shattering false notions that *grace* is a license to live any way we choose. Being judged is a foreboding thought, but it definitely *encourages* us to live holy lives!

What name do we call our judge? (v. 17)

Fortunately for those in Christ, our Judge is also our Father! He may judge our *works* impartially, but He can't be impartial to *us!* That's Good News! We needn't be alarmed when we stand before Him. We can know exactly *what* and *how* we will be judged.

Remember the dreaded "pop quiz" of our school days? Why did we hate them so?

If you are like me, you hated pop quizzes because they revealed you were not doing the work the teacher had assigned. We scored much better when we had the opportunity to prepare.

Our heavenly Textbook contains many worthy assignments for us to be "bothering about." Our Teacher has warned us that an examination of our assignments is scheduled. We will even receive a grade. Will it matter how we score?

Grades always mattered to me. Unfortunately, being a "bookworm" was not considered "cool" and several kids in elementary school teased me. (I'm sure the pointy, thick glasses didn't help.) Even though their rejection hurt my feelings, I couldn't change my desire for good grades. It was too strong. So I learned to cope with being considered "strange" by some.

Glorious rewards are promised to those whose strong desire to please God results in being considered "strange" by the world. "Good grades" at our final examination will more than make up for any rejection on Earth. We will study these rewards in *Week Seven*. So stayed tuned!

2. *The lavish love by which we were redeemed is ample reason to revere God.*

To be "redeemed" means to be "released by the payment of a ransom." We are *released* from the grip of Satan into the grip of God (Acts 26:18). Our *ransom* is the precious blood of the Son of God. The word "precious" means "valuable, costly, esteemed, beloved."

When was such a transaction made? (v. 20)

What does such knowledge teach you about God's love for you?

Why do you suppose God paid the highest possible price to make you His own?

Before the *creation* of the world, before you or I or *any* human being was born, before we ever did anything right or wrong, God made the decision to redeem us. He never intended for us to *earn* His approval. He loved us while we were yet enemies, when we were committing our foulest sin (Romans 5:8–10). *Now that's grace!*

Heaven is a reward suitable to the price paid for it.

For a long time, I struggled with why Jesus had to die such a horrible and painful death. Why didn't God provide a ransom of silver or gold? Over the years, God has taught me many reasons why it had to be this way. For one, He wants us to *marvel* over His love. God chose such an extravagant display of forgiveness to deprive us of any excuse for not believing His love for us—and to make it oh so difficult to deny Him our love. His exorbitant love attracts our love and demands our all.[14]

The cross also teaches us the devastating consequences of sin while emphatically demonstrating that there is no sin God is unwilling to forgive. To think otherwise would devalue the sacrifice. It would be like saying, "You didn't pay enough, Jesus." The horrendous pain and humiliation Jesus suffered on the cross declares there is *no* life too sinful, too broken, or too shameful that His blood will not forgive and restore. He would rather die *for you* than live *without you.*

And consider this: *Heaven is a reward suitable to the price paid for it.*

3. *Lastly, Peter motivates us to live as strangers on Earth because our faith and hope are now in God.*

Like Abraham, we are to look forward to the City of God (Hebrews 11:9–10). We are to live in "tents" as we pass through this life—unhindered by our possessions and free to move as God commands. We trust God to supply every need and satisfy every desire rather than striving to find them in the world.

John Wesley said it best:

For what end is life bestowed upon the children of men? Why were we sent into the world? For one sole end, and for no other, to prepare for eternity. Your life is continued to you upon earth for no other purpose than this, that you may know, love, and serve God on earth, and enjoy him to all eternity. Consider! You were not created to please your senses, to gratify your imagination, to gain money, or the praise of men; to seek happiness in any created good, in anything under the sun. On the contrary, you were created for this, and for no other purpose, by seeking and finding happiness in God on earth, to secure the glory of God in heaven. Therefore, let your heart continually say, "This one thing I do,"—having one thing in view, remembering why I was born, and why I am continued in life,—"I press on to the mark." He shall be my God for ever and ever, a guide even unto death![15]

Therefore… live your lives as strangers here in reverent fear.

The positive side of living like a stranger now is we won't be one in Heaven! Our hearts will have resided there long before our bodies arrive!

Do you agree that we've been given plenty of motivational material to possess a reverent fear of God? Knowing that God will judge our lives motivates us to live according to His instructions. Knowing that Christ's precious blood was spilled to purchase our entry into Heaven motivates us to honor the God who would dare display His love so poignantly. I shudder to think of how we disregard His commandments and abuse His gift of grace, treating "as an unholy thing the blood of the covenant" that sanctifies us (Hebrews 10:29).

Ponder it. Respond to it. *It's worth bothering about.*

DAY 3 *the only thing that counts*

IF YOU ARE LIKE ME, you are chomping at the bit to get going on our adventure into Heaven! But before we go riding off into the sunset, we need to pack our bags with a few more supplies. Hopefully you've loaded up on self-control, holy behavior, and reverent fear. Have you remembered to begin with prayer? If not, please stop and do so! It is essential nourishment for each day's ride toward the True Country.

Let's look at the seventh outcome of a life mesmerized by God's great salvation and our incorruptible inheritance. Please begin by reading *1 Peter 1:13–25.* We're going to know this passage by heart!

What is our seventh exhortation? (v. 22)

Look closely at verses 22–23. There is good news tucked into these verses.

(?) **How do we come to have a sincere love for the brethren?**

When we obey the truth by believing in Jesus Christ, our souls are made pure; with our new birth comes a new love. What a great birthday gift! Immediately upon being adopted into God's family, our Father places within us a love for our new brothers and sisters. This love is sincere; it is "undisguised and without hypocrisy." And although this love has come to us as a gift, Peter calls us to act upon it.

Paul speaks a similar word in 1 Thessalonians 4:9–10:

> Now about brotherly love we do not need to write to you, for you yourselves have been taught by God to love each other.... Yet we urge you, brothers, to do so more and more.

There is a natural affection for the body of Christ given to us when the Holy Spirit moves into our hearts. However, we are encouraged to go a level deeper; to take what God has planted and reap a harvest.

Read *1 John 3:14–24.*

(?) **What is one way that we *know* that we are a child of God?** (v. 14)

(?) **How is love expressed?** (vs. 16–18)

(?) **Why can't we claim to be unable to love certain people?** (v. 20)

(v. 22)

(v. 24)

(?) **What two things are "worth bothering about"?** (v. 23)

In this week's search to discover what we need to be "bothering about," we should take a clue from God's commands. Faith in His Son and love for one another are at the *top* of His list. There is no greater proof of belonging to God than possessing a sacrificial love for others. The Apostle John gave us three good reasons why we can have great confidence in our ability to love, even when our hearts seem unable to do so. First, God is greater than our hearts. Second, He will give us what we ask for in prayer. Third, the Holy Spirit lives in us. (And God's unconditional love comes with Him!)

(?) **Fill in the blanks with the word "love" or "loved," noting what they teach about the importance of love.**

1 Cor. 13:1–3 If I speak in the tongues of men and of angels, but have not

_____, I am only a resounding gong or a clanging cymbal. If I

have the gift of prophecy and can fathom all mysteries and all knowledge,

and if I have a faith that can move mountains, but have not _____,

I am nothing. If I give all I possess to the poor and surrender my body to

the flames, but have not _____, I gain nothing.

John 13:34–35 A new command I give you: _____one another.

As I have _____you, so you must _____one another. By

this all men will know that you are my disciples, if you _____one

another."

The way we love one another will matter in eternity. Read *Matt. 25:31–46.*

(?) **What do these verses teach you about how faith-driven love expresses itself?**

Jesus takes our love for others personally, doesn't He? Not only will *others* know we are Jesus' disciples by our love for one another, *Jesus* recognizes us by our works of love. We are saved by faith alone, yet real faith expresses itself in unselfish and loving acts for others.

Galatians 5:6 says it well: "The only thing that counts is *faith* expressing itself through *love*" (emphasis mine).

That's quite a revealing declaration, isn't it? It makes me want to get busy bothering about "the only thing that counts!" Most of us have spent a considerable amount of energy "bothering about" love. We were all created with a God-given need to give love and to be loved. Loving and being loved is an essential, wonderful, difficult, and risky part of living.

(?) **Have you ever determined to love someone better? What did you do?**

C. S. Lewis suggested that we not waste time bothering about *whether* we love our neighbor, just act as if we do. "As soon as we do this we find one of the great secrets. When you are behaving as if you loved someone, you will presently come to love him."[16] Christian love is an *action*, not an emotion. Emotions often follow, but they are secondary. The great challenge then, is being willing to *act* on the behalf of another. This is where heavenly-mindedness comes to the rescue. Peter claims we can enlarge our hearts to love others by setting our hearts upon Heaven.

Paul echoes his encouragement in Colossians 1:4–5:

> . . . we have heard of your faith in Christ Jesus and of the love you have for all the saints—the faith and love that spring from the hope that is stored up for you in heaven.

(?) **What "springs up" from our hope in Heaven?**

(?) **Why would hope in Heaven result in more love for the brethren?** (Remember that love is an action!)

(?) **Why would hope in Heaven result in greater faith?**

We are most apt to believe, or put our faith in, those things that are the most "real" to us. Heaven becomes a real place to us as we construct a detailed mental image using the revealed Word of God. Knowledge creates expectancy; expectancy builds faith. Therefore, we must *know* and *cherish* the promises of the marvelous inheritance of Heaven. Otherwise, how will we ever choose Heaven over this world? If our thoughts of Heaven are few and far between, we will be occupied with what is pressing, living for ourselves instead of for others.

As we contemplate Heaven, we realize the immeasurable worth of man to God. We are inclined to love even our enemies when we are mindful of the eternal destinies of all people. Few of us would wish Hell on anyone.

Our hope in Heaven frees us from the insecurities and selfishness that limit our faith and love. We risk outlandish faith and extravagant love when we're safe and secure in God's grip of grace. We live knowing we've little to lose and much to gain.

Lastly, read *2 Corinthians 3:12* and *4:13–15*

(?) **Record how our hope in Heaven expresses itself.**

☺ Think for a moment about how our hope in Heaven can give us greater boldness in sharing the gospel. **What hinders us from sharing the gospel at times?**

Many things hold us back—fear of rejection, fear of failure, a lack of knowledge, or a lack of love. But perhaps we hesitate to be truly bold in sharing the Good News because we aren't actively considering what truly *good news* Heaven is. If we think little about Heaven, or if we envision Heaven as some ghostly and boring place, why would we dedicate our lives to telling others this "Good News" that Jesus died for us to inherit?

Which brings us back to our beginning premise: Heavenly-minded people are of the most earthly good. For what greater good could come from our life than the salvation of another human being? Setting our hope upon Heaven *does not* mean we neglect this present world. Quite the contrary: In seeing life as it *will* be then, we begin to see life as it *should* be now. We sacrifice and labor to meet people's needs. We share the Good News. We surrender our lives into the hands of the One who so loved the world that He gave His only Son… and that's the only thing that counts.

DAY 4 *losers keepers*

I HOPE YOU ARE BEGINNING to grasp Scripture's clear mandate to set our sights on Heaven. The saying "He (or she) is too heavenly-minded to be of any earthly good" is directly opposed to the teaching of Scripture. Perhaps you imagine a heavenly-minded person as someone who goes through life unconcerned with the needs of this world, living "above the fray," and escaping into a dream world. That is not the kind of heavenly-mindedness the Bible encourages! Scripture defines a heavenly-minded person as one who accomplishes the *most* earthly good—the sort that results in *eternal* good.

C. S. Lewis wrote:

If you read history you will find that the Christians who did most for the present world were just those who thought most of the next. The Apostles themselves, who set on foot the conversion of the Roman Empire, the great men who built up the Middle Ages, the English Evangelicals who abolished the Slave Trade, all left their mark on Earth, precisely because their minds were occupied with Heaven. It is since Christians have largely ceased to think of the other world that they have become so ineffective in this. Aim at Heaven and you will get earth 'thrown in': aim at earth and you will get neither.[17]

It is an amazing and surprising concept: When we take our eyes off of this world and set them upon the world to come, we actually experience the fullest measure of life in *this* world. Jesus taught this concept repeatedly. Let's look at a couple of examples.

Read *Matthew 13:22–23*. The seed sown is the message of the Kingdom of God (Matt. 13:19).

(?) Is the focus of the person described in verse 22 on earthly things or heavenly things?

(?) How is the effectiveness of the Word in his life described?

(?) How about the one who takes to heart the message of the Kingdom? How is his effectiveness described?

(?) How would you describe a fruitful life?

When we are unencumbered by earthly things, our lives produce fruit, and it is fruit that endures (John 15:16). A fruitful life is rich in good works. A fruitful life impacts other lives for eternal purposes. A fruitful life relies upon the power of the Holy Spirit and is much more productive than the one consumed with worldly cares and worries.

Let's pick back up in *1 Peter 1:23–25.*

(?) **How have we been born into the Kingdom?** (v. 23)

(?) **How is that good news?** (v. 25)

In these verses, Peter quotes Isaiah 40:6–8. It would help us to see the context. Mark your place in 1 Peter (it probably falls open to this passage without your help!) and read *Isaiah 40:1–11, 21–31.*

(?) **What news is Isaiah proclaiming?** (vs. 9–10)

(?) **What does Isaiah contrast in verses 22–26?**

(?) **Do Isaiah's "good tidings" comfort you as he claims they should? How?**

Look again at *1 Peter 1:23–25.*

(?) **What is Peter's conclusion as to how we should respond to so great a salvation?**

Isaiah describes with great flourish the vast contrast between our great God and every created thing. Our God can lift up every valley and lay low every mountain. He makes the mortal immortal. We have this immeasurable comfort and absolute assurance: We shall see the glory of the Lord! The mouth of the Lord has spoken and His words stand forever. He *is* coming! He is coming to rule the Earth, and He is bringing His reward with Him.

Therefore, Peter proclaims, although you are as frail as the grass and flower, you need not be afraid of the future. You are eternal! *Therefore*, Peter concludes, live your life for God!

Jesus confronts us with His own version of this truth. Read *Matthew 16:24–25.*

(?) **Write down His words to us in verse 25.**

Think about Jesus' words not only as the way to *eternal* life, but as the way to a *fruitful* life.

(?) **How do we attempt to "save our life"?**

(?) **How do we "lose our life" for Christ's sake?**

(?) **What do we "find" as a result?**

When we decide to live for Jesus instead of for ourselves, we "lose our lives." We find life again in Him, not only in eternal life to come, but also in the truest meaning of *this* life. When we become wholly His, we become more ourselves than ever before.[18] Our distinctiveness is *not* lost. To the contrary, our personality shines the brightest when selfish aims dim. As we commit to live as His Word instructs, we discover paradoxical truths: It is more blessed to give than to receive, to serve than to be served, to be rich in deeds rather than rich in possessions. The key to victorious *living* is in successful *dying*. In losing, we win!

But how do you decide to lose your life? It's easy to say I must "die to self," but very hard to do. Fortunately, Jesus points the way in the two scriptures that follow His directive.

Read *Matthew 16:26.*

Jesus asks two thought-provoking questions. Take a moment and visualize Him looking directly at you, asking you for an answer. How would you respond?

1. *"What good will it be for you if you gain the whole world, yet forfeit your soul?"*
2. *"What can you give in exchange for your soul?"*

How do these two questions relate to Jesus' call to "lose your life"?

Jesus' questions make us squirm, don't they? We like to live in denial of the certainty of death and we do all we can to avoid the subject. We just keep living… sometimes without even facing the finality of death and struggling through the hard questions of life. Then someone we love dies, or we get bad news from the doctor, or we barely escape a car accident. We tend to examine the *purpose* of life only when confronted with the *frailty* of life. But Jesus' words cut straight to the heart of the matter. We are forced to compare the temporal with the eternal, the value of the world compared to the value of the soul. What matters the most to us? Where are we spending our energies? What are we trying to gain?

I think it's helpful to examine His questions from another angle. What if you could "purchase" eternal life? What would you be willing to give? Imagine if eternal life went on sale at an auction! What would be your highest bid? Would you stop short of bidding all you possess? Would you be willing to go into debt? Think about how you spend your time. Is there anything you would not be willing to forsake in exchange for eternal life?

"Losing our lives" becomes a very sensible and wise response when you consider what is "found." Paul called the laying down of our lives a "reasonable service" in view of the great mercies of God (Romans 12:1, KJV). The word "reasonable" means rational and logical. What Jesus is asking of us surely passes the test of reason. Jim Elliot said it well: "He is no fool who gives what he cannot keep to gain what he cannot lose."

Now let's look at verse 27 to find another persuasive reason to "lose our lives." **What does Jesus promise?**

How does His promise encourage you when you consider what it means to "lose your life"?

Jesus gives us two future events to set our hope upon:
- He is coming again.
- He is going to reward every man according to his deeds.

The Greek word translated "reward" is *apodidomi*, which means "to give up or back; restore; return." In other words, whatever we "lose" or sacrifice in this life, Jesus will restore in the life to come. Therefore, in God's economy, losers are keepers!

If we make it our aim to "sacrifice" our lives, we can easily become self-imposed martyrs, sacrificing the joy and pleasure of life God desires for us. We can come to possess a "grin and bear it" type of Christianity that does not honor God. Instead of focusing on what we'll *give up*, Jesus tells us to rejoice in what we will *find*. Then comes the surprising result—the lives we "lose" become fruitful, abundant, purposeful, and of much earthly good. The only time God asks us to give something up is to make room for something better! As we pour our lives out to God, He pours His life in to us. And what a life it is!

It fills my heart with amazement. Our God is God after all. He can demand whatever He wants from us. What He says should be believed and obeyed, solely because He is in charge! Yet, He reasons with us, He motivates us with reward, and He encourages us to make the right decisions. He is so very gracious toward us. He doesn't love us *because* we are good, but He knows His love will *make* us good. The hope of Heaven has a *powerful* effect upon our life.

Heavenly-minded people are fruitful, faith-filled, people-loving losers of life… and losers are keepers!

DAY 5 *fine linen*

I LIKE EXAMPLES. ROLE MODELS. People who have worn this life of faith well. It helps me to see how Scripture looks on someone else before I put it on myself. My husband Don likes to people-watch at airports. I particularly enjoy people-watching from the pages of God's Word. I can admire their successes and gawk at their failures without being rude. I can see if their beliefs unraveled or stood the test of time.

Today we'll examine a life that models all seven of Peter's exhortations. So far in our study, we've been inspired by Paul and by Peter. Let's look at the life of a man who inspired them. Scripture gives him quite a recommendation:

> Since then, no prophet has risen in Israel like Moses, whom the LORD knew face to face, who did all those miraculous signs and wonders the LORD sent him to do in Egypt—to Pharaoh and to all his officials and to his whole land. For no one has ever shown the mighty power or performed the awesome deeds that Moses did in the sight of all Israel.
>
> (DEUT. 34:10–12)

If you have some extra time today, read the biography of Moses' life in *Acts 7:17–44.* **Jot down the highlights.**

Moses had his ups and downs, didn't he? He logged forty years with the Egyptian Ivy League, forty years with Midianite sheep, and forty years with stiff-necked Israelites. Moses experienced the magnificent, the monotonous, and the miraculous. His journeys led him from a papyrus basket to a palace to a pasture to a panoramic view of the Promised Land. (Try saying that five times fast!) His faithfulness landed him a place of honor in the Hall of Faith (Hebrews 11), alongside many other role-model types.

Let's turn to *Hebrews 11:23–29*. It's the focus of today's lesson.

(?) **What did Moses give up when he "refused to be known as the son of Pharaoh's daughter"?** (Check your notes on Acts 7 if needed.)

(?) **What did Moses choose over the pleasures of sin?** (v. 25)

(?) **What did he regard as a greater value than the treasures of Egypt?** (v. 26)

That makes little sense, if we are using our earthly senses! Moses was educated in the wisdom of the Egyptians and was a man with great power. For forty years he lived among the privileged of the richest empire in the world. Yet one day he chose poverty over wealth, suffering over pleasure, slavery over freedom, misery over ease, and disgrace over acclaim.

(?) **How in the world and why in the world did he do so? What was he thinking?** (v. 26)

(?) **What can the eyes of faith see?** (v. 27)

(☺) **Such a sight of God enables one to do what, according to this verse alone?**

Moses is an excellent example of how the expectancy of future grace can influence a life. He weighed his choices: On one side of the scale, he placed the *best* the world had to offer—the treasure of Egypt. On the other side of the scale, he placed the *worst* God had to offer—disgrace for the sake of Christ. Even still, the scales tipped in favor of Jesus. He weighed the temporal against the eternal; the *passing* pleasure of sin against *everlasting* pleasure with God; a short-lived rule on Earth versus a never-ending rule in Heaven. In each instance, Heaven won out. The future gain was worth the sacrifice. He could wait.

But still, Moses was as human as the rest of us. To live above the lure of earthly riches and sinful temptations required Moses to intentionally and continually set his hope upon the reward to come. He exercised monumental self-control and refused to be conformed to evil passions. He fought his fear of an earthly king and persevered by trusting the Invisible King. Moses followed Peter's instructions to a T, didn't he? And Peter hadn't even written his epistle yet!

I imagine Moses experienced enough of the world's best in his first forty years to realize that it wasn't all it was cracked up to be. The pursuit of earthly pleasure and riches never fulfills the deep yearnings of the human soul.

(☺) **Have you ever set your sights upon an earthly goal and then found it lacking once you attained it? What did you learn?**

I haven't had the opportunities for fame and fortune to the extent Moses did, and you probably haven't either. But I have climbed the proverbial ladder to the top of many a wall, only to discover that what was on the other side was *not* what I had hoped for. It was *not* what the world had promised it would be. There was always something lacking.

There is a perfectly good reason for that. God fashioned our hearts, so only He can satisfy them! The only ladder worth ascending is the one leading to Him. God's ladder may sometimes feel like it's leaning against thin air…but that is the nature of faith. In actuality, there is no safer or sturdier "wall" to lean your full weight against.

If you know the rest of Moses' story, did God bless his earthly life? How?

Our God *rewards* faith (Heb. 11:6). And even though Moses was looking to *heavenly* reward, his faith and obedience had its own reward on Earth. He didn't have to wait until Heaven to see God's wonders. He became the servant through which God miraculously delivered the Hebrew people from the hand of Pharaoh, resulting in the mighty exodus that set over one million people free. He received the Law at Mount Sinai, recording the Ten Commandments that have guided countless lives. Under the inspiration of the Holy Spirit, he wrote the first five books of the Bible, called the Pentateuch. He was the architect for the Tabernacle, where God Himself chose to dwell. He was a judge over the people and led them to the Promised Land. He had such an intimate relationship with God that his face shown from their encounters. Heavenly-mindedness resulted in much earthly good in Moses' life!

You might wonder how Moses knew of Christ and the rewards of Heaven at this particular time in history, long before Jesus was born. We can get a short answer to that question by looking up a few scriptures.

Let's read the verses that flank our chapter on faith, *Hebrews 11, vs. 1–2, 39–40.*

How were those who died before Christ's coming commended?

God accepted those who lived before Christ's coming on the basis of faith. Faith in what, you ask? Faith in the *coming* Redeemer, the Messiah, the seed of Abraham, promised as far back as the fall of man, as recorded in Genesis 3:15. Actually, the gospel was preached beforehand to Abraham (Gal. 3:8) and foreshadowed in a way that folks would talk about for a very long time! God painted a vivid picture of the coming sacrifice of His only Son, Jesus, through Abraham's offering of his son Isaac (Gen. 22).

Read the following scriptures about Moses' understanding of Christ and Heaven and answer the questions that follow:

John 5:46 (Jesus is speaking.) "If you believed Moses, you would believe me, for he wrote about me."

Who did Moses write of?

Acts 3:21–22 He (Jesus) must remain in heaven until the time comes for God to restore everything, as he promised long ago through his holy prophets. For Moses said, "The Lord your God will raise up for you a prophet like me from among your own people; you must listen to everything he tells you."

Who did Moses prophesy of?

Hebrews 8:5 They serve at a sanctuary that is a copy and shadow of what is in heaven. This is why Moses was warned when he was about to build the tabernacle: "See to it that you make everything according to the pattern shown you on the mountain."

What was the Tabernacle a copy and a shadow of?

Moses knew of the promise of Christ. He wrote of Him! He prophesied of Him, calling Jesus "a prophet like me." It's not clear how much he knew *before* he walked away (or ran away!) from Egypt. But he responded in faith to what he knew and he believed in a coming Deliverer. God honored whatever understanding Moses possessed with more and more understanding as he walked in faith.

I marvel to think of all the ways God taught Moses about Christ and His Heaven. Surely as he assumed the role of delivering the Hebrew people from the power of Pharaoh, he longed for the One who would deliver the world from the power of Satan. Surely as he led the people to the land flowing with milk and honey, he longed for the heavenly Promised Land. The layout of the Tabernacle foretold of the pathway to God through Jesus and was a pattern of God's Heavenly Throne. The list could go on and on.

What's my point? *Step out in the faith you have.* God will grow it up! Those who earnestly seek after Him are rewarded with greater revelation. As you look ahead to the reward to come, your earthly life will be rewarded as well. Intimacy with Jesus is the ultimate reward on Earth.

Moses was convinced: No power on Earth, no pleasure of Earth, no possession or palace or comfort on Earth was worth his Christ. All of Egypt could have been his. But Moses, like Paul, considered worldly gain *rubbish* compared to heavenly gain. Instead of earthly treasure, Moses laid up the heavenly kind.

Which leads us to *Matthew 6:19–21.*

(?) **Have you ever lost an earthly treasure to decay or theft? If so, how did you feel about it?**

(?) **What type of treasure could we store up for ourselves in Heaven?**

(?) **Why would heavenly treasure make a good investment?**

Jesus is always after our hearts! When we invest our time, money, abilities, prayers, and possessions for God's purposes on Earth, our hearts go to Heaven. When our treasure lies in Heaven, we never need to fear loss! It will be waiting for us when we arrive.

🙂 **You won't believe** *Revelation 14:13.* **What follows those who die in the Lord?**

And you thought you couldn't take it with you!

Moses modeled the exhortations of 1 Peter 1. Mentally girded for action and sober in spirit, he refused the fleeting pleasures of sin and embraced mistreatment with God's people. He put his hope in the grace to come, choosing disgrace for the sake of Christ over worldly acclaim in Egypt. He was obedient, not being controlled by his desires, but living a holy life. His faith and hope were in God. And Moses deeply loved the people he led. He endured forty long years of their complaining, backsliding, blame, and rejection. Yet time and again he graciously interceded for them, even when God threatened to destroy them and make Moses into a great nation. Moses' love for God's people was so deep he cried out to God, 'Please forgive their sin—but if not, then blot me out of the book you have written " (Exodus 32:32).

When our treasure lies in Heaven, we never need to fear loss! It will be waiting for us when we arrive.

Did the fabric of Moses' life endure? Absolutely! We can read about it in Rev. 19:7–8 (NAS):

> "Let us rejoice and be glad and give the glory to Him, for the marriage of the Lamb has come and His bride has made herself ready." And it was given to her to clothe herself in fine linen, bright and clean; for the fine linen is the righteous acts of the saints.

Righteous acts—the works of our earthly lives that were done in the power of God for the glory of God—are described as clothing of *fine linen.* The works that followed Moses to Heaven he would now model forever. And hopefully, so will we. *Righteous deeds will endure for all eternity.* Once again, it's something worth bothering about!

WEEK 3
Lost and Found

*O*nce upon a time there lived a man and a woman. Their home was a lush and beautiful garden which God Himself had planted. In the garden were *all kinds* of fruit-bearing trees. Only one tree's fruit was forbidden to them. The couple's job was to tend the garden, care for the animals, and begin a family. Most of all, they were to enjoy the companionship of their Creator. He joined them for strolls down lush green carpeted paths. It was Paradise.

But hold on…a serpent (the devil in disguise) slithered onto the scene and insinuated that God was withholding something good from them. What could it possibly be? They swallowed his lies (along with the forbidden fruit). And, just that quickly, Paradise was lost.

We have no idea how long Adam and Eve enjoyed the Garden of Eden. We aren't told if it was one day, one month, one year, or one hundred years. It may have lasted no more than one hour! Try as we might to read their story, there is no text between Genesis 2:25 and 3:1. (Take a look.) However long their stay, it was much too short. Adam and Eve were forced to leave Paradise and an angelic guard was enlisted to conceal the way back in.

But the God who declared the works of His hands as "very good" was not abandoning them. What *God* creates endures. His desire for human beings to fill the Earth and rule over it was not a failed experiment! Our merciful God has a "Grand Plan" for both mankind and the Earth, which Scripture promises will be far greater than the original. One day all will be right with the world again—this time forever! Paradise *will* be found!

DAY 1 *plan "R"*

HAVE YOU EVER WONDERED WHAT life would have been like if Adam and Eve hadn't messed up the whole paradise thing? What a world! No shame, no pain, no blame... oops. Seems I'm guilty of blaming them. They probably resisted temptation longer than I would have. It seems a prideful, rebellious human race forced God to abandon Plan "A" (Absolute Paradise) and substitute Plan "F" (Free-for-all). But the whole of God's Word reveals what I've chosen to call (drum roll, please)... *Plan "R."*

(?) **Any ideas what the "R" might stand for?**

(?) Hold on to your "R" and let's look and see what God's Word reveals. Open your Bible to *Genesis 1:1.* **What did God create?**

To rightly understand God's future plan for Heaven, we need to go back to the beginning. The Bible opens with God creating a physical world out of nothing. The first chapter of Genesis doesn't give us specifics on where God came from, or how He did what He did. He simply *spoke* and it happened. Just like that! It is by faith we believe the universe was formed at God's command (Heb. 11:3). I doubt I could understand it even if He had elaborated!

The Father, Son, and Spirit all participated in the creation of the world (Gen. 1:2, 26 and John 1:1–3). I wonder how much time and discussion went on before the actual moment of declaration. In my work as a home designer, I enjoyed the schematic stage the most. It was challenging and rewarding to create a space uniquely suited to my client's desires and needs. Undoubtedly, God took great joy in designing an environment in which the human race could thrive. Just imagine the committee of Three discussing every detail—smiling and crying and nodding in agreement as they formalized Their plan.

In the first two days of Creation, God spoke light, water, and the sky into being. On the third day, God created the land, seas, and vegetation—

our Earth! Upon the creation of our planet, God "saw that it was good." It's truly amazing to think that this *tiny* planet is the focus of God's attention! The universe is so huge, so vast—and yet, Earth, *our* Earth is "full of His glory" (Isa. 6:3). The fourth, fifth, and sixth days brought forth the sun, moon, and stars; the fish, birds, and animals of the Earth. These too, God declared "good." But God was just getting warmed up. His final creation caused Him to step up His praise and proclaim it was *"very good."*

❓ **Discover what caused Him such delight, according to** *Genesis 1:26–31.*

❓ **What was God's original intent for mankind?** (v. 28; see also *Gen. 2:15.*)

For more about our creation, read *Genesis 2:7–25.*

❓ **Describe how you visualize the Garden of Eden.**

Before the foundation of the world, God anticipated you and me. He dreamed us up, so to speak. Essential to our appreciation of what awaits us in Heaven is our understanding of God's loving attentiveness in creating a world just for us. God "did not create it to be empty, but formed it to be inhabited" (Isa. 45:18). Perhaps He held off on declaring His creation "good" until it started to look like a place you and I could inhabit. He intentionally gave us a physical body to live on a physical Earth. It was all made for us—awesomely spun out of His deep desire to capture our hearts.

Adam was formed from the dust of the Earth. The Hebrew word "formed" means to mold by squeezing into shape. God "made" Eve from a rib taken out of Adam. The Hebrew word for "made" used in Gen. 2:22 means "to build." Imagine that! God didn't *speak* us into existence; we are hand-made, fashioned with love. Visualize Him bending over us, breathing life into us. These images communicate how personally and deliberately God created you and me. There is *nothing* accidental about our beginnings. What's more...

> ...thou hast created all things, and *for thy pleasure* they are and were created.
>
> (REV. 4:11, KJV; EMPHASIS MINE)

We were created for the *pleasure* of the Lord. But the human race has been slow to comprehend such an awesome and humbling truth. If you are unfamiliar with the fall of mankind as recorded in *Genesis 3*, please read it.

What were the consequences of Adam and Eve's disobedience to God? (2:17 and 3:16–21)

How do the consequences relate to God's original purpose and plan for mankind?

How did the consequences of sin affect the Earth? (3:17)

Adam and Eve were given the Earth to cultivate and inhabit; sin resulted in a curse upon God's creation. They were to be fruitful and fill the Earth; sin resulted in pain in childbirth. Sin altered the relationship between husband and wife and adversely affected their work and purpose. Worst of all, God created us in His image for fellowship with Him; sin forfeited that great privilege. Death was not a part of God's Plan "A." Adam and Eve's rebellion against God's authority resulted in death—*immediate* spiritual death and *eventual* physical death.

Unfortunately, more judgment was to come. The full story can be found in Gen. 6–8. The evil of human beings was so far-reaching and so continual, "The LORD was grieved that he had made man on the earth, and his heart was filled with pain" (Genesis 6:6). Even still, He gave man 120 years to repent. Nary a soul responded. So the Lord sent a forty-day downpour to wash away the stench of rampant wickedness. He could have started from scratch, but He didn't. One man, Noah, had captured His heart. God saved Noah, his family, and two of all living creatures from destruction. (Never underestimate the value of one solitary person who is sold out for God!)

Let's pick up the story after the waters had receded: *Genesis 9:1–3, 8–13.*

What did God promise to never do again? (v. 11)

Who is His covenant with? (vs. 12–13)

Although it was man who corrupted the Earth, thousands upon thousands of innocent animals died in the flood. The land lay barren and uninviting. We see a shift in the relationship between man and animals after the Flood. Animals God once paraded in front of Adam to name now would live in fear and dread of man. When Noah departed from the ark, he offered an animal sacrifice to God (Gen. 8:20). The first animal sacrifice may have been at Adam and Eve's expulsion from the Garden of Eden, when God gave them skins for clothing (Gen. 3:21). Animal sacrifice was God's way to "cover" the sins of mankind until the Ultimate Sacrifice, the Lamb of God, would come. Sin has dreadful and far-reaching consequences.

Even still, God blessed Noah and his sons and reiterated His desire for mankind to increase in number and fill the Earth. I particularly appreciate that God's covenant extended to all living things *and* to the Earth. God graced the sky with a rainbow to declare His covenant with His creation.

Let's fast-forward to *Romans 8:18–23.*

What will happen to all of God's creation when Jesus returns to Earth? (v. 21)

(⚇) **How is creation described in its present state?** (v. 22)

Have you ever thought about how Jesus' return to Earth will liberate *nature*? Since the fall of mankind, creation has been in bondage to decay. But a Day is coming when the curse on the Earth will be lifted forever. Perhaps that is why the Psalmist writes:

> Let the sea roar... let the rivers clap their hands; let the mountains sing together for joy before the LORD; for He is coming to judge the earth...
>
> (Ps. 98:7–9, NAS)

Won't that be a sight (and sound!)? Nature will rejoice! All of God's creatures will live in harmony! Until then, we *groan* together... and we *hope* together.

Let's look at some scriptures that will encourage us to join creation in *eagerly awaiting* this glorious Day. They reveal what the "R" stands for in our Plan "R."

(⚇) **Read the scriptures and circle the words beginning with the letter "r" that could represent God's plan.** (You'll find several.)

Acts 3:21 He (Jesus) must remain in heaven until the time comes for God to restore everything, as he promised long ago through his holy prophets.

Matt. 19:28–29 Jesus said to them, "I tell you the truth, at the renewal of all things, when the Son of Man sits on his glorious throne, you who have followed me will also sit on twelve thrones, judging the twelve tribes of Israel. And everyone who has left houses or brothers or sisters or father or mother or children or fields for my sake will receive a hundred times as much and will inherit eternal life."

Rev. 20:6 Blessed and holy are those who have part in the first resurrection. The second death has no power over them, but they will be priests of God and of Christ and will reign with him for a thousand years.

Isaiah 35:9b-10 But only the redeemed will walk there, and the ransomed of the LORD will return. They will enter Zion with singing; everlasting joy will crown their heads. Gladness and joy will overtake them, and sorrow and sighing will flee away.

With just this small sampling of Scripture, we discover God's grand plan: He will *R*estore, *R*enew, *R*esurrect, *R*edeem, *R*ansom—take your pick. I wish I could count how many times these words appear in the Bible. No doubt they occur hundreds of times, for our *R*edeemer is the topic of conversation in each book of the Bible, from Genesis to Revelation.

For a further treat, reread the first two scriptures and draw a box around what God is going to restore or renew.

Everything will be restored. He will make *all* things new. God doesn't leave anything out, does He? The ramifications of such action are mind-boggling. Wickedness, sorrow, and sighing will be replaced with purity, gladness, and joy. Anything lost for the sake of Christ will be regained with increase. And a nice long reign with Christ sounds mighty fine as well!

We deserve a quick peek at what a redeemed world looks like:

Then will *all your people be righteous* and they will *possess the land forever*. They are the shoot I have planted, the work of my hands, for the display of my splendor.

(ISA. 60:21, EMPHASIS MINE)

God's Plan "R" is to fully redeem His people and restore this Earth for the display of His splendor! Don't miss the great promise of Scripture concerning Planet Earth. She's not going anywhere! She will be made new, but she will never be obliterated. God declared her "very good" as a place for His children to dwell. So often we envision Heaven as a non-solid, cloud-like environment where no one can put their feet up and feel at home. Wrong! Scripture is happy to announce that in the Eternal Heaven, we will once again enjoy the Earth! And what's more, the Earth will enjoy us! *Forever.*

There is so *much more* to say. We'll pick up that subject tomorrow! For now, revel in this knowledge: Coming soon, made possible through faith in Jesus, is a *R*enewed and *R*estored Earth for a *R*esurrected, *R*edeemed, *R*ansomed, and *R*eclaimed human race. *Plan "R" is in full operation!*

But the plans of the LORD stand firm forever, the purposes of his heart through all generations.
(Ps. 33:11)

DAY 2 *much more*

WITH THE FALL OF MANKIND came a fallen Earth. God's magnificent creation was now subject to sin and death and decay, along with her caregivers. But God did not abandon His plan or purpose for human beings to live on the Earth and rule over all living creatures. Plan "R" was put into place. Paradise would be *Re*gained. What's more, Scripture declares that Plan "R" is even greater than Plan "A."

Read *Romans 5:8–21*. If you mark in your Bible, underline every occurrence of the phrase "much more" or similar wording.

Fill in the blanks with the name ADAM or JESUS:

1. Sin entered through_____ and spread to all men.

2. Through one man,_____ , death reigns.

3. Through one man,_____ , life reigns.

4. The trespass of_____results in condemnation to all men.

5. The righteousness of_____ results in justification to all men.

6. Through the disobedience of_____many were made sinners.

7. Through the obedience of_____many will be made righteous.

Despite the enormous consequences of man's disobedience to God, we have reason to rejoice. God has done a work that far surpasses even His original work! What awaits us in Plan "R" is *much more* than what was lost in Plan "A." Grace outdoes sin. Redemption is *much more* than innocence; restoration is *much more* than the former condition; reconciliation is *much more* than what was originally lost. God made mankind upright (Eccl. 7:29). Yet the cross of Christ has ushered in something far greater, far deeper, and far stronger.

What provision and gift did Jesus bring? (v. 17)

Contemplate this for a moment: If we had remained innocent, we would never have experienced God's grace. Christ died for us although we did *nothing* to deserve it. In fact, many of us spent years resisting, rejecting, and even despising His offer of forgiveness. He loved us anyway. Love like that does something to you, doesn't it? Being the recipient of grace causes a breaking in the heart that results in a lasting and powerful sense of being loved. It creates a loyalty that binds you to the One who loves you unconditionally. Such grace grows in its impact upon the human heart—strengthening us and empowering us to move forward in our relationship with the Lord. From Heaven, Jesus continues to "save" us—drawing us near to God through His prayers for us (Heb. 7:25). God's grace performs a work that results in *righteousness.*

To be righteous means we are "right" with God; our hearts conform to God's divine law. We are *declared* righteous upon faith in Jesus Christ, but amazingly, one day we will *become* righteous. What has been imputed to us will one day be perfected in us.

I like the visual picture of being *clothed* in righteousness. We were all born wrapped in cloths of sin, an unwelcome inheritance passed on to us from the first parents. Scripture calls our vain attempts to make ourselves righteous "filthy rags" (Isaiah 64:6). Christ, who is sinless, put on humanity's garment of sin and wore it to the cross (2 Cor. 5:21). When you and I accept the sacrifice made on our behalf, Jesus removes our cloak of sin and places His robe of righteousness upon us (Isaiah 61:10).

What does this mean for us? Adam and Eve were naked in the Garden of Eden, innocent and without shame. But we have been *clothed*—clothed in the *very righteousness of God* because of the blood of Jesus Christ. Therefore, unlike Adam and Eve, when we enter the Paradise of Heaven we will never sin. We will never rebel against God, and we will never desire anything above His love. Redeemed and righteous, we will never lose what Christ has gained for us. Something *huge* has happened to us by the powerful and inexplicable sacrifice of the very Son of God. In God's plan for the ages, a redeemed sinner is *much more* than an innocent one. He is God-graced and righteous. We will be sinless, *but we will still possess our free will*—just like Jesus. *That* is quite an accomplishment!

So, to Plan "R" we can add *R*ighteousness.

Let's further examine this *much more* plan of God's by comparing the "beginning" with the "end." I think you'll enjoy discovering a promising continuity to God's grand plan.

☺ On the chart below, note what God will restore, make new, or fulfill.

The Beginning	The Much More
Gen. 1:1 In the beginning God created the heavens and the earth.	Rev. 21:1
Gen. 1:16 God made two great lights-- the greater light to govern the day and the lesser light to govern the night.	Rev. 21:23-25
Gen. 2:8-10 God had planted a garden…in Eden…In the middle of the garden were the tree of life and… A river watering the garden…	Rev 22:1-2
Gen. 3:8 Then the man and his wife heard the sound of the LORD God as he was walking in the garden in the cool of the day…	Rev. 21:3
Gen. 3:14-15 So the LORD God said to the serpent, "… he will crush your head, and you will strike his heel."	Rev. 20: 2-3, 10
Gen. 3:19 By the sweat of your brow you will eat your food…	Rev. 7:16
Gen. 3:19 …you return to the ground, since from it you were taken; for dust you are and to dust you will return.	Rev. 21:4
Gen 8:21…every inclination of man's heart is evil from childhood.	Rev. 21:26-27
Gen. 9:2 The fear and dread of you will fall upon… every creature…	Isaiah 11:6-9

☺ What do these mirror images tell you about God's plan for the ages?

In Matthew 19:28, Jesus claims "the renewal of all things" will occur at His return. The word "renewal" or "regeneration" is the Greek word *palingenesia,* which means "new birth." *Palin* means "again," and *genesis,* "birth."[19] In other words, Jesus is going to bring about a "new genesis."

God is *good* at completing tasks. Even seemingly impossible ones, like putting this world back together again! He has a plan and you are a part of it. Hang in there in this study. You will find amazing comfort and strength in learning what God has planned for your life.

(⸛) **What do you most desire God to make new in your life?** (Go ahead and give Him your "impossibility" or your "too late now"! He is as creative as He is powerful, and redemption is His specialty.)

Glance back at the chart. See the narrow column sandwiched between "The Beginning" and "The Much More" columns? That's where we're living— we're in-between-ers! It's tough being in such a world, isn't it? Something inside each of us longs for a harmonious, perfect world—a place where God is so close you can literally walk with Him in your backyard! As Romans 8 declared, we groan in this present environment as we long for the day when suffering will end and peace will reign. Throughout history, mankind has attempted to create a utopian world, struggling to recreate the paradise we forfeited in the Garden of Eden. But only Jesus can do that. *And praise God, He will!* We were created for Paradise. And when we believe upon Jesus, one day we will return to Paradise.

Since our Paradise-to-come includes a new and restored Earth, you may be wondering where Heaven is today. Do all those who have died in the in-between time have to wait until the New Earth to experience Heaven? We'll discover the *Present Heaven* tomorrow—a very real place with the very real presence of God.

For now, I want to hammer home Scripture's deliberate and obvious message: Mankind's *final* and *ultimate* destination—the *Eternal Heaven*— includes the Earth. We were made *from* the Earth and *for* the Earth. It is part of God's overall plan of redemption. Redemption extends not only to man, but also to *all* of God's creation. What Satan has stolen, God will recover.

What sin has cursed, God will bless. What death has destroyed, God will resurrect... all with increase and greater glory. That's God's style. He's a *much more* kind of God.

DAY 3 *heaven or bust*

WHEN I WAS A CHILD, my family took a road trip to kid heaven: Disneyland. The five of us—my mom, dad, brother, sister and myself—piled into the station wagon and headed west. It took us three days to travel from Houston, Texas, to Anaheim, California. There were precious few stops along the way. My dad had a schedule to keep—it was Disneyland or bust. If you were hungry, thirsty, or in need of a bathroom stop—too bad. Like I said, my dad had a schedule to keep!

Much to my chagrin, twenty-some years later he made a similar trip with his grandson, my first-born. Hungry? Thirsty? Need a bathroom stop? *No problem!* Captain Granddad was happy to oblige. Nary an ice-cream opportunity was passed up. They even had picnic lunches at scenic turnouts!

Today we will begin a road trip across the pages of God's Word to get a quick overview of God's plan for the ages. It'll be a three-day whirlwind with few rest stops. Although I'd love to take scenic turnouts and sit awhile, that will have to come later. (Next week, I promise!) So hang on to your questions. For now, it's Heaven or bust.

A timeline will be our roadmap. Although we don't have to be experts on end-time events, we do need to have an idea of what is behind and ahead to understand different passages on Heaven in the Bible. As we learned yesterday, there is a *Present Heaven,* where believers now reside with Jesus. And, there is an *Eternal Heaven,* our final and ultimate residence.

There are three periods of time to discuss:
1. The time prior to Jesus' first coming and resurrection: **the Age of Promise.**
2. The time between Jesus' resurrection and His Second Coming: **the Church Age.**
3. The time following Jesus' Second Coming: **the Age of Righteousness.**

(?) **For now, label the three periods in the corresponding numbered blanks on the timeline below.** (We'll add others as we go.)

I. _____

4. _____

5. _____

First Coming ✝

Ascension ⇧   2. _____

6. _____

Second Coming ☁   3. _____

OK! Ready to take off from Creation and head for the hills? From the moment of Adam and Eve's rebellion in the Garden of Eden, God put Plan "R" into operation. He promised a Redeemer even as the curse of sin and death came upon the Earth (Gen. 3:15). Through Abraham, Isaac, and Jacob, He established the nation of Israel, from which the Redeemer would come.

God then sent prophet after prophet to proclaim the promise of a Redeemer and to entreat Israel to prepare for His arrival. The prophets foretold of Jesus' first and second comings without distinguishing them as two separate events. Therefore, when Jesus came, His disciples believed that He had come to *rule* the Earth, unaware that He must first *save* the Earth. After His resurrection from the dead and ascension into Heaven, Jesus sent forth the Holy Spirit and the Church was born. Even though Israel provided the Redeemer, as a nation they rejected Jesus. Therefore, "the times of the Gentiles" (Luke 21:24) were ushered in. The Church was now the vehicle to spread the message of redemption.

Before we move further down our timeline, let's examine the first time period, the *Age of Promise*. As we learned last week, those who died *before* Jesus' coming were saved by faith in God, believing in His promise to provide a Redeemer. References to Heaven in the Old Testament primarily focus upon the Messiah's future reign upon the Earth during the *Age of Righteousness*. Therefore, little is said about where the saints reside *until* that time. Upon the death of a saint, Scripture often states he was "gathered to his people." Jesus gives the most thorough depiction of the dwelling place of Old Testament saints upon their deaths in His illustration of Lazarus and the rich man (Luke 16:22–31). Jesus clearly defines two destinations. There was a place of comfort we will call "Abraham's Side." And there was a place of torment, called "Hell" or "Hades." We'll study this passage next week.

Label these two destinations in the numbered spaces provided on your timeline:
4. Abraham's Side
5. Hell

After Jesus' resurrection, He ascended into Heaven. Was this Heaven the same place as Abraham's Side, the place the Old Testament saints inhabited? Or was it a different place?

Read *John 3:13*. What is Jesus' claim concerning Heaven?

The Heaven that Jesus ascended to upon His resurrection is not the same place inhabited by the saints who had died prior to His coming. As Jesus claimed, He was the only one who had ever been in the presence of the

Father in His Heaven. He had to come to Earth as the Sacrifice for the sins of the world before Heaven could be opened and access to the Father made possible! Chapters 8–10 of the book of Hebrews beautifully compares the Old (First) Covenant initiated under Moses to the New (Second) Covenant initiated by Jesus Christ. *Let's take a look at selected verses.*

1. Hebrews 8:1–6. The earthly Tabernacle was built according to the plans God gave to Moses on Mt. Sinai. The children of Israel carried the Tabernacle through the wilderness into the Promised Land. Later, King Solomon built the Temple according to a similar layout.

What is the earthly Tabernacle, or sanctuary, a copy and shadow of? (v. 5)

Which covenant is superior, the first or the second, and why? (v. 6)

2. Hebrews 9:1–9 describes the Tabernacle's floor plan and function. Since it was a copy of Heaven, we need a general understanding of the layout.

What two rooms were in the Tabernacle, and what articles were in each? (vs. 2–3)

What separated the Holy Place (outer room) from the Most Holy Place (inner room)? (v.3)

Who was permitted to enter the inner room, or Most Holy Place? (v. 7)

What did he always carry into the Most Holy Place? (v. 7)

What were the sacrifices unable to do? (v. 9)

3. Hebrews 9:11–15, 24–28. These verses compare what Jesus accomplished to the ministry of the earthly priests.

What did Jesus take to the Most Holy Place of Heaven? (v. 12)

What did He obtain for us? (vs. 12, 14)

What did Jesus' death do for those under the first covenant? (v. 15)

4. Hebrews 10:11–22

Why has Jesus sat down at the right hand of God? (vs. 12–18)

What did His sacrifice accomplish?
(v. 14)

(v. 16)

(v. 17)

According to verse 19, where can we now enter, and how?

According to verse 20, what opened for us?

(?) Who do we have in Heaven, and what does that allow us to do and have? (vs. 21–22)

There are so many glorious truths in these passages! The author of Hebrews underscores the superiority of Christ by using key words such as "more," "better," and "much more." It wonderfully illustrates yesterday's lesson. I'm glad I'm on the *much more* side of the timeline, aren't you? I can't imagine always needing an innocent animal to be slain because of my sin. Thank you, *thank you*, dear Jesus—our Great High Priest, our Mediator of a new Covenant—a *better* Covenant, enacted on *better* promises.

As we learned, the earthly Tabernacle served as a copy and symbol of the Present Heaven. It consisted of three parts: the Courtyard, the Holy Place and the Most Holy Place (or Holy of Holies). The Levitical priests would make daily, continuous offerings in the Courtyard and in the Holy Place. The Most Holy Place was utilized only once a year to make atonement for the entire nation of Israel. This sacred room housed the Ark of the Covenant. It represented the Throne of God in Heaven, for it was where the *glory of God* met with man on Earth. God's presence in the visible form of the "Shekinah glory" hovered over the Ark between two cherubim of gold (Exodus 25:22).

The Ark of the Covenant in the Most Holy Place was separated from the Holy Place by a heavy, ornate veil, or curtain. The High Priest of Israel was the only person permitted to enter behind the veil. On the Day of Atonement he would sprinkle the blood of a sacrificed animal upon the Mercy Seat (which covered the Ark). Forgiveness, or atonement, comes only through the shedding of blood because "life… is in the blood" (Lev. 17:11).

Upon His resurrection, Jesus "passed through the heavens" to the Throne of God (Hebrews 4:14). Interestingly, the Hebrew people considered the heavens to have three realms: the first heaven was the atmosphere, the second heaven was outer space, the third heaven was God's Dwelling Place. Picture Jesus making His way through the heavens—passing through the Courtyard, the Holy Place, and then entering the Most Holy Place, God's Dwelling Place. He presented *His* blood at God's Throne. A *one-time* offering, it was adequate to forgive *all* the sins of *all* time. Jesus then sat down at the right hand of God the Father. This was the consummation of God's plan for the ages. *The mission was accomplished!* Sin was paid for; God was satisfied. It was a world-changing, covenant-making, earth-shattering event.

Keeping your place in Hebrews, turn to *Matt. 27:50–53*.

(:?) **What happened when Jesus died on the cross?**

The people in Jerusalem had quite a weekend, didn't they? Jesus of Nazareth is crucified. Then the Earth quakes. Rocks split. Tombs break open! And three days later, just when they thought things had settled down, Jesus' tomb is reported empty! What's more—*He was reported to be alive!* And if that wasn't enough to get your heart racing, deceased "holy people" were seen *all about the city!* They were raised to life and came out of their tombs after Jesus' resurrection. I just bet Simeon and John the Baptist were among them! Unfortunately, we're told very little about this amazing occurrence. I think the Earth split open with joy and propelled a few saints out of their graves and on to their feet! What a fitting way to underscore that the Son of God had conquered the grave.

Other events testified to the magnitude of the moment as well. As Jesus' flesh was torn upon the cross, the veil in the Temple was ripped apart, exposing the Most Holy Place. Similarly, in the heavenly realm, the way to the Father was opened. Jesus said, "I am the way and the truth and the life. No one comes to the Father except *through* me" (John 14:6, emphasis mine). Because of Jesus' death, those who die in Christ pass *through* the veil into the very Dwelling Place of God.

Jesus opened a *new and living way* to God—not only in Heaven, but also on Earth. By His sacrifice, we are invited to boldly come to the throne of grace through prayer and find mercy and help in time of need (Hebrews 4:16).

So... how did Jesus' blood offering affect the Old Testament saints who resided in Abraham's Side? And what happened to the saints who came out of their graves at Jesus' resurrection?

We can catch a glimpse of them in *Hebrews 11:39 -12:2*.

(?) **How are they described? (12:1)**

(?) **Where are our eyes to be?** (A good reminder from *Week One* and *Two*!)

The Old Testament saints have joined Jesus in the Present Heaven! Jesus was the first to ascend into Heaven, yet I assume He didn't wait long before opening the gates to the troops gathered together with Abraham. I don't know if the saints who rose from their graves at Jesus' resurrection had to die again, or if God just took them straight to Heaven, body and all. Perhaps they followed on the heels of Jesus, as described in Ephesians 4:8, "When he ascended on high, he led captives in his train and gave gifts to men."

Tomorrow we will add to our cloud of witnesses *all* believers who have died in the current *Church Age*. Together they eagerly wait for the Day when Jesus will return to Earth and gather up the rest of the Church. In the mean-time, isn't it encouraging to have fans in the Present Heaven cheering you on to victory?

(?) **Before we quit today, let's make a few more marks on the timeline:**
   6. Label the **Present Heaven.**
   → Draw an arrow from Abraham's Side to the Present Heaven to remind you that the Old Testament saints have joined Jesus in Heaven.

Whew! We just traveled across thousands of years in one quick trip! Rest up; we have more distance to cover tomorrow. If you have more questions than answers at this point, that's OK. Make a note of them in the margins. Our plan is to put this picture of Heaven together like a puzzle, piece by piece, examining each unique shape to glean all we can. It won't be until the end that a final portrait is revealed. I believe the completed picture will be more than worth our effort.

We've taken in a great deal. Revel in the knowledge that at the end of the ages, Jesus' sacrifice will *banish sin forever.* It will *perfect* you and me forever! No need to worry about sin or temptation in Heaven. The *Age of Righteousness* will reign. I can't wait! It's Heaven or bust—and I'm about to bust just thinking about it!

DAY 4 *rising to the occasion*

ARE YOU READY TO HOP back in our station wagon and drive towards the Eternal Heaven? This week we are visiting the major events on God's roadmap. Yesterday we visited the saints who died prior to Jesus' resurrection. We discovered that during the *Age of Promise,* believers were gathered together in a place of comfort called *Abraham's Side.* However, they are not there today! Their quarters were drastically upgraded when Jesus ascended to the *Present Heaven* and opened the new and living way to God. We will study the details of the Present Heaven beginning next week. For now, it's still Heaven or bust! Our final destination is the *Eternal Heaven.* It will begin with the creation of a *New Earth.* God has a plan to reestablish Paradise upon *this* planet!

Leg two of our journey will concern those who die during our present period of time, the *Church Age.* Scripture refers to a believer who has died as "asleep." God's Word also describes a time when they will "wake up" and rise from the grave. Some scholars believe that the body *and* the spirit "sleep" until the Great Resurrection at Jesus' return. They believe that all believers of all times will meet Jesus at the exact same moment. Others believe that although the *body* "sleeps" until the Resurrection Day, the *spirit* goes immediately to be with Jesus in the Present Heaven. We will study scriptures that address these questions today and in the weeks ahead. It is important for us to know where our deceased loved ones are today and what awaits us upon our deaths.

Let's begin at the time following Jesus' ascension. Persecution of the newly formed church has begun. Stephen, a dauntless and Spirit-filled believer, was causing a stir. Dragged before the Sanhedrin (the Jewish court), he gave a bold testimony in defense of Jesus, citing the long history of Jewish resistance to God's truth.

Let's pick up the story in *Acts 7:54–60.*

(❓) **What does Stephen see?** (v. 56)

(?) What two things does he ask Jesus to do? (vs. 59–60)

(?) Do you believe Stephen immediately went to be with Jesus upon his death? Why or why not?

This passage gives us a rare glimpse into the Present Heaven. You might recall from our study yesterday that upon His ascension, Jesus entered the heavenly Temple and *sat down* at God's right hand. For Stephen's eyes only, God rolls back the curtain that veils Heaven from sight. And there is Jesus, *standing* at the right hand of God!

(?) Let's speculate for a moment. If you were in Stephen's sandals, what would Jesus' *standing* rather than sitting signify to you?

How good God is! He may not always deliver us from trouble, but He never deserts us, extending to us the grace we need to endure even the worst of situations. Seeing Jesus on His feet must have given Stephen much needed courage. Stephen "stood up" to the Sanhedrin for Jesus, so perhaps Jesus was returning the favor. But I tend to believe that Jesus rose for the occasion of Stephen's homecoming, just as you or I would rise to welcome a friend. Stephen's request for Jesus to receive his spirit indicates that he anticipated *immediately* being with Jesus.

☺ Let's study a few other scriptures that address the moment of death for the believer. Underline *where* a person goes at death and note *when* he arrives, whether stated or inferred.

Luke 23:42–43 Then he [the repentant thief on the cross] said, "Jesus, remember me when you come into your kingdom." Jesus answered him, "I tell you the truth, today you will be with me in paradise."

Phil. 1:23–24 I am torn between the two: I desire to depart and be with Christ, which is better by far; but it is more necessary for you that I remain in the body.

2 Cor. 5:8 We... would prefer to be away from the body and at home with the Lord.

☺ What do these scriptures teach concerning *when* a believer will be with Jesus? Check which answer you agree with.

- ❑ When the body dies, the spirit immediately joins Jesus in Heaven.
- ❑ The spirit remains with the body in the grave until a future resurrection of both body and spirit.
- ❑ It's unclear what happens to the spirit at death.

I doubt that Paul (the author of the latter two scriptures) would be eager to die if he believed he would be "on hold" in the grave. Notice that being home with the Lord means being *away* from the earthly body. If *both* body and spirit "slept" until the Resurrection Day, we would never be "away from the body." Jesus reminded the Sadducees, who did not believe in the resurrection of the dead, that the God of Abraham, Isaac, and Jacob is "not the God of the dead but of the *living*" (Matthew 22:32, emphasis mine). Other scriptures confirm that Abraham, Isaac, and Jacob are alive and well with Jesus in the Present Heaven.

Yet, the *body* does "sleep" until it is raised to life at the Resurrection. Stephen's earthly body is *asleep* today—it remains in the grave—but a day is coming when his body will be *awakened!*

We must never forget that resurrection always involves the *body*. The word "resurrection" literally means "a standing up again; raised to life again; raised from the dead." To believe that the spirit lives on after death is *not* the same as believing in the resurrection of the dead. A *resurrected* person has a *body and a spirit*, like the Risen Christ. As we will study later, the pattern for our bodily resurrection is Jesus Christ. Just as His tomb was empty, so ours will be one day.

(?) Let's study a few scriptures concerning the future Resurrection Day. **Record what you learn.**
Job 19: 25–27

Isaiah 26:19

John 5:28–29

John 11:21–26

(?) What did Martha believe, according to verse 24?

(?) How does Jesus define Himself? (v. 25)

(?) We can't miss what Jesus does for Martha's brother. Glance down to verses 38–45. **What does Jesus do, and how does He do it?**

God has a plan to resurrect our earthly bodies. One day—on "the last day"—we will be given glorified bodies to live on the New Earth in the Eternal Heaven. This has long been the hope of God's people. It sustained Job, comforted Martha, and impassioned Jesus.

If our "sleeping" bodies reside somewhere other than a tomb, that is no problem for God. Just as God *spoke* and the world came forth, when Jesus speaks our bodies will come forth. Resurrection is *not* the creation of some non-human, unrecognizable body. If that were so, why would God bother to call our old bodies up from the grave? Job knew that even though his skin would be destroyed, in the end in *his* flesh, *his* eyes would see his Redeemer upon the Earth. What will be "resurrected" in the last day is *your earthly body*—restored, revived, redeemed, *raised*—**Plan "R"!**

From Adam to this present time, when death comes, the body dies and "returns to the ground it came from and the spirit returns to God who gave it" (Eccl. 12:7). But the day is coming when all bodies now "sleeping" will *rise to the occasion!* Does this mean those in the Present Heaven are a spirit without any sort of body? We will deal with that question later in our study.

Let's take a look at how this amazing resurrection will happen. In 1 Thessalonians 4:13–18, Paul is comforting the Thessalonians who feared their deceased loved ones would miss the Resurrection. He assures them that the dead in Christ will have a *bird's eye view* of this momentous occasion!

Please read *1 Thessalonians 4:13–18* carefully. Pay close attention to verse 14.

Who will God bring with Jesus when He returns to clothe His followers with their eternal bodies? (v. 14)

Where does Jesus come from? (v. 16)

Therefore, where must those who have previously died in Christ be at the present time?

Where will this event take place? (v. 17)

Now, let's nail the order of this Day down. Reread the passage and try to put the following events in chronological order:

___ We will all be with the Lord forever.

___ The Lord will come down from Heaven with those who have fallen asleep.

___ Those who are living on Earth will be caught up in the clouds to meet Jesus in the air.

___ The bodies of those who come with Jesus from Heaven will rise from the grave.

The day we meet Jesus in the sky is referred to as the Rapture of the Church. The term "rapture" comes from the Latin word for the term translated "caught up" in verse 17. It means "to seize; to take to oneself." Jesus will come *down* from Heaven, bringing with Him the believers residing in the Present Heaven, and their "sleeping" bodies will rise. In the next moment, all of the believers living upon the Earth will be "caught up" with Jesus in the sky and instantly changed, never experiencing death. Then we will all be with the Lord forever! (Answer: 4, 1, 3, 2)

What happens next? Stayed tuned... we'll conclude our road trip tomorrow. Let's end our time today with a quick stop for some food for thought. Continue reading *1 Thessalonians 5:1–11.*

How will the Day of the Lord come to those in darkness (non-believers)? (vs. 1–3)

Should the Lord's coming surprise the sons of the light, or the believers in Jesus, in the same way? (v. 4)

Why? How are those who believe in Jesus supposed to be living? (v. 8)

What did God NOT appoint us to? (v. 9)

Don't miss verse 10. Whether we are awake (alive) or asleep (dead), where will we be?

Are you seeing how *good* the Good News of Jesus Christ truly is? Let me encourage you as Paul instructed! A Day is coming when *all* who believe in Jesus Christ—from the first to die to the last standing—will be *instantly* changed; clothed in immortality and made ready to dwell with their Creator forever. Be comforted to know that the believers who have died before you are alive and well and with Jesus in the Present Heaven!

> *Be comforted to know that the believers who have died before you are alive and well and with Jesus in the Present Heaven!*

If you die before Jesus returns, He will rise to welcome you to Heaven. And if you remain alive until Jesus returns, you will rise to meet Him in the air! Only God the Father knows when that glorious Day will be (Matthew 24:36). I think God keeps it a secret so that every generation will be on their toes *and* on their knees! It's *wonderful* to know that Christians will not suffer the wrath of God when His judgment comes upon the Earth. We must not be duped by the world's false sense of "peace and safety." Clothed in faith, love, and hope, we live "in the light of day" for the entire world to see—living holy, self-controlled, God-honoring lives. We live on Earth as *heavenly-minded* people, knowing our Savior may come at any moment. *Let's rise to the occasion.* Our Redeemer comes!

DAY 5 *life on the line*

ON THIS FINAL LEG OF our journey, I'm reminded of my friends who promised their children a trip to Disney World. It took a little time to make the arrangements to go, so their children were quite anxious by the time the big trip arrived. Upon entering the gates of the Magic Kingdom, their five-year old son fell to his knees and dramatically exclaimed, "*Yes!* We're *finally* here!"

You may feel like exclaiming the same today, for we will at last arrive at the Eternal Heaven! We are in for quite a ride, so buckle up! At times you may want to shut your eyes and cover your ears. Other times you may want to stop and stay awhile. The view will be both frightening and marvelous as we journey through the Great Tribulation, the Second Coming, and the Millennium. But all these travels make it possible to arrive at the New Heaven and the New Earth. Are you up for the challenge? Just one more day to go!

Yesterday we were left hanging in mid-air, as we halted our trip at the Rapture of the Church. Recall that at the Rapture, all believers (those in the Present Heaven and those on Earth) receive their eternal, glorified bodies. Unfortunately for purposes of our time-line, we don't know exactly *when* this event will take place, only that it will occur sometime during "the Day of the Lord." The Day of the Lord is not one single day. It is a *period of time* that encompasses the Rapture, the Tribulation, and Jesus' Second Coming. It would take another Bible Study or two to adequately address the various opinions concerning these end-time events. Since our purpose is to understand them in the context of Heaven, we need to just hit the highlights. Let's head out and see what we can discover.

1. The Tribulation

The Tribulation is the period of time when God pours out His wrath upon all ungodliness on the Earth. His judgments are described in Revelation 5–18 and in the books of the Old Testament prophets. Jesus warned of the Tribulation: "For then there will be great distress, unequaled from the beginning of the world until now—and never to be equaled again" (Matt. 24:21). Jesus revealed that this hour of trial will come upon the "*whole world*" (Rev. 3:10). Devastating plagues, wars, earthquakes, and famine bring about catastrophic death and suffering. It is believed to last seven years with the worst calamities occurring in the last 3½ years, referred to as the Great Tribulation (Daniel 9:24–27).

Let's take a brief view of the Tribulation and see if we can't discover why such devastation must come. **Read the scriptures below and answer the questions that follow.**

Joel 2:31–32

How do some people respond to the "great and dreadful day of the Lord"? (v. 32)

Revelation 19:1–2

What does God condemn and avenge, and how are His judgments described?

During these horrible days, God judges those whose "sins are piled up to heaven" (Rev. 18:5). He avenges the blood of the saints. But with God, there is mercy even in His wrath. God is willing to save *any* that are willing to repent. Yet sadly, passages in Revelation report that multitudes dig in their heels and reject God's saving hand. (See Rev. 9:20–21; 16:9, 11.) Scripture warns that people who have repeatedly rejected God's truth will find themselves horribly deluded, believing the lies of the devil (2 Thes. 2:10–12). It serves as a sober reminder that we should never ignore the tug of the Holy Spirit, or we may become hardened to His voice (Heb. 3:15).

2. The Second Coming of Jesus

The Tribulation comes to an end (hurray!) by the coming to Earth of our Deliverer, Jesus Christ. This event differs from the Rapture, when Jesus comes *in the air* to remove believers from the Earth and outfit His believers with eternal bodies. The Second Coming is when Jesus' feet actually set down on Planet Earth! Scholars disagree upon how much time separates these two events (the Rapture and the Second Coming), varying from a few moments to several years.

Read *Zechariah 14:1–9.*

According to verse 4, where does Jesus first appear upon His return?

What is His ultimate reason for His return? (v. 9)

Jesus returns to rescue Jerusalem and to set the entire world free from Satan's rule. He comes back just as He left—in the clouds, on the Mount of Olives (Acts 1:9–12). Zechariah's account is affirmed and expanded upon in *Revelation 19:11–20:3.* (Read it if you have time.) Here's a quick summary: Jesus returns to Earth with the armies of Heaven, consisting of throngs of angels and glorified saints. He defeats His enemies in the great battle of Armageddon. Satan is bound and thrown into the abyss for 1000 years. Jesus begins His reign over the physical Earth.

Before we move on to the Millennium, let's consider the timing of the Rapture, the Tribulation, and Jesus' Second Coming. Some scholars believe the Rapture will *precede* the Tribulation in order for the Church to escape the time of wrath. The Rapture and the Second Coming would be like bookends on either end of the Tribulation (7 years) or the Great Tribulation (3½ years). Others believe the Rapture will occur at the *end* of the Tribulation, *at the same time* of Jesus' Second Coming. In this time sequence, Jesus would gather His church in the sky just prior to setting His feet upon the Mount of Olives.

No matter when the Rapture comes in relation to the Tribulation, we have Good News! (Could you use some?) Yesterday we read in *1 Thessalonians 5:9* that "God did not appoint us to suffer wrath . . ."

🕮 **Read the following scriptures and underline what else is promised:**

1 Thessalonians 1:10… wait for his Son from heaven, whom he raised from the dead—Jesus, who rescues us from the coming wrath.

Revelation 3:10 (a word to the faithful church from Jesus): Since you have kept my command to endure patiently, I will also keep you from the hour of trial that is going to come upon the whole world to test those who live on the earth.

2 Peter 2:9… the Lord knows how to rescue godly men from trials and to hold the unrighteous for the day of judgment…

Noah and his family were saved from the flood because Noah found favor with God (2 Peter 2:5). Lot and his family were also rescued from God's wrath upon Sodom and Gomorrah because the Lord promised He would not slay the righteous with the wicked (Gen. 18:23–32). Similarly, Israel was protected from the plagues God sent upon Egypt (Exodus 8–11). These believers were not taken *off* of the Earth, but they were spared God's judgment upon the wicked. During the Tribulation, 144,000 from the tribes of Israel are given a seal on their foreheads to protect them from harm (Revelation 7:3–8, 9:4).

Believers in Jesus Christ are "marked in him with a seal" at salvation (Eph. 1:13). Scripture is clear: *God knows His own.* If the Church is *not* taken to Heaven before the Tribulation, she *will be protected* from the wrath poured out upon the unrepentant. God has promised that when we align ourselves with Jesus and keep His Word, He will rescue us from His wrath. It's helpful to remember that part of the reason *for* the trial is to save a multitude of hard-to-reach souls. We who already believe in Jesus need no such convincing. *Whew.* Thank you, Jesus!

3. The Millennium

The great distress of the Tribulation ends when Jesus returns to Earth and sets up His Kingdom. Those who died for Jesus' sake during the Tribulation are raised to life and reign with Him for 1000 years. Although Satan is bound, he is released at the end of the Millennium and once again wrecks havoc. However, this final rebellion is quickly extinguished by fire from Heaven. Satan is then thrown into the lake of fire "forever and ever." (See Rev. 20:1–10.) The Millennium is a time characterized by peace and abundance, *a foretaste of the New Earth to come.*

For a preview, read *Isaiah 11:6–9* and *Isaiah 65:20–25.* **Record what life will be like.**

Sounds like a nice neighborhood doesn't it? You may be confused over how people die and have children during this period. Remember that this is *not* Heaven! *It is life on Earth with Jesus as King.* Death has not yet been destroyed.

There are many opinions concerning the Millennium. One school of thought contends that it is not a literal kingdom but a spiritual kingdom, in which the 1000-year time span is symbolic of Christ's reign in the hearts of believers until His return. Regardless of whether the Millennium is a literal kingdom or a spiritual one, Scripture clearly describes a time when God's people will literally reign upon the Earth—not just for one thousand years, but *forever.* For "Judah will be inhabited forever and Jerusalem through all generations" (Joel 3:20).

4. The New Heaven and the New Earth

"Yes! We're *finally* here!" After traveling all this way we must take at least a quick look at the beginning of our Eternal Home.

Revel in *Revelation 21:1–5.* **What sounds the best to you?**

"These words are trustworthy and true." Amen!

If you aren't too road-weary, let's complete our timelines. Review the information (#1-#6) that we identified on *Day 3*. Then add the following to the corresponding number on the timeline on page 104:

> 7. **The Rapture.** Add a few stick figures to remind you that we get our new bodies at this time.
> 8. **The Millennium.** Draw the devil underneath it and bind him up good!
> 9. Identify the **lake of fire** beneath the creation of the New Earth. With a mighty swooping arrow, throw Satan in! (Go ahead and enjoy it.)
> 10. **The Eternal Heaven.**

Lastly, place a dot on the line representing your life and an "x" signifying your death. You get to pick the time.

Congratulations on completing our "Heaven or Bust" road trip. We've come a long way in just three days! However inadequate our timelines are in capturing the magnitude and mystery of God's grand plan for the ages, we can still celebrate and glory in Plan "R." When I read about end-time events, it always comforts me to remember Jesus Christ is the same yesterday, today, and forever (Heb. 13:8). Our future is safe in Him.

Take one last look at your timeline. Look at your dot. Seems kind of small, doesn't it? Timelines put things into perspective. They remind us we will spend a lot more time *on the line* than *in the dot*. Do you live for the dot or for the line?

It's a bit unnerving to mark the time of our death. It reminds us that we don't have much time... or control! In Luke 12:15-21, Jesus tells a story about a man who lived his life with little thought of eternity. He said to himself, "You have plenty of good things laid up for many years. Take life easy; eat, drink and be merry." But God said to him, "You fool! This very night your life will be demanded from you. Then who will get what you have prepared for yourself?"

Heavenly-minded people do not live foolishly. They are aware that the things of this world are passing. They are alert to the fact that Jesus might return at any moment. They live as if their life is on the line... the *Infinite* Line of eternity with Jesus.

1. The Age of Promise

4. Abraham's Side

5. Hell

First Coming

Ascension   2. The Church Age

6. Present Heaven

7. _____

Second Coming   3. The Age of Righteousness

8. _____

New Earth   9. _____

10. _____

WEEK 4

Blueprints of Heaven

his week we are going to roll out the blueprints of Heaven to discover all we can about its physical layout. We've already seen sketches of the Present Heaven through the floor plan of the earthly Tabernacle. We caught a quick look behind the veil into the Throne Room of Heaven through Stephen's eyes. Our aim is to increase our desire of Heaven through Scripture's eyewitness accounts.

C. S. Lewis wrote:

> Most of us find it very difficult to want "Heaven" at all—except in so far as "Heaven" means meeting again our friends whom have died. One reason for this difficulty is that we have not been trained: our whole education tends to fix our minds on this world. Another reason is that when the real want for Heaven is present in us, we do not recognize it.[20]

Do you recognize the "real want for Heaven" in you?

So many times it's hard to put our finger on the elusive cry of our hearts. There is an ache in our souls that is hard to define and even harder to satisfy. For the next two weeks we will examine Heaven in light of such longings. Perhaps we'll find what our hearts are searching for in Scripture's blueprints of our Eternal Home with God.

DAY 1 *Homesick*

HAVE YOU EVER BEEN OVERWHELMED with homesickness? Maybe as a child your parents sent you to camp. Even though you knew you should be having fun, your heart was longing for the familiar. I don't remember being homesick as a child, but I have experienced an odd sort of homesickness as an adult.

Every now and then on a car trip I'll see a white shotgun house tucked back in a grove of trees—and oh the stirring in my heart! It takes me right back to long summer days spent at my grandmother's house. I remember every inch of her home. I can hear how the floor creaked in the living room. I can smell the musty single-car garage with the dirt floor. I loved to pass the time in the wide wooden swing on the screened-in porch. My sister and I would spy on the quiet neighborhood from the sturdy branches of the magnolia tree out front. It was a simple time. I felt safe and secure, warm and welcome.

Sometimes the sound of a cricket or the smell of a fragrant summer breeze will stir longings in me for something I can't quite identify.

Sometimes the sound of a cricket or the smell of a fragrant summer breeze will stir longings in me for something I can't quite identify. My heart seems homesick for a far-away place in a far-away time. A safe, secure, snug place, where all cares cease and I live in childlike wonder.

(?) **What causes you to feel such longings?**

Smells, sounds, music, and seasonal changes have the uncanny ability to create a sense of nostalgia, reminding us of someone or some place from our past. Perhaps many of the hopes and desires deep within us are an inexplicable longing for the world we were created to dwell in, where we walked with God in the cool of the day.

Read *John 14:1–4.*

(?) **Where is Jesus going?**

⊙ According to verse 1, why was Jesus telling the disciples about His Father's House?

⊙ What does Jesus want His friends to know about their future?

Although Jesus affectionately called the earthly Temple His Father's house (John 2:16), the context of this passage is Heaven. Since the earthly Temple was a *copy* of the heavenly one (Heb. 8:5), both are truly His Father's House.

His death imminent, Jesus began to prepare the disciples for His departure. The dark path to the cross was ahead. Through it all, Jesus wanted His followers to know that one day they would be together again. Even after His resurrection, Jesus would eventually leave them and ascend to Heaven. How difficult it would be for the disciples, after experiencing the constant companionship of *God* in human skin, to be separated from Him. Our deepest human need is to be united with our Creator. St. Augustine said it so well: "Thou hast made us for thyself and our hearts are restless until they rest in thee."[21]

- The KJV of John 14:2 begins: "In my Father's house are many mansions…" ﹘
- The NAS: "In My Father's house are many dwelling places…"
- The NIV: "In my Father's house are many rooms…"

The Greek word *oikia* translated "house" means "a residence, an abode; by implication a family." The Greek word *mone,* translated "mansions" in the KJV, also means a residence or abode and communicates the idea of "staying." The only other time *mone* is used in Scripture is later in this same discourse when Jesus says, "If anyone loves me, he will obey my teaching. My Father will love him, and we will come to him and make our home (*mone*) with him" (John 14:23). God makes His home with us *on Earth* until we make our home with Him *in Heaven!*

⊙ When you consider Heaven as "the Father's House," what images come to mind?

😊 **List what you learn about the Father's House in John 14:1–4.** Consider it in terms of recognizing the "real want for Heaven" in you.

Remember the chorus to the song "Big House"?

> It's a big, big house, with lots and lots of room.
> A big, big table with lots and lots of food.
> A big, big yard where we can play football.
> A big, big house, that's my Father's House.[22]

This simple chorus communicates an important truth—God is all about relationship and fellowship! His Heaven will be an environment suitable to such activities. We identify love, family, laughter, familiarity, and belonging with the ideal home life. If you long for a warm and loving home, God will provide it in Heaven. Heaven is not an abstract idea! It is not a cold, sterile, foreign habitat. It is the place God has created to gather His children together under one roof.

Just as we personalize our homes to reflect our personalities, so God's House reflects His taste, His creativity, and His nature. Romans 1:20 declares that God's invisible qualities—His eternal power and divine nature—are clearly seen in all He creates. The most beautiful site Earth has to offer—from Pikes Peak to Niagara Falls to an Oklahoma sunset—provides just a glimpse of the creative ability of our Heavenly Architect. Do you long for a beautiful place to live? In the Father's House, we won't merely *see* beauty, we will be "united with the beauty we see...pass into it...receive it into ourselves...bathe in it...become part of it."[23]

In Jesus' brief words of comfort to His disciples, we can glean several insights into Heaven:

1. First of all, Jesus underscores the reality of such a place. Heaven is a *place*. He *would have told us* if it were not true. Do you long for life to never end? Jesus entreats us to *believe* in God and to *believe* in Him! When we do, our troubled hearts find peace in the promise of eternal life.

2. Heaven is a large House with *many* rooms. It has many rooms because there will be many residents! In Revelation 7:9, Heaven is filled with "a great multitude, which no one could count." Do you long for a large family in which everyone knows you and loves you? Heaven will fulfill that desire in ways "no one could count."

3. Heaven is a *prepared* place. Jesus goes before us and makes Heaven ready for our arrival. He *personalizes* a place for you. Individuality is not lost in Heaven!

On a recent visit to out-of-town friends, I spent the night in a new addition to their home, which was a beautiful apartment above the garage. Towels were laid out in the bath, fresh linens were on the bed, drinks were in the fridge, a box of candy was on the coffee table, and best of all, coffee packets were provided for the morning. They know me well and their preparations communicated their love for me. I felt so welcomed and pampered that I didn't want to leave.

Jesus tells us twice in these three verses that He is personally preparing a place for us. What an amazing act of love. Do you long to feel special? There is no telling what Jesus will have waiting for you upon your arrival! He knows you better than you know yourself. It will be *His* delight to see *your* delight as He leads you to the "mansion" He has made ready for you.

4. Jesus assures us that *He* will come for us. There will be no awkward moments of wondering if we are in the right place! Although multitudes will be in Heaven, no one will be lost in the crowd or overlooked. Do you long to belong, or to be someone important? You will be welcomed in Heaven by the very *Son of God* (2 Peter 1:11).

5. Lastly, Jesus assures us that *where He is, we will be.* Just as His resurrection demonstrates the surety of our resurrection, so His ascension into Heaven assures our ascension into Heaven. We go the way He goes. Do you long for eternal security or eternal purpose? In Heaven, you will dwell in safety with your Creator and find complete fulfillment in Him.

Holding your place in John 14, flip over to *John 17:24.*

What does Jesus tell the Father He wants?

Heaven is all about being together with Jesus. Somehow, someway, we aren't going to have to wait in a long line to get in our five minutes with Jesus. Think about it! He loves us now as though we are the only one on Earth. Would His love be less personal or accessible in Heaven?

If Jesus' primary purpose in telling His disciples about Heaven is to comfort them—and comfort comes in the assurance that they will be where He is—then the Father's House describes the Present Heaven, where Jesus presently resides. This is important to know as we distinguish between the Heaven believers enjoy at present versus the Heaven we will all occupy for all eternity. The present tense of the verb "come," used when Jesus says He will *come* back to take us to be with Him, suggests Jesus' *continual* coming to individual lives. He gathers us *one by one* and takes us home with Him.[24] The ultimate fulfillment of this passage will occur at the Rapture, when He gathers all believers together.

Jesus' words in verse 4 ought to make our ears perk: "You know the way to the place where I am going." One thing is for certain—we need to be sure that we have *good* directions to the Father's House!

Continue reading *John 14:5–6.*

(?) **How do we find our way to God and His House?**

(?) **Can anyone come to the Father apart from faith in Jesus?**

(?) **Read** *John 14:7–11* **to discover why this is so. What is Jesus' explanation?**

We can't leave John 14 without at least reading Jesus' words of assurance concerning our temporary "separation" from Him. Read *verses 15–20.*

(?) **What has Jesus given us so that we do not feel like orphans?**

The mystery of the Trinity is simply that…a mystery! There is *one* God who is *Three* Persons: Father, Son, and Holy Spirit. We cannot say that we believe in God but not in Jesus, for Jesus *is* God. The Father and the Son are One. By putting on flesh and blood, God the Son became the means by which we are redeemed and reconciled to God the Father. The only way to enter the Father's House is by accepting a personal invitation from the Son.

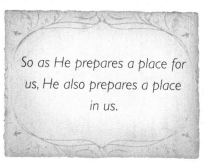

So as He prepares a place for us, He also prepares a place in us.

Jesus gives us assurance that although we are separated physically from Him, we are NOT separated in spirit. He gives us the Holy Spirit to live in us and be with us so that we are constantly in God's company. While on this Earth we are able to communicate with Him and partner with Him to continue His work. He will reveal Himself to us as we love Him and obey Him. So as He prepares a place *for* us, He also prepares a place *in* us.

> But Christ is faithful as a son over God's house. And we are his house, if we hold on to our courage and the hope of which we boast.
>
> (HEBREWS 3:6)

Later this week we will tour God's House. Let's end today with a favorite: *Psalm 23*.

How does David begin? Write down verse 1.

How does David conclude? Where will he dwell forever?

Recently some friends returned from a mission trip to Mexico where they built small homes for the poor. One very plain concrete-block house had a compelling message written on the wall: "I have no want." What a thought-provoking statement of faith. Could you claim the same?

Before I became serious about following Jesus Christ, I would fall asleep at night planning my dream home. Being in the home design business, I was anxious for the day when my husband and I could afford to build our first home. From time to time, a client would describe the house they wanted and I'd use one of the plans I had dreamed up for myself. And then I'd design myself a new one. I was a walking book of house plans!

You can imagine my delight when my new, believing heart beheld the promise of John 14:2. When I read how Jesus was preparing a mansion for me in Heaven, I took it literally and personally. Some time later I noticed something had changed in me. I was no longer dreaming of house plans! Without any concerted effort on my part, I had become content with the home I had. In fact, I was no longer remotely interested in designing one for myself. It was nothing short of miraculous to me. I knew that one day I was going to live in a home designed by Jesus Himself! Talk about your ultimate Dream Home! He's a *way* better architect, *way* more creative, with a *way* bigger budget. Therefore, I could wait. And I could even be happy in the wait! I continued to enjoy designing homes for others without envy in my heart.

God's promises about Heaven have the power and the purpose of loosening our grip on this Earth and putting our anxious hearts to rest. When we trust in Jesus and look forward to the Home He is preparing for us, we have no want. Our souls are full. Death is but a shadow. It simply leads to Home.

Are you homesick for God's House? It's OK… you're supposed to be! God has set eternity in your heart and Paradise in your soul. Revel in the beauty of a sunrise, a cool autumn breeze, the smell of the rain, the surprise of a rainbow. In those nostalgic moments, know that *your* God is filling *your* heart with desire for Himself and His Home. And even though you may ache for what is beyond your reach, remember Jesus' urging: *"Let not your heart be troubled. Believe in God. Believe also in Me."*

DAY 2 *indelible impressions*

YESTERDAY JESUS COMFORTED US WITH His description of Heaven as "My Father's House." In the passages we will explore today, Jesus' intention is not to comfort, but to confront and convert. He is more concerned with the "who" and "how" of Heaven than with "what" Heaven is like. Yet within these powerful messages, Jesus gives us marvelous word-pictures that help us visualize eternal life.

Jesus came to Earth with an incredible, glorious promise: Heaven. He came to Earth with an incredible, glorious mission: to take us to Heaven! But Jesus needed us to know not only what He came to save us *to*, but also what He came to save us *from*. For He also came to Earth with a horrible and violent warning concerning Hell. And He suffered a horrible and violent death to save us *from* Hell.

Hell is rarely spoken of today. It's as though it is impolite to even discuss it. But Jesus spoke of Hell often—more than any other person in the Bible. We will take a fuller look at what Scripture teaches about Hell in *Week Six,* but it's an unavoidable subject in the passages we are studying today. Jesus often referred to Heaven and Hell in the same illustration and we dare not cut Him off in mid-sentence! Try as we might, we simply can't believe Jesus about Heaven and dismiss what He says about Hell. He did not make empty promises *or* idle threats. To comprehend the incredible gift of Heaven, we must know the reality of Hell. If anything can make Heaven more appealing, it is the horror of Hell.

The Scripture passage we will read today describes Heaven and Hell *before* the resurrection and ascension of Jesus Christ. *Abraham's Side* was the "place of comfort" for all of God's children before Jesus' coming. We learned last week that upon His ascension, Jesus opened the way to Heaven, taking Abraham and Co. with Him. Although this story depicts the after-life in Old Testament days, we can apply the principles to our understanding of life-after-death.

Read *Luke 16:19–31.*

In reading illustrations such as this one, we should first look for the emphasis of the story. Jesus has a point and He intends for us to get it! His primary purpose in this passage is not to teach *details* about Heaven and Hell. However, neither is His intention to mislead. The detail in the passage is there for a purpose. As far as we know, Lazarus and the rich man were real people—possibly people that Jesus' audience knew. As we gather information from other scriptures during our course of study, we will be able to better discern what is to be taken literally and what is to be interpreted figuratively in this illustration. We don't want to limit Jesus' teaching *or* stretch it too far.

(ツ) **What do you believe to be Jesus' main message?**

☺ **Going verse by verse through this passage, list all you learn about:**

Abraham and Lazarus	Hell and the rich man

Let's consider Jesus' main emphasis.

Two points Jesus makes perfectly clear: 1) there is a Heaven and 2) there is a Hell. There are two, and only two, destinations—with no crossing over. Jesus' illustration emphatically states the eternal consequences of our earthly lives. Once we die, our earthly choices stand, no matter how anguished our regret.

Addressing the Pharisees' love of money (16:14), Jesus uses the illustration of the rich man in Hell and a poor man in Heaven to dispel the prevalent thinking that wealth was proof of a person's righteousness and poverty proof of God's disfavor. Jesus is *not* saying that wealthy people go to Hell because they are wealthy! Jesus had many wealthy friends. Abraham himself was a very rich man (Gen. 13:2).

Neither did the rich man go to Hell because he failed to help Lazarus. However, it does indicate an arrogant, hardened heart and a flagrant disregard for the clear message of the Law to care for the poor. A life lived for God could not be "gaily living in splendor everyday" (v. 19, NAS) when one so horribly in need was right before his eyes.

Why did the rich man end up in Hell? We can discern that he knew about repentance and that he knew the writings of Moses and the Prophets. He obviously rejected them, either trusting in his wealth and status to get him to Heaven, or preferring this life over the one to come. The rich man did not heed the revelation God gave him. Neither did his brothers. Therefore, they would not receive a greater revelation of someone rising from the dead.

Abraham's final words allude to Jesus' own resurrection, indicating the fate of those who refuse to believe the ultimate proof of Christ's Lordship.

Jesus' story also emphasizes that we cannot warn others of Hell after we die, though we will desperately want to. We may be "too polite" to speak of Hell or "too sophisticated" to believe such a place exists. But we won't be either if we find ourselves there! We often fail to consider how our relationship with the Lord (or lack thereof) influences those we love. The worst example to others could be a lukewarm relationship with God. It sends a message that although we profess God exists, we don't consider Him worthy of sacrificial love, time, and devotion. Jesus implores us to consider our loved ones' eternal destinies—as well as our own—while we still have time.

Let's compare lists of what we observed about Heaven and Hell. Remember— Jesus came from Heaven! He would not give us a wrong *impression* of what we are to expect.

1. Death meant immediate passage to either Heaven or Hell. Jesus indicates no "waiting period" between death and the after-life. The rich man's brothers were alive and able to be warned, so those in Heaven or Hell had not slept through thousands of years until the "Last Day."

2. Angels carry Lazarus away at death, indicating care in the journey to Heaven.

3. Heaven is a place of comfort and companionship.

4. Hell is a place of torment and agony.

5. Jesus describes those in the story as having bodies that seem human (eyes, fingers, tongue).

6. Those in Heaven retained their earthly name and identity.

7. There is recognition and knowledge of one another, even with Abraham, who lived much earlier. There is communication between people in Heaven and Hell and remembrance of their earthly lives.

8. The rich man begged for mercy but received none. After blatantly ignoring Lazarus' great need on Earth, he entreats his favor now that the tables are turned. He does not demonstrate regret for his ill treatment of Lazarus. It appears his arrogance entered Hell with him.

9. A great chasm separated Heaven and Hell; and no one could pass over. However, the rich man could see into Heaven, adding to his anguish.

Abraham could see into Hell, knew what had transpired on Earth, and believed justice had been served.

(·?) **Do you question any of these observations? Which one(s), and why?**

(·?) **How does Jesus' message speak to the injustice existing upon the Earth?**

Do you ever wonder why some people seem to get away with anything? Jesus' story teaches us that a day of accountability is coming. Our God is a *just* God, and Heaven will right earthly wrongs.

Holding on to your impressions from this passage, let's compare them to another portrait of Heaven and Hell from Jesus. Read *Luke 13:22–30*.

(·?) **What similarities do you see between this passage and the former?**

(·?) **What would you consider to be Jesus' main point?**

(·?) **What was Jesus' answer to the question posed in verse 23?**

(☺) Once again, Jesus emphasizes that our decisions on Earth concerning our salvation are *final*. **Why wouldn't the door to Heaven open?** (v. 27)

The latecomers to Heaven's door were not "known" by Jesus and are called "evildoers." We cannot fool God. There are no magic words to open the gates to Heaven. We enter only as the Owner has provided. He warns that many people will try to enter Heaven on their own terms. But the way in is narrow; access to Heaven is only possible through faith in Jesus. The people in this passage knew *of* Jesus—they had eaten with Him and heard His teaching. But knowing *about* Jesus and simply hearing His teaching is NOT saving faith. We must believe Him and receive Him as our Lord and Savior. Only when we give Him *our* life does He give us *eternal* life.

Notice how Jesus entreats us to "make every effort" (v. 24) to know the way to Heaven during our tenure on Earth. The phrase "make every effort" (NIV) or "strive" (NAS) comes from the Greek word *agonizomai* meaning "to agonize, struggle or wrestle; to compete for a prize; to labor fervently." Jesus is again emphasizing the enormous importance of our earthly quest of God and His Heaven. Our eternal destinies deserve our *diligent* investigation.

Jesus came first to His own people, the Jews. Yet Israel as a nation would not listen. In a similar message (Matthew 8:5–13), Jesus marvels at the faith of a Gentile centurion and the lack of faith of His own people. In both passages, Jesus speaks of the anguish the Jews will suffer when they see their forefathers in the Kingdom with believers from all over the world, yet they, God's chosen ones, are cast out. As with the rich man of Luke 16, the occupants of Hell see into Heaven. Their regret is so intense they gnash their teeth. Part of the torture of Hell is the knowledge of being excluded from Paradise. The prophet Isaiah indicates that those in the *Eternal Heaven* will be able to see those in the *Eternal Hell* (Isaiah 66:22–24). If these passages are not to be taken literally, the message is still horrifying. The time to accept Jesus and the time to proclaim Jesus is *now*.

(☺) **Need some good news? What are those in Heaven doing in this passage?** (v. 29)

Jesus gives us a glimpse of the great fellowship in Heaven—the grand gathering of believers from all over the Earth. Often He speaks of our eating and drinking together in the Kingdom. (How's that for good news? I'm always cheered up by the thought of a "feast," especially one I did not have to prepare!) Again, Jesus portrays Heaven as a *physical* place and His children as *physical* beings.

Jesus doesn't indicate the number of people in Heaven will be *few*, but that many who expect to be present *will not be*. He is anguished over Israel's rejection of His love. Glance down at verse 34.

What did Jesus want to do?

What was Jerusalem's response?

Our Savior desperately wants "all men to be saved and to come to a knowledge of the truth" (1 Tim. 2:4). Is there someone you know and love who is "unwilling" to come to Jesus?

List their name(s) below:

Be diligent for their sake! If we believed Jesus' message concerning Hell—fully and ardently believed it—we would never be bashful in sharing God's truth.

Has Jesus' message made an "indelible impression" upon you today? How?

The image of the rich man pleading for the opportunity to warn his brothers about his fate in Hell is emblazoned upon my heart. The vision of people looking longingly into the Great Feast—yet being cast out—has made its mark as well. Jesus has painted an unforgettable portrait of eternal consequences and etched His message across the canvas: *Choose Heaven. Choose now. Then choose to tell the world.*

DAY 3 *holy visitations*

THIS WEEK WE ARE GATHERING scriptures that describe Heaven. Although Jesus is the only one who came *down* from Heaven, there are a few Biblical accounts of God's people going *up* to Heaven, or of having visions of Heaven. Isaiah, Ezekiel, Daniel, John, and Paul all had such experiences. All but Paul were directed by the Holy Spirit to record them. Don't you wish that video cameras had existed back then? Undoubtedly, human words and imagery are unable to capture the fullness of such holy visitations. But really, neither could the best recording device! I get the sense from reading their accounts that you really *had to be there* for the full impact! However, the word pictures they paint certainly inspire a longing and excitement for the majesty of God's Holy Habitation.

Let's take a quick peek at a few of these holy visitations and record the highlights. Don't linger too long because there is a lot of material to read. Just allow mental images to fill your mind.

Isaiah 6:1–8 (Interestingly, John 12:41 reports that Isaiah's vision was of Jesus!)

Ezekiel 1:1–9, 22–28

Daniel 7:9–10

Revelation 4–5:14 (We'll come back to this passage.)

☺ **Do these visions stir your heart with a particular longing?**

☺ **Do any portions of these visions cause you concern? If so, what?**

☺ **Even without studying these passages in detail, we learn several important truths:**

1. There is a *Throne of God* in the *Temple of God* in the Present Heaven.

2. Most importantly, there is One sitting on the Throne! And He is indescribable!

3. Majestic angelic beings surround the Throne. They, too, seem indescribable! (And perhaps a bit scary. It's no wonder with each angelic message to Earth, the first words spoken were "Do not be afraid"!)

4. Intense worship is taking place. "Holy, holy, holy" never ceases to be uttered. No one is able to remain emotionless. No one is even able to remain standing!

5. Brilliance, jewels, crowns, rainbows, lightning, crystal seas and rivers of fire describe the scene. The Throne Room reflects its King—full of light, power, splendor, mystery, awe, and beauty.

6. A multitude of sounds fill the air: angels' wings and rushing waters, passionate praise and irrepressible sobs, trumpet blasts and harp strings, thunder bolts and holy hushes. The foundations tremble and hearts

pound. Thousands sing with a loud voice. (I like that... I'm anxious for the day when I can sing loudly without offending my own ears!)

The sounds of Heaven intrigue me. Don Piper wrote about them in his book, *90 Minutes in Heaven*. Proclaimed dead following a car accident, Piper experienced his own holy visitation to the gates of Heaven:

> My most vivid memory of heaven is what I heard. I can only describe it as holy swoosh of wings. But I'd have to magnify that thousands of times to explain the effect of the sound in heaven... The celestial tunes surpassed any I had ever heard. I couldn't calculate the number of songs— perhaps thousands—offered up simultaneously, and yet there was no chaos, because I had the capacity to hear each one and discern the lyrics and melody . . ."[25]

Perhaps you've read similar accounts from people who have had afterlife experiences. Although we must be discerning of contemporary accounts of heavenly visits, we also need to remember our God is the same God today as in the day of Ezekiel and John. His ways and His heart and His ability have not changed. Neither has our need for hope, comfort, and powerful reminders of our future with Him! I praise Him for the glimpses of glory He allows.

Let's catch back up with John as the Spirit transports him to the Throne of God in Revelation 4 and 5. We'll work our way through these two chapters, primarily picking up on the sights and sounds of the Throne Room in Heaven.

The first thing John mentions when he enters Heaven's door is a Throne "with someone sitting on it." **For a visual reminder, fill in the scriptures below with "Lord."**

Psalm 11:4 The_____is in his holy temple; the_____is on his heavenly throne. He observes the sons of men; his eyes examine them.

Habakkuk 2:20 But the_____ is in his holy temple; let all the earth be silent before him.

Psalm 103:19 The_____ has established his throne in heaven, and his kingdom rules over all.

God is *always* on His Throne, ruling over all His creation. I am *so thankful* that He doesn't take breaks, leaving the Throne unoccupied! Sometimes we may feel as though our lives and this world are spiraling out of control, but Scripture testifies that God's eyes are upon us. He *is* in charge!

In our scene in Revelation, the One on the Throne is God the Father, distinct from God the Son (5:13).

How is God the Father described? (4:2–3)

How is the Holy Spirit described? (4:5)

How is Jesus described? (5:5–7)

Interesting, isn't it, that our one God is described in Three specific forms? The Father is Brilliant Jewels; the Holy Spirit is Seven Blazing Lamps; the Son is the Lion of Judah, the Root of David, the Triumphal Lamb. God is seated on the Throne; the Holy Spirit is before the Throne; and Jesus is standing in the center of the Throne.

Although the Holy Spirit is described as seven spirits, He is *one* Spirit with seven distinct ministries. God the Spirit takes on many forms throughout Scripture and it appears He will continue to do so in Heaven. Here He manifests Himself as "seven lamps." Interestingly, the lampstand in the Tabernacle had seven lamps (Exodus 25:37). It was fueled by pure olive oil (Exodus 27:20), another symbol of the Holy Spirit. Again we see the pattern of Heaven displayed in the earthly articles of the Tabernacle.

Jesus appears as the sacrificial Lamb of God, "looking as if it had been slain" (5:1). You might recall that the resurrected Jesus showed Thomas his scars.

Why do you think Jesus will eternally bear the marks of His crucifixion?

John says the One on the Throne "had the appearance" of jasper and carnelian. Jasper in ancient days was more like a diamond or a crystal than it is today. It was clear and cast colors as a prism. Carnelian, or sardius, was blood red.

(?) **Why might God appear as these two stones?**

Truly, there is no describing God! Although He appears as Brilliant Jewels on His Throne, Scripture often describes God in human terms. In this passage, John refers to God's "right hand." Moses and others beheld God's "back" and His "feet." God declared no one should see His "face" and live (Exodus 33:20). Amazingly, one day we *will* see God's face—but not until our glorified feet land in the Eternal Heaven (Rev. 22:4). Even then, I doubt we will find the words to adequately describe Him.

(?) **What might be the significance of the rainbow around the Throne?** (Remember, Heaven houses the *originals*; Earth displays the copies!)

When God judged the Earth and sent the flood in Noah's day, He chose the rainbow that *encircled His Throne* to be the sign that He would never again destroy the Earth. Think of it... the Throne, the place of rule and judgment, is surrounded by God's covenant promise toward us. His promises to us are inseparable from Him. We are ever on His mind!

Did you notice how everything in this passage is described according to its proximity to the Throne? I can't help but think about how the back rows seem to fill up first at a church service or Bible study! It's as though the closer we sit to the front, the greater our accountability. We can't sneak out if we're up front! Don't you imagine that in Heaven we will all want front row seats? Imagine being within arm's reach of the Holy Trinity in all Their collective glory! Even now, the closer we are to God's Throne, the fuller the measure of God's power and grace in our life. Don't hang in the back! Bring all of your life, everything and everyone in it, under God's eye and rule. There is no safer place!

In the center of the Throne are four creatures, or angelic beings, similar to those in Isaiah's vision of Heaven. They cry out "Holy, holy, holy" night and day. These are the only two occurrences of the threefold "holy" in Scripture, both coming from the mouths of angels in the Throne Room in Heaven. Recall that in the earthly Tabernacle there were two rooms separated by the veil. The outer room of worship was called the Holy Place or literally "the Holy" (the word *place* is added for clarity). Only the Levitical priests, who had gone through an extensive cleansing ritual, could enter. Beyond it was an inner room of worship called the Most Holy Place or literally "the Holy Holy." So holy was the room that the High Priest could only enter with a blood sacrifice. He wore bells on his garment so that those outside the veil could tell if he was still alive (Exodus 28:35).

Another veil hinders us from seeing into a third room: God's Throne Room in Heaven. But through these holy visitations, we are allowed to venture in and behold the holiest place of all, "the Holy Holy Holy." The impact of the presence of God in Heaven has no earthly comparison. It is *three times holy!* The angels can't help but cry out, "Holy, holy, holy!" It's no wonder the elders couldn't stay in their seats!

Rev. 4:4, 9–11 describes 24 thrones with 24 elders upon them. The elders most likely represent the 12 tribes of Israel plus the 12 apostles. Perhaps there are truly 24 men, but most likely they are representative of all of God's redeemed—Jew and Gentile, Old Testament saints and New Testament believers.

What are the elders wearing and what are they doing?

Now glance back over *Rev. 5:8–14*, noting the activity of the elders.

From reading the elders' declarations and songs, what filled their hearts?

Later we will learn about the crowns they are wearing and laying before the Throne. But what a scene John witnessed! Did you notice how many times the elders fell down? I counted three times!

(?) **Have you ever been so moved in worship that you were compelled to lay low? If so, describe what was happening in your heart.**

(?) **According to *Rev. 5:13*, who is praising God?**

Do you suppose that every created thing would include *every* created thing? In past lessons we learned that nature will praise God and animals will ascribe Him honor. Add them to the scene surrounding the Throne, along with thousands of angels, every redeemed man and woman, every child and babe, from the Garden of Eden to the present day. What a diverse group, worshipping as one! It sounds like a wonderful fairy-tale, doesn't it? Perhaps that is why those stories so blessed our child-like hearts—they reflected a want of Heaven deep in our souls.

A friend of mine recently told me that Heaven didn't excite him because it would just be a long praise and worship service. I hope today's lesson revealed that there is *nothing* ordinary about Heaven's praise! It will be so thrilling, so spectacular, so compelling that no one will want it to end. And it won't! An unlimited variety of activities is and will always be taking place in Heaven. But how could we be in the presence of God and *not* worship? We were created for it! Mankind has invented all kinds of gods to bow down to, attempting to satisfy the vacancy in their souls God carved out for Himself. But only God is worthy of worship. Only He can thrill our souls for all of eternity. It's *amazing* that we will be permitted to be so close to the Awesome God of the Universe. *Thank you*, Jesus.

What better way to end today's lesson than with a holy visitation of your own? Turn on your favorite praise music. Close your eyes and see the multitudes of worshippers around you. Majestic angels, every sort of animal, people from every tribe and nation—even the mountains and trees join you in song. Thunder, lightning, and brilliant rainbows surround you. Picture Jesus beckoning you forward. Walk toward His Throne, if your legs are able. Gaze upon the Brilliant Jewel, the Blazing Lamp, and the Triumphal Lamb. Declare (loudly if you are able!) the songs of praise from the pages of Revelation 4 and 5. Fall down and worship God. He is oh so worthy!

DAY 4 *no more*

YESTERDAY WE PEEKED INTO HEAVEN'S door with Isaiah, Ezekiel, Daniel, and John. We stole a glimpse of "the Holy Holy Holy" Throne of God. Hasn't it been amazing to see Heaven through the blueprints of the earthly Tabernacle? It's no wonder God commanded Moses to build the Tabernacle *exactly* as He instructed! God was bringing a bit of Heaven down to Earth. I once thought it odd that the construction plans for the Tabernacle and the Temple filled so many pages of the Bible. I should have known God would only fill precious real estate with a precious picture for us to behold!

Today we'll again roll out the blueprints of Heaven. But this time we will be examining the layout for what is NOT there. I think you'll rejoice equally in the "**no more**" of Heaven as in the "much more" of Heaven. I must warn you, we will be flipping back and forth in our Plan Book! So warm up your fingers! We've got Heaven to explore!

Let's begin by rejoining the Apostle John as he reports loud voices and the sound of a trumpet in Heaven's corridors...

Read *Revelation 11:15–19.*

What is about to happen? (vs. 15, 18)

What was seen inside the Temple in the Present Heaven? (v. 19)

Heaven's clock is about to strike midnight! The Kingdom has come! God's enemies will be judged. God's servants will be rewarded. The Earth will be reclaimed. And, of course, the 24 elders are face down, worshipping! Where else would they be? The final judgments were about to be poured out upon the Earth.

As the Earth shakes below, the Temple in Heaven opens above! For the first time in a *long* time, the sacred Ark of the Covenant is seen. The last sighting of it on Earth was during King Josiah's reign, when Solomon's Temple was repaired (2 Chron. 35:3). A few years later, the Babylonians seized Jerusalem and destroyed the Temple. Its furnishings were broken into pieces and carried to Babylon, as were the Jews (2 Kings 25:9–14). The exile ended when King Cyrus allowed the Jews to return to their homeland and rebuild the Temple. He even gave back some of the stolen articles from the Temple (Ezra 5:13–15). But no mention is made of the Ark of the Covenant during the Temple's decimation or restoration. Some believe it was destroyed and some believe it was hidden. But it's comforting to discover it *safe and sound* in the Present Heaven! While in exile in Babylon, the prophet Ezekiel had a vision of God's glory leaving the Temple upon the wings of the cherubim (Ezekiel 10:18). I think God whisked His Ark to the safety of Heaven on the cherubim's wings!

Now back to our excitement in the Present Heaven. When the Tribulation on Earth draws to a close, a loud voice from the Throne says, "It is done!" (Rev. 16:17). Hallelujahs roar from Heaven's multitude. The day they have longed for has finally arrived (Rev. 19:1–4). Soon Jesus will return to the Earth and begin His Millennial reign.

Let's fast-forward 1000 years to the completion of the Millennium. The last enemy, death, is destroyed (Rev. 20:14).

(?) What happens next, according to *Revelation 21:1–4?*

The word "new" used to describe the Earth and sky does not mean totally *different*, but rather totally *superior*. Scripture even tells us how this "makeover" is accomplished. Keeping your place in Revelation, turn to *2 Peter 3:10–13.*

😀 How will the first heaven (or atmosphere) and the Earth pass away?

😀 What do heavenly-minded people look forward to? (v. 13)

This present world will be destroyed by fire. The heavens will disappear with a roar and the Earth and everything in it will be laid bare. Even the sky must be cleansed from sin, for Satan, the "ruler of the kingdom of the air" (Eph. 2:2), has defiled it. No trace of evil can remain! *Everything* is purified. The "home of righteousness" will emerge from the ashes.

C. S. Lewis describes this phenomenal moment, when the new replaces the old:

> Then the new earth and sky, the same yet not the same as these, will rise in us as we have risen in Christ. And once again… the birds will sing and the waters flow, and lights and shadows move across the hills, and the faces of our friends laugh upon us with amazed recognition. Guesses, of course, only guesses. If they are not true, something better will be.[26]

Oh for the Day! Let's return to *Revelation 21*.

😀 Where does the Holy City come from? (v. 2)

The New Jerusalem is the "dwelling" or "tabernacle" of God that comes down from Heaven. We don't go *up* to live with God! He brings His Tabernacle *down* to the Earth. Heaven and Earth merge together. Jesus has bridged the two in His role as both God and Man. Most likely this Tabernacle of God from Heaven is the same dwelling as the "Father's House" Jesus has been busily preparing (John 14:2–3). Construction is complete only when God's family is complete!

Tomorrow we will take the grand tour of this dwelling and explore the scriptures that describe it more fully. For the rest of today, let's focus on *Revelation 21:22- 22:5.*

🔖 **List what will *not* be in the New Jerusalem.**

There is no Temple in the New Jerusalem, for the Lord God and the Lamb *are* its Temple. Let's think about that for a minute. At the present time, believers in Christ are God's Temple (2 Cor. 6:16). Yet in the City of God, God will be *our* Temple. It will be as if we enter and pass *into God* as we would a dwelling! He will spread His tabernacle over us (Revelation 7:15) and completely envelope us with His love. Wow!

Although there is *no more* Temple in the New Jerusalem, the Throne of God remains. Make no mistake—God will still rule! We will not become little gods or ever know all He knows or do all He does. But we will reign *with* Him!

There seems to be a Camelot-like atmosphere to the Holy City. Earthly kings come and go through the gates. Recently I received a picture postcard of majestic castles from my sister who was traveling overseas. Just the photographs of them captured my heart! Do you suppose the "real want for Heaven" in us causes us to love castles and kingdoms and such? Think of how *noble* life will be in the New Jerusalem. Nothing impure will *ever* be present. *No more* vile words or acts… *no more* harm or injury… *no more* fear or worry. Only safe streets and safe hearts will reside within the Kingdom's walls!

Why will there be *no more* night? "God is light; in him there is no darkness at all" (I John 1:5). Symbolically speaking, we will never again be "in the dark," outside of God's presence and glory. It's hard to imagine *no more* sun or moon in our Eternal Dwelling. But don't fret—the same Artist who paints today's sunrises and sunsets will radiate our New Light. Besides, the scripture only states that there is *no need* for the sun and the moon. Just as a flashlight isn't needed in the daylight, the sun and moon may still be *present* but *out-shined* by God's glory. I'll bet we will still enjoy the twinkle of stars! One thing we know for sure—God will light our world!

Look back at *Revelation 21:1.*

(?) **What else will no longer be on the New Earth?**

Could this mean a *literal* sea? I hope not! My favorite place on Earth is seaside! Other scriptures indicate there *will* be bodies of water on the New Earth. Jesus will reign "from sea to sea, and from the River to the ends of the earth" (Zech. 9:10). So what could this scripture mean?

There are several possibilities. For one, the sea depicts evil and death in the book of Revelation. Surely there will be *no more* evil and *no more* death in the Eternal Heaven. Also, since John is in exile on the island of Patmos, the sea could represent separation. In the Eternal Heaven there will be *no more* separation ever again—from each other or from God. Others have suggested that there will be *no more* salt-water bodies because its purifying properties will no longer be needed.

But we know of a special sea that is in the Present Heaven. Look back in *Revelation 4:6.*

(?) **What is before the Throne?**

Knowing that the earthly Temple is a copy of the heavenly Temple, let's search the blueprints for something that might be a foreshadowing of the sea of glass, or Crystal Sea.

Read *Exodus 30:17–21.* (I warned you we would be all over the Bible today! Hang in there!)

(?) **What was the basin (or laver) used for in the Tabernacle?**

(?) Check out *Exodus 38:8.* **What was the basin made out of?**

Now take a look at its Temple counterpart in *2 Chronicles 4:2–6.*

(?) **What was the basin called?**

Lastly, read *Hebrews 10:19–22*.

⟨☺⟩ **How is our approach to God similar to the instructions given to the priests?**

The "Sea" in the earthly Temple was a large basin of water used by the priests to wash in before they approached the altar of God. In the Tabernacle, the bowl was even *crystal-like* in appearance! Perhaps then the Crystal Sea is the *heavenly* basin that symbolizes how we are washed with pure water upon our acceptance of the sacrifice of Jesus Christ. My swimmer's heart can imagine plunging into God's Crystal Sea on my way to His Throne—washing all my sins away! Perhaps there will be "no more sea" in the Eternal Heaven because sin is finally destroyed and we are eternally clean! In Heaven, we will always be welcome into the presence of God! *What grace!*

Do you remember reading in Revelation 22:4 how God's Name will be on our foreheads? The High Priest of Israel wore a turban with the words "Holy to the Lord" on the front (Exodus 39:30). Perhaps that is what will be on our foreheads. *We will finally be fully His.* What a reminder to us! We worry about so many things in our relationship to God, but He is after our love, our attention, and our fellowship. In Heaven, He will have it. We will spend eternity exploring His heart and mind—learning from and being thrilled by the God who created us, forgave us, and called us to His side.

Let's close by considering the other "no mores" we discovered today that we've yet to mention. On the New Earth, there will be *no more* mourning, crying, or pain. *No more* shame. *No more* lies. *No more* shut gates. Revelation 7:17 would add *no more* hunger, thirst, or scorching heat.

⟨☺⟩ **What additional "no mores" would you like to add to Heaven's list?**

The Eternal Heaven ushers in the greatest "*no more*" of them all: *No more* death! We could add *no more* devil or demons! Neither will there be any envy, greed, selfishness, hate, anger, frustration, loneliness, or depression. How about having *no more* headaches, backaches, stomachaches, earaches, or heartaches? We'll never again suffer from a lack of love, lack of time, lack of sleep, lack of money, lack of space... *no more* lack, period.

I'll miss none of the above, except I'm curious about *no more* tears. As one who cries over sappy TV commercials, I *know* I'll be crying when I first see my loved ones in Heaven! How will any of us be able to hold back tears of joy and gratitude? Perhaps "happy tears" are still permitted! As we stand before God, pure and holy and free... and look upon *His face* for the very first time... well, I just hope the Lord has a Heaven-sized hankie! I need to blow my nose already.

DAY 5 *the shining city*

WELCOME BACK TO OUR TOUR of Heaven! I hope this week's homework has enabled you to better recognize the "real want for Heaven" in you through Scripture's description of Heaven's layout. We've examined the Heaven before Jesus' ascension called *Abraham's Side*. We visited the *Present Heaven* through Jesus' portrait of His Father's House and through the visions of the prophets and apostles. Yesterday we witnessed the descent of the New Jerusalem at the dawning of the *Eternal Heaven*. Today we are going to return to the New Jerusalem and zoom in for a closer look.

Have you ever taken a city tour in a double-decker bus? I had the opportunity to do so while vacationing in Vancouver. It was fun to sit back and take in the sights as the driver explained the history of the city. It was the perfect way to enjoy a large city in a short time—with no risk of getting lost!

Let's take our tour of the New Jerusalem in a similar fashion. The Holy City Bus Line is ready to depart to the most beautiful city on Earth... the *New* Earth, that is. Take a seat on the upper deck, where the view is best. The Apostle John's angel will be our driver and John will be our tour guide. Hear his excitement as he shows off the place that Jesus has diligently and lovingly prepared for you. But before we go, let's do a little pre-trip research so we can better appreciate our tour.

Read the following scriptures about Heaven and circle the words used to describe it:

Hebrews 11:10, 16 For he was looking forward to the city with foundations, whose architect and builder is God.... they were longing for a better country—a heavenly one. Therefore God is not ashamed to be called their God, for he has prepared a city for them.

Hebrews 12:22, 28 But you have come to Mount Zion, to the heavenly Jerusalem, the city of the living God. Therefore, since we are receiving a kingdom that cannot be shaken, let us be thankful, and so worship God acceptably with reverence and awe...

Rev. 2:7 To him who overcomes, I will give the right to eat from the tree of life, which is in the paradise of God.

Heaven is a *physical place*. It's a truth that bears repeating until our former images of Heaven come down to Earth! Sometimes we envision Heaven as "less than" Earth rather than "more than." In C. S. Lewis' novel, *The Great Divorce*, Hell is described as a vaporous ghost town. Heaven, on the other hand, is a solid, tangible, and vibrant place. We need a physical habitat because in the Eternal Heaven we will be physical beings. (Which will be our topic of discussion next week.) Nowhere in Scripture is Heaven described as ethereal. Concrete terms such as kingdom, city, country, mountain, and paradise are always used to describe Heaven.

Keeping these images of Heaven in mind, let's climb aboard our bus and head out for the New Jerusalem. Roll down the window and take in the clean, fresh air. All things are *brand new* on the New Earth! It all smells new, too! We never want to forget that the Eternal Heaven includes a renewed and *glorious* Earth. If this present world was undefiled, can you imagine the beauty? The canyons, waterfalls, and rainforests are but a *sneak preview* of what God has planned for our New Earth.

Please read *Revelation 21:9–22:5*.

What is your first impression of the Holy City?

What about it makes you desire to live there?

(?) Is there anything about it that you don't find desirable?

(?) Do you think that this description of the New Jerusalem is symbolic, literal, or both? Why?

My first impression of the Holy City is that it is a Kingdom fit for a King! But not an earthly king; such extreme extravagance only befits the Eternal God, the *Maker* of Heaven and Earth. It is pure and clean and brilliant—perfect for Perfection!

The New Jerusalem appears to be a real city, doesn't it? The mighty wall with its many gates is reminiscent of the great cities of the past. We see the familiar—foundations, streets, gates, rivers, trees, leaves, and fruit. Yet the walls and foundations are jewels, the streets are golden, the gates are pearls, the rivers are crystal clear, the trees are life-giving, and their leaves bring healing. And the *people!* The people *all* belong to God. The New Jerusalem offers all that is good and enjoyable about city life, without any of the ugliness or evil.

But I've lived in a small town far too long to get overly excited about a big city. I tend to get lost in metropolitan areas and I panic on crowded overpasses. I'm most drawn to cobblestone main streets, wide-open spaces, and casual living. I've always wanted to live on the water, sip coffee on the deck, and watch the sunrise.

(?) How about you? If you could live *anywhere* on the Earth, where would it be?

Because I implicitly trust my Architect and Builder, I need a closer look at my new residence. So let's work our way through these verses, looking for both the literal *and* symbolic meaning. Although we shouldn't miss the symbolism of our Heavenly City by limiting it to a literal interpretation, neither do we want to miss the obvious by spiritualizing what is meant to be factual. There is great comfort in

> One reason we fail to recognize the "real want for Heaven" in us is that we fail to acknowledge the simple truth that we like our physical state.

the familiar! One reason we fail to recognize the "real want for Heaven" in us is that we fail to acknowledge the simple truth that we *like* our physical state.

So let's pull over at the scenic turnout at the top of John's mountain (21:10) and look out over the city. (Aren't you glad we will continue to enjoy the mountains in the New Earth?)

How is the city described from a distance? (vs. 11, 16, 18)

Even from our mountain perch, the glow from the Holy City is brilliant, reflecting light like a giant crystal. Heaven is the Father's House, so it will undoubtedly reflect His beauty and attributes. The city sparkles of transparent gold, as does the great street of the city (21:21). Sadly, some people are willing to sell their souls on this Earth for what will be trod underfoot in the Kingdom of God!

The city is laid out in a square. It is as high as it is long and wide. In the earthly Temple, the Most Holy Place was a perfect cube (1 Kings 6:20), the three equal measurements illustrating our Triune God. But I don't think we need to conclude that the New Jerusalem is *cubical*. A very high mountain may define its height! After all, the Heavenly City is also called *Mt. Zion*, the mountain of God.

Numbers are often figurative in Scripture. Undoubtedly, the measurements of the city are meant to communicate its perfection, exactness, and enormity. Surely it causes one to think, "How wide and long and high and deep is the love of Christ" (Eph. 3:18). Also, the measurements of both the city and the wall are multiples of 12, the number for God's people. (There were 12 tribes of Israel and 12 apostles of the Church, representing the complete body of Christ.) We can't miss the symbolic message that this city has room for *all* of God's children.

However, the fact that an angel *measures* the city emphasizes that our heavenly habitat takes up a real amount of space. To help put 12,000 stadia or 1,500 miles into perspective, the continental United States averages 2,500 miles from east to west and some 1,200 miles from north to south. It's difficult to know whether the angel measured one side of the city, or the perimeter. If the angel measured the perimeter to be 1,500 miles, then each side would be 375 miles long. Either way, it's a spacious place!

The wall surrounding the city is thick and high, made of sparkling, crystal-like jasper. There are three gates per side, each one honoring a tribe of Israel. Interestingly, the tribes of Israel surrounded the earthly Tabernacle while marching and camping in the wilderness. Three tribes were on the east, three on the north, three on the west, and three on the south (Numbers 2) just as in our New Jerusalem. The tribe of Judah (Jesus' lineage) camped at the Tabernacle's sole entrance on the east. I imagine the same configuration will surround the heavenly Tabernacle.

Let's leave our scenic turnout and drive down the mountain to get a closer look at the gates and the foundation wall.

What are the foundations of the wall made out of, according to verse 19?

According to verse 21, what are the gates made of?

Keeping your place in Revelation, look up *Matthew 13: 45–46* and *John 10:9.*

Considering these scriptures, what might the gates of pearl symbolize?

I love how the gates are made of a single, gigantic, magnificent pearl! Just as the beauty of a pearl is formed through the oyster's pain, the beauty of eternal life was born through Christ's pain on the cross. Christ *is* the pearl of great value. He *is* the gateway to Heaven. Every coming and going from this capital city of Heaven will remind us of the price our Savior was willing to pay for our admittance.

During the days of the earthly Tabernacle, the High Priest wore a breast-plate decorated with jewels similar to those in the Holy City's foundation wall. Since the New Jerusalem is the heavenly Tabernacle, let's read *Exodus 28:15–21, 29* to see a possible correlation.

What might the jeweled foundation around the City represent to God? (v. 29)

Ephesians 2:19–22 also sheds light on the wall's costly foundation. **Record what you learn.**

The High Priest's breastplate was square (just as our city) and had twelve precious stones mounted in four rows. Each stone was engraved with the name of a tribe of Israel, just as the foundation stones are engraved with the names of the apostles. The breastplate was worn each time the High Priest entered the Holy Place, covering his heart as a memorial before the Lord. In a similar way, the rows of jewels in the foundation surrounding the *ulti-mate* Holy Place are a continuing memorial before God. What a tribute to the work of the apostles, to whom all the church is indebted. The apostles carefully and sacrificially laid the foundation of our faith upon the chief cornerstone of Christ.

You and I have the opportunity today to add our own stones to the wall's foundation! The apostle Paul likens our Spirit-empowered earthly works to gold, silver, and precious jewels (1 Corinthians 3:12). We are to build upon the apostles' solid foundation with good works and sound doctrine, creating a spiritual dwelling of God. The New Jerusalem, as the Bride of Christ, is the literal fulfillment of the completed work of God's household. Each stone embedded in the wall reflects the uniqueness of every believer, giving glory to the God who claimed each one.

(◔‿◔) It's time to drive through the pearly gates and onto the street of gold. Reacquaint yourself with *Rev. 22:1–3*. **Describe or draw what you see.**

Are you encouraged to see that the New Jerusalem is not all metal and stone? Once beyond the extravagant wall and gates, a garden awaits us! Let's not forget God's promise to restore Paradise on Earth! The word "paradise" is of Persian origin and means a park or a *walled* garden, shady and well watered.[27] Isn't that terrific? I feel more at home already! The city may gleam of gold, but I trust the earth is just what we'd expect—marvelously rich, fertile soil.

Perhaps the Throne of God sits on top of the majestic Mt. Zion, for all to behold. Picture the river of living water cascading down the mountain, splashing into a wide pool at the base. Fruit-bearing trees line its banks, creating a lush and pristine park. Just as the beauty of Heaven will delight both the eyes and the soul, so will the food of Heaven. We will be both physically and spiritually healthy, for the leaves on the trees assure healing and wholeness for all.

And could I add a moat around our city? After all, it is a *Kingdom*. And feast your eyes on Zechariah 14:8–9:

> On that day living water will flow out from Jerusalem, half to the eastern sea and half to the western sea, in summer and in winter. The LORD will be king over the whole earth.

The prophet Ezekiel described a similar scene in *Ezekiel 47:1–12*. (If you have extra time today, you'd enjoy reading it.) He saw a river flowing from the Temple. It grew deeper and wider as it exited through the gates. Fruit trees of all kinds, with leaves for healing, lined its banks. Everywhere the mighty river flowed, everything came to life. Salt water became fresh. Fish of every kind swarmed the waters. Fishermen lined the river's banks with their nets. (Don't you know the Apostle Peter will be among them? So much for manning the pearly gates! He'll really be "in heaven" then—on the banks of the Great River, hauling in the fish!)

Did you notice the mention of "months" in Rev. 22:2? Look back at Zechariah 14:8-9. The seasons will change as well! When the curse upon the Earth is lifted, there will be *no more* devastating storms, frigid temperatures, or excruciating heat. Yet we will enjoy changes in scenery and temperature! Heaven will *never* be monotonous—even in its perfection!

Heaven will never be monotonous—even in its perfection!

As our bus drives down the main thoroughfare of the City of God, go ahead and daydream a bit. Picture yourself on a walk with the Lord... in the "cool of the day" of course. You pick the season. The path by the water's edge is strewn with leaves—the leaves of healing. Why not stop and have a picnic? Drink deeply of the water of life. Eat freely of the fruit of any tree. Enjoy the company of your Savior. Plan "R" is accomplished: Paradise has been regained!

As we depart the Holy City, I can't help but remember the book *Return From Tomorrow*. The author George Ritchie writes of an after-death experience in an army hospital in 1943. During the nine minutes he was pronounced legally dead, he went on a journey with Jesus to Heaven and Hell. Near the end of his experience, he was allowed one tiny glimpse of a "glowing, seemingly endless city . . ." *Our New Jerusalem!* When he realized he was about to return to life on Earth, George pleaded with Jesus:

> Desperately I cried out to Him not to leave me, to make me ready for that shining city, not to abandon me in this dark and narrow place... The light of Jesus had entered my life and filled it completely, and the idea of being separated from Him was more than I could bear.[28]

The Shining City. Can you see it? Has its promise filled your heart? One day we will have more than a fleeting glimpse of it. We will call it Home. The light of Jesus will fill our lives completely and we will never be separated from Him again.

We've always wanted to live in a perfect world. One day we will.

WEEK 5
A Change of Clothing

*O*ver the years I have had the enormous pleasure of designing houses for friends. It's a marvelous process! A "dream home" moves from the imagination, to a drawing, to a three dimensional space. A vague wish list becomes a custom-designed house. The best moment comes when the owners move in with all their unique treasures and transform their dream into a real home.

One such couple held a dinner party to celebrate their new house. I was excited to be included. Surely I would enjoy the "oohs" and "aahs" as others toured this beautiful home for the first time. It would be a big moment for me.

I did receive much attention that evening, but not due to my architectural ability! Mid-way through the evening, the hostess came over to my side and called for the guests' attention. With laughter in her eyes, she directed everyone to look at my feet. To my horror, I was wearing two different shoes! Worse still—they were not the least bit alike. One was a blue flat; the other was a multicolored pump. How did I even walk without a limp? So much for my big moment. My faux pas was the cause of much laughter over the years, my own included.

Last week we toured the glorious residence of God. Our vague wish lists became Three-dimensional. Our heavenly home could not be more spectacular, yet it is custom-designed just for us. And did you know that Jesus is planning to host a dinner party at the completion of His Father's House? Invitations are still going out! Preparations are being made. People from all over the world—*from all over time*—will be in attendance. Talk about a *big* moment! Not only will we be *in* glory—we will be *with* Glory!

Which makes me want to look at my feet. What will I be like in such a place, in such company? Will I feel awkward and horribly out of place in such beauty and perfection? What will I wear? What will I feel like and be like? Since I can't even get my act together on this Earth, how will I ever fit in Heaven?

God has some good news for those of us with miss-matched shoes! A change of clothing has been ordered. Our Father plans to outfit us from head to toe. Our new wardrobe will include new hearts, new minds, and new bodies. In the biggest moment of our lives, God will present you and I "without fault and with great joy" (Jude 1:24). Let's discover how!

DAY 1 *no-body or some-body?*

FOR THE NEXT THREE DAYS we are going to study scriptures that describe what our bodies will be like in Heaven. All kinds of possibilities fill our minds. Will we be like ghosts, angels, or (gulp) the four creatures? Maybe we will be like superheroes, able to leap tall buildings in a single bound! As a child, I had a recurring dream in which I could fly. I would be in some sort of danger and right when my would-be captors were going to grab me, I would bound from the Earth to the sky! (Nowadays I'd be happy to simply bound out of bed in the morning!)

(☺) **How about you? What would you like your eternal body to be able to do?**

Our culture puts such an emphasis on physical beauty. We often long to look like someone else, especially when we are young. Being tall, I wanted to be short. Having wavy hair, I tried to straighten it. Being fair-skinned, I scorched myself to get a tan. As we grow older, we work hard to keep our bodies healthy and in shape. Yet often our goals are unrealistic and our efforts are in vain. I'll never forget my mom asking my sister and I to never allow her out of the house in sleeveless shirts once her arms started to sag! Our bodies rarely look like we wish they would. Will we ever approve?

When considering what our bodies will be like in Heaven, we must divide Scripture rightly between the *Present Heaven* and the *Eternal Heaven*.

As we studied in *Week Three*, at the Rapture all believers on Earth and in Heaven receive their *resurrected, eternal* bodies. We also learned that instantly upon the death of a believer, his or her spirit goes to be with Jesus. But it is not clear what sort of body, if any, is given to those who die in Christ prior to the Rapture. Are we given some sort of "intermediate" body, or are we bodiless spirits until the Resurrection Day?

We've tackled this question to a degree in previous lessons. In Jesus' illustration of Heaven and Hell, Lazarus, the rich man and Abraham seemed to have ordinary human form and were recognizable to one another. Our observations of the elders in the book of Revelation gave us a similar impression. Does Scripture provide more insight?

Let's begin with *2 Corinthians 5:1–5.*

(💬) **How does Paul contrast our earthly body to our heavenly body?** (v. 1)

(💬) **How does Paul feel about the prospect of being "naked," or without a body?**

(💬) **How do you feel about it?**

As far as we know, the human soul has never existed in a disembodied state. God gave Adam a body *before* He breathed in His spirit (Gen. 2:7). We can only assume that God follows the same pattern as He knits each babe in the mother's womb (Ps. 139:13). Would God leave us unclothed in the Present Heaven while we await our eternal, glorified bodies? Plato believed the spirit was imprisoned in the body and would be liberated at death. Paul seemed to consider an unclothed state abhorrent. Christianity teaches that we become *more* than we were before death*, never less.*

We do have an eyewitness account of two men, Moses and Elijah, who visited Earth long after their "deaths." They appear with Jesus at His transfiguration. Interestingly, both men had unusual departures from the Earth. Moses was buried by God Himself (Deut. 34:6) and Elijah was taken to Heaven in a chariot of fire (2 Kings 2:11). We assume both men came from *Abraham's Side* where all the deceased believers dwelt before Jesus' resurrection.

Read of the account in *Luke 9:28–36.*

How does Jesus appear? (v. 29)

Describe Moses and Elijah. What do they do and what do they know? (v. 31)

Although Moses and Elijah appeared in "glorious splendor," they were identifiable as men. It's interesting to consider how the disciples could have recognized them—there were no "Kodak moments" in their day! Perhaps God disclosed who they were, or perhaps something about their appearance revealed their identity. It is entirely possible that God created earthly bodies for Moses and Elijah to inhabit just for this trip to Planet Earth. It's even possible that Elijah never lost his body! But it is also likely that after our deaths, God outfits us in "intermediate" bodies that look entirely human, making us recognizable to one another.

It's interesting to note that Moses and Elijah *knew what was about to take place on Earth.* Remember the songs of the elders in the Present Heaven? They possessed knowledge of God's plan for mankind and were anxious for Jesus' Second Coming. Scripture also indicates that those in Heaven are aware when each person on Earth repents of their sins and joins the family of God (Luke 15:10). It's safe to conclude that those in Heaven aren't ignorant of *God's work on Earth.* They probably *do not* know and see every detail of our earthly lives—that's God's business alone. But they *do* know about eternal matters and add their prayers to ours. It seems God continues to enlist the assistance of the saints in His redemptive work, even while in Heaven.

Peter's idea of building three shelters to have a sleepover with the men from Heaven is "peter-esque." He often didn't quite "get it" and would speak out of turn! "He did not know what to say, they were so frightened" (Mark 9:6). Who can blame them for being frightened? In Peter's defense, however, his desire for heavenly people to live on Earth was prophetic! On the New Earth, Peter *will* be able to camp on Mt. Tabor with Moses, Elijah and Jesus! He was just ahead of God's schedule.

Did you notice how Moses and Elijah suddenly disappeared? It appears as though our heavenly state allows for miraculous transport—like in my childhood dreams!

We see a glimpse of Jesus' splendor in this passage. "His face shone like the sun" (Matt. 17:2) and His clothes become dazzling white, bright as lightning. The light seems to radiate from *within* Him. Such a revelation gives us understanding as to why there will be no need of the sun in the New Jerusalem. It also gives us a sneak preview of how dazzling *we* will be one day, when we become like Him! (We'll study more about it on *Day Three* and *Four*.)

We can learn more about what our heavenly bodies will be like from the descriptions of those in the Present Heaven in the book of Revelation. Keep in mind, John's recorded vision concerns "what will take place later" (Rev. 1:19). In other words, John was seeing into the *future* Present Heaven. The two scenes we will read about today take place *after* the Tribulation on Earth has begun, but *before* Christ returns. If the Rapture has *not* yet occurred, or if these martyrs were killed during the Tribulation, we have an account of our pre-resurrection state.

Read *Revelation 6:9–11.*

(?) Describe those under the altar. How do they appear?

(?) What does this scene reveal about those in the Present Heaven?

At first glance, it seems those "under the altar" are disembodied spirits because the text refers to them as "souls." The Greek word (*psuche*) may also be translated "life, mind, or heart." It carries the meaning of "the breath of life," or of a "living being," referring to the total person. Paul used it to describe our earthly state: "So also it is written, "The first man, Adam, became a living soul" (1 Cor. 15:45, NAS).

Adam became a *psuche* when God breathed life into his *body*. Therefore, the use of the word "soul" does not prove we will be bodiless in the Present Heaven.

Regardless of whether these martyrs have a physical body, this passage confirms that the *soul* does not sleep until the Resurrection. The martyrs speak, pray, think, learn, and interact with one another and with God. They remember what occurred on Earth and are passionately involved in God's unveiling plan. They are aware of the passage of time and are anxious for God to act on their behalf. Although their white robes are symbolic of their purity, righteousness, and deeds, their clothes also suggest a physical body.

I'm struck by the desire of the martyrs to have their blood avenged. Have you ever wondered how we will be completely happy and at peace in Heaven knowing that many people refuse to repent and receive God's love? It seems the occupants of Heaven have God's mind on the matter and understand His justice.

Let's study one more passage. Read *Revelation 7:9–17.*

How are the occupants of the Present Heaven described? (vs. 9, 14)

What are they doing? (vs. 9- 10, 15)

Some scholars believe this great multitude to be the martyrs of Revelation 6:9, joined by others who died during the Tribulation days on Earth. The Apostle John describes them as being from "every nation, tribe, people, and language," which leads us to believe that we will retain our racial and ethnic identity in Heaven. In the same vein, we will very likely remain male and female in Heaven. God's plan is to keep you *you*—and your nationality, race and gender are a part of *who* you are, not just what you look like. In Heaven, humanity won't become one skin color or one sex. But we will become one in our praise to God! One fine day we will at last celebrate our differences instead of fighting over them.

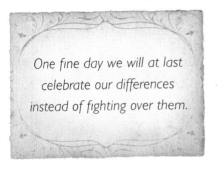

One fine day we will at last celebrate our differences instead of fighting over them.

Did you notice the *palm branches* in the multitude's hands? Palm branches were an important symbol to Israel. The walls of the Temple were adorned with them (1 Kings 6:29). The palm tree was a symbol of victory and the prosperity of the righteous (Ps. 92:12). It also represented the healing presence of God. While in the wilderness, God revealed Himself to the Hebrew people as the God "who heals you" (Exod. 15:26). He then led them to Elim, a place of twelve springs and seventy palm trees. Similarly, in this scene in Heaven, God leads His people to "springs of living water" and wipes every tear from their eyes. Heaven is a place of *rest* and *healing*.

But it is also a place of great celebration! With the giving of the Law, God instituted several annual festivals for the Hebrew people. The final festival of the year was the Feast of Tabernacles (or Booths). It was celebrated after the crops had been gathered. God commanded His people to cease work and celebrate His goodness for seven days. (God knows you and I need a break every now and then!) Each family would construct and live in a tabernacle made of branches and palm fronds in remembrance of God's protection and guidance in the wilderness (Lev. 23:39–43). The booths represented God's shelter from the heat, storms, and rain (Isa. 4:6). During the last day of the feast, known as the great Hosanna Day, the Israelites would rejoice before the Lord, celebrating His goodness, shaking their palm branches before an altar decorated with willow branches.[29]

In Revelation 7, the Lord of the Harvest has gathered His harvest of souls before Him. This great family *celebrates God's goodness* with palm branches in hand. They have arrived safely in the ultimate Promised Land. God spreads *His* tent (or tabernacle) over them and they will dwell inside the joy of God's canopy forever—free from heat, hunger, and thirst. Isn't it amazing how much we learn about Heaven just from the presence of a palm branch?

We'll continue our study of our heavenly bodies tomorrow. Although we may not be able to conclusively determine what sort of bodies we will have in the Present Heaven, a body seems necessary for the described activities. I'm relieved to know that I won't be invisible or unrecognizable! Simple common sense tells us that if the Present Heaven contains a city with streets of gold, its occupants would need feet to walk upon them! However, there is also a mighty good reason why God plans to outfit all His children with eternal bodies at the same moment. God is saving something incredibly special until everyone in the family arrives Home. Therefore, a major change of clothing is in store for those in the Present Heaven at the Rapture. And even *if* we have no bodies until that day, we'll never be a *no-body* in Heaven! We are preciously *some-body* to our Father God, our Lord Jesus Christ, and the Blessed Holy Spirit. God will care for us.

DAY 2 *a body to die for*

OFTEN WE HEAR SOMEONE COMPLIMENT another by saying, "He/she has a body to die for." It's a rather funny saying in light of Paul's words in 1 Corinthians 15. Paul claimed that each of us *will* have a body to die for—but we will have to die for it! Hmm… it's no wonder that the Corinthian church had difficulty understanding the resurrection of the dead! The Greek culture accepted the immortality of the *soul* but not the immortality of the *body*. They considered the body to be sinful and weak and reasoned that death would set the soul free. Such influence caused the Christians in Corinth to believe that a bodily resurrection would enslave the soul again. They misunderstood the gospel's hope and God's ability to produce a heavenly body. Paul addressed their confusion in a portion of his first letter to them, now known as the "Resurrection Chapter" of the Bible. We've studied parts of this chapter. Let's take a fresh look at it today.

Please read *1 Corinthians 15:35–49* and answer the following questions:

What does nature teach us about the resurrection of our bodies? (vs. 36–39)

Based on Paul's illustration, will our spiritual bodies differ from our earthly ones? (v. 37)

Will our spiritual bodies be related to our earthly ones? (v. 38)

How would you answer Paul's questions: "How are the dead raised?" and "With what kind of body do they come?" (vs. 42–45, 49)

Let's consider Paul's points concerning our resurrection:

1. Although we cannot explain how life comes forth from death, we see it demonstrated in nature. When a seed "dies," a new plant begins to grow. What is true in the physical realm is also true in the spiritual. Our earthly bodies will die, yet new resurrected bodies will come forth. (The exception being those alive at Jesus' return.)

2. Just as the plant differs from the seed, so our heavenly bodies will be different from our earthly ones. Yet the plant has absolute identity with the seed. An acorn becomes an oak tree, not a palm tree. God has set us apart on Earth through fingerprints and DNA. He isn't about to throw our uniqueness out in Heaven! There *is* continuity between our earthly bodies and our heavenly ones. We do not become someone or something else! That would be reincarnation, not resurrection. Yet...

3. Verses 42–44 declare the *superiority* of our eternal bodies. Our present bodies die because of the "dishonor" of sin. Our new bodies will *never* be weak or sick or age! Flesh and blood cannot inherit the Kingdom of God (1 Cor. 15:50) for eternal life requires eternal bodies. A new system will replace the old.

4. God will give us a body as He has determined. He is clearly able to create bodies ideally suited to each species and each environment. All possess their own unique splendor. Our earthly bodies, made from the earth, are suited for earthly conditions. In like manner, our spiritual bodies will be just right for the *Eternal Heaven* (which includes a New Earth). And during the interim, God will provide the perfect outfit for the *Present Heaven*.

   Just like a seed contains the blueprint for a plant, so our natural body contains the blueprint for our spiritual body. Joni Eareckson Tada writes:

Somehow, somewhere within you is the pattern of the heavenly person you will become, and if you want to catch a glimpse of how glorious and full of splendor your body will be, just do a comparison. Compare a hairy peach pit with the tree it becomes, loaded with fragrant blossoms and sweet fruit. They are totally different, yet the same. Compare a caterpillar with a butterfly. A wet, musty flower bulb with an aromatic hyacinth. A hairy coconut with a graceful palm tree… You and what you will one day be are one and the same—yet different.[30]

5. We will bear the likeness of the man from Heaven! This is our greatest clue to our heavenly outfit. We will look to Jesus as our example in our next two lessons.

So how are the dead raised? What kind of body will we have? Mark your place in 1 Corinthians, for we will be coming back. **Let these scriptures add to your understanding:**

Romans 4:17 **What can God do?**

Phil. 3:20–21 **What kind of body will we have? How is resurrection accomplished?**

The God who spoke and worlds were created, the God who formed us from the dirt, the God who raised His Son from the dead… *this* God will resurrect *your* body. He can call things into being that do not exist. *All things*—inanimate or animate, in the sea, or sky, or under the Earth are subject to Jesus. God has the power to *breathe life* into anything or anyone:

> "… if the Spirit of him who raised Jesus from the dead is living in you, he who raised Christ from the dead will also give life to your mortal bodies through his Spirit, who lives in you."

> (Rom. 8:11)

In *Day Four/Week Three* we studied the Resurrection Day of the church, also called the Rapture. But there is more to learn! Let's return to *1 Corinthians 15* and read *verses 50–54* for additional insight into this spectacular day.

(⟳) **What will herald our transformation?** (v. 52)

The Hebrew people annually celebrated the Feast of Trumpets two weeks prior to the Feast of Tabernacles. It was a time for remembrance and new beginnings. When the new moon rose in Israel in the month of Tishri (September-October), watchers would blow the trumpet from hill to hill until the signal reached the Temple. From the Temple Mount the High Priest would blow the ram's horn to announce the beginning of the New Year, Rosh Hashanah.[31] The people were to remember when trumpets sounded the alarm of war and how the Lord saved them from their enemies (Numbers 10:9).

(⟳) **In light of the Feast of Trumpets, what might the trumpet call at the Rapture represent?**

Just as the trumpet was used to announce or call forth an assembly in Israel, Heaven's trumpet blast will call forth an assembly—in the air! The "sleeping" bodies of those living in the Present Heaven will be raised imperishable. The mortal bodies of believers living upon the Earth will be made immortal. Picture the sound of the heavenly trumpet moving from hill to hill throughout all the Earth as Jesus gathers each believer. What a *new* year it will be as we are clothed in *new* bodies. And just as the Feast of Trumpets preceded the Feast of Tabernacles, the Rapture precedes Jesus' return to Earth, when He will dwell—or *tabernacle*—among us. Isn't God's Word grand? And there's more...

1 Thessalonians 4:16 informs us that not only will there be a *trumpet* call at the Rapture, Jesus will also descend with a "shout." According to Thayer's Greek Definitions, the Greek word translated "shout," *keleuma*, means "an

order, command, a stimulating cry... that by which animals are roused and urged on by man, as horses by charioteers... "[32]

(?) **Do you recall how Elijah was transported to Heaven? (If not, read** *2 Kings 2:11–12*.)

Could Elijah's rapture be a preview of the Rapture of the Church? Wouldn't it be awesome to be whisked away to Heaven in our very own horse-driven chariot of fire? Visualize the sky lit up with God's own version of fireworks! And, contrary to popular thinking, the unbelievers left on Earth *may* observe this phenomenon.

I think it's worth the trip to *Revelation 11:7–12* to read about the rapture of two prophetic witnesses during the Tribulation. (But don't lose your place in 1 Corinthians!) During the last days on Earth, these two men will continually and powerfully testify of God and therefore will be hated by the Antichrist and those who align themselves with him.

(?) **How will God revive the dead bodies of the two prophets and how will they be taken to Heaven?** (vs. 11- 12)

(?) **Will there be witnesses to the prophets' death, resurrection and ascension?** (vs. 9–10, 12)

(?) **Why might God do such an extraordinary thing?** (Reading *verses 13–15* may give you some insight.)

During the Tribulation days on Earth, the occupants of Earth have precious time left to accept God's offer of redemption. Maybe that is why God opens the heavens for all to see! The news of the death of the two prophets in Jerusalem reaches *all* the inhabitants of the Earth. (Most likely it will be played and replayed on TV!) Then, before a watching world, God demonstrates His resurrection power. Two lifeless bodies stand to their feet and ride a cloud to Heaven! *Wow!*

Our God can do *anything!* He can *breathe life* into the most hopeless situation. And we don't have to wait until the Rapture to experience His resurrection power. God *delights* to take what is meant for evil and turn it into good (Gen. 50:20).

(:?) **What seemingly dead situation in your life needs God's breathe of life?**

Ask Him for what only He can do! There can be no *permanent loss* in our lives if we invite God's resurrection power to bring forth a victory of His making.

It is time for one last trip back to *1 Corinthians 15*. Read Paul's words of hope recorded in *verses 55–58*.

(:?) **What is the Good News of this passage?**

(:?) **According to verse 58, how are we to live in light of such news?**

(:?) **Once again, heavenly-mindedness leads to earthly_____ !**

Years ago, I was designing a house for a married couple who made an unusual request. They wanted a large eastern window in their bedroom. Normally people don't want to be awakened at dawn, so I voiced my concerns. I've never forgotten their response! They told me that they wanted to open their eyes each morning to see if the Lord had returned! "For as lightning that comes from the east is visible even in the west, so will be the coming of the Son of Man" (Matt. 24:27). What a way to start every day! No doubt their attitude for the day ahead was affected by those first few moments of expectation. Those who have the greatest *hope* respond to life with the greatest *diligence*.

For two thousand years the faithful have hoped their generation would be the one that never died—the generation that would hear the trumpet sound and be caught up to Heaven in a whirlwind. But *every* person who has trusted Jesus as their Lord and Savior, whether they reside in Heaven or upon the Earth, will be a part of this spectacular homecoming in the sky. Jesus *is* coming again and His first order of business is to give every follower a resurrected, immortal body. In the twinkling of an eye, you and I will have a body to die for!

> *Therefore we do not lose heart. Though outwardly we are wasting away, yet inwardly we are being renewed day by day. For our light and momentary troubles are achieving for us an eternal glory that far outweighs them all. So we fix our eyes not on what is seen, but on what is unseen. For what is seen is temporary, but what is unseen is eternal.*
>
> (2 COR. 4:16–18)

DAY 3 *"it is I Myself!"*

YESTERDAY WE LEARNED THAT OUR heavenly bodies will bear the likeness of Jesus, for He "will transform our lowly bodies so that they will be like his glorious body" (Phil. 3:21). I like the word "glorious" defining my "to die for" body, don't you? My desire for Heaven is growing stronger by the minute! The Greek word *doxa* translated "glorious" denotes "an appearance commanding respect, magnificence, excellence, or manifestation of glory."[33] Sounds like we're in for an extreme makeover of the Divine kind!

Yet I still can't help asking, "Just what does a glorious body *look* like?" So today we will fix our eyes upon the resurrected Jesus to find the answer. We will read the resurrection account in two of the gospels, answering *lots* of questions before we draw conclusions as to what sort of body we will receive. As you read, keep in mind that Jesus' tremendous suffering on the cross was for this very gift—to bestow upon you an eternal body for eternal life with the Eternal God. The gift was given in joy. Open it with faith!

1. John 20:1–18

(?) Did the disciples and Mary immediately understand what the empty tomb meant? (v. 9) Why might that be?

(?) What was Mary's frame of mind when the angels and Jesus spoke to her? (vs. 11, 13, 15)

(?) Who did Mary initially think the Risen Christ was? What made her recognize Him? (vs. 14–16)

(?) What did Mary do when she recognized Jesus? (v. 17)

2. John 20:19–20, 24–30

(?) Locked doors did not prevent Jesus from entering the room where His disciples hid. What can we infer about His resurrected body? (vs. 19, 26)

(?) Jesus showed the disciples, and later Thomas, His hands and His side. Why did He do so? (v. 27)

How does Jesus desire for us to respond to His resurrected state? (vs. 29, 30)

3. John 21:1–14

What caused the disciples to recognize Jesus? (You might want read *Luke 5:4–7* to help with the answer.)

What did Jesus have waiting for them on the shore? (v. 9)

4. Luke 24:13–35

Why did the two disciples not recognize the Risen Jesus? (vs. 16, 31)

When and why were they able to recognize Him? (vs. 30–32)

5. Luke 24:36–43 (This account corresponds to and adds information to John 20:19–20.)

What was the disciples' first reaction to Jesus' appearing? Why? (v. 37)

(?) What was Jesus' response to them? (vs. 38–39)

(?) In what additional way did Jesus prove He was not a ghost? (vs. 41–42)

(?) *Finally*, the disciples believed in the bodily resurrection. **What was their ultimate response to the Good News, according to Luke 24:50–53?**

Good work! Now, let's see what conclusions we can come to.

(?) **From all you read, how would you describe Jesus' resurrected body?**

(?) **What was Jesus' main concern for His disciples?**

Let's begin with the tender encounter between Mary and Jesus. Mary Magdalene was the first one Jesus blessed with the glorious news of His resurrection. Jesus had freed her from seven demons, and she had thereafter been devoted to Him. Mary was one of the few followers present at Calvary. Jesus had seen her anguish as she witnessed His. Surely this meeting was part of "the joy set before Him" as He endured the cross (Hebrews 12:2). Imagine His delight as her mourning gave way to *gladness* and her despair became *praise* (Isa. 61:3).

If Jesus hadn't given Mary the task of telling the disciples that He was alive, she very likely would have never let Him go. Jesus' request for her to stop clinging to Him may at first seem a bit harsh. But the Greek word *haptomai* translated "hold on to" or "touch" means "to fasten or attach oneself to, to adhere, to exert influence upon."[34] Get the picture? Mary was holding on to Him for dear life! She had lost Him once and *did not* want to lose Him again. Jesus had to gently remind her that He still must go to the Father.

Recently I witnessed a soldier's homecoming on TV. The soldier's mom held him in a death grip and repeated over and over in his ear, "I'll never let you out of my sight again!" Don't you know that is how Mary felt? We may react just the same when we first see Jesus—holding on to Him with all our might, never wanting to let Him go.

When Jesus first appeared to the disciples, they are afraid. But after He convinces them that He is *not a spirit,* they are overjoyed.

(?) **Why might that be?**

Beside the fact that ghosts are just plain scary, the disciples would not have doubted Jesus would "live on" as a spirit in Heaven. What they couldn't comprehend, even after Jesus' repeated revelations to them, was that His *earthly body* would rise from the dead and live forever. This was *truly* victory over death! *Eternal* life was a *physical* life!

We can only imagine how much this first moment with the disciples meant to Jesus. *At last* His companions would understand what had been accomplished for their sakes. Jesus declared to them, "It is I Myself!" Imagine Jesus telling His friends:

> "It's really *Me*! I am *risen*! My body is *real!* No, no, I promise I am *not* a ghost! Ghosts don't have flesh and bones. Touch Me and see! Look at My scars! Watch Me eat! Listen to what the Scriptures say of Me… don't you see? It says I will *rise from the dead.* And so shall *you!* Believe this! Preach this! Teach this! Not only is the soul immortal, your *body* shall be as well."

Jesus leaves no room for doubt concerning the reality of His resurrected body. Once the disciples finally had their eyes and minds open to the truth of resurrection, they were full of joy and praise. *This was their Jesus! He was alive!*

Yet Jesus' body seems so human and so ordinary that at times His followers did not even take notice of Him. Mary thought that He was the gardener. The two on the road to Emmaus thought that He was a fellow traveler. The disciples-turned-fishermen thought that Jesus was just an interested bystander on the beach. His "glorious body" was not full of light like at His transfiguration. Will our bodies be so unchanged? In the book of Revelation, we get a glimpse of Jesus after His ascension into Heaven. His appearance in those accounts is anything but ordinary. But it's vital for us to understand that the hope Jesus gave the world was that the *human body*, even though seemingly destroyed by death, would rise and live forever.

Does the fact that Jesus' closest friends were slow to recognize Him mean that He no longer looked like Himself? Let's think about each instance, because recognition in Heaven is an important issue. When the disciples were fishing, they had seen the Risen Christ on two previous occasions. So they either had sleep in their eyes, or fish on their brains! Jesus' fishing tip tipped them off as to who He was. Then the race was on to get to Jesus' side. This time no one had to ask, "Who are You?"

Mary had tear-flooded eyes. She was so distraught at the tomb, she didn't even react to the sight of the angels! Have you ever been in such a state? So dazed by grief or disbelief that you barely took notice of your surroundings? It was only when Jesus spoke her name that she turned toward Him and recognized her Lord.

The Emmaus travelers' had veiled eyes, supernaturally preventing them from recognizing the Risen Christ. Jesus knew just the way to expose their doubts and expand their faith. What a moment it must have been when He broke the bread and their eyes were opened! I'm so thankful that God still enjoys surprising us with His presence! The Holy Spirit is always willing to open our minds and explain the Scriptures to us. And we have a standing dinner invitation with the Son (Rev. 3:20). If we'll but walk and talk with Him, Jesus will set our hearts on fire and our feet to running, just as the Emmaus boys.

In each of Jesus' appearances, recognition came quickly when He said or did something familiar. I think the failure of His followers' to recognize Him had to do more with their state of mind than with any change in Jesus' appearance. They were so shocked by His physical resurrection that it took some time for their brains to register what their eyes were seeing. Finally, at Jesus' patient insistence, the unbelievable was believed. As a result, their shouts of joy could not be silenced. Two thousand years later, their excitement is still music to human ears.

How does Jesus' physical state impact your expectation of Heaven?

Are you curious as to why nearly every appearance of the Risen Christ involved a meal? No doubt it was intended to prove that Jesus was not a ghost. But food is the focus of several of Jesus' comments about Heaven. He comforted His disciples at the Last Supper with the news that this would *not* be their last meal together (Luke 22:15–18). We will be "at the table" with Abraham, Isaac, and Jacob (Matt. 8:11, NAS). Although Scripture suggests that our eternal bodies may not require food as our present bodies do (1 Cor. 6:13), it does imply that food will nourish our souls (Rev. 22:2). Mealtimes inspire good conversation and fellowship. Heaven will be an eternity of both!

Although Jesus' body looked ordinary and did ordinary things like eating, it was nonetheless extraordinary! He could do all the things a spirit could do—He appeared and disappeared and walked through locked doors! It's no wonder that the disciples thought He was a ghost. But even before His resurrection, Jesus demonstrated His ability to overcome laws of nature. (When He walked on water, His disciples thought He was a ghost then too!) But in His resurrected state, Jesus purposely displays His power over earthly elements. Perhaps it was to demonstrate how *our* humble bodies will be changed upon our resurrection. We are promised "glorious freedom" in our glorified state (Romans 8:21). Acts 8:39–40 records that the Spirit of God snatched up Philip and transported him to a different city! In Heaven, we will be *completely enveloped* by the presence of the Spirit. Who knows what new abilities will be possible?

Jesus spent *forty days* upon Earth before ascending to Heaven. He put to death fear and doubt. He resurrected faith and joy. He made *absolutely sure* that His loved ones knew what had been accomplished through His death and resurrection. We will share eternity with a God we can see and touch! We will share it with a God we can hug and who will hug us back! We will share it with a God who fixes breakfast for us by the Sea and walks with us along the road. *How incredible.*

Jesus jubilantly proclaimed to all who would listen, "It is I Myself!" I grin as I picture us on glory's side, pinching ourselves in joyful discovery, exclaiming, "It is I myself! It is really me! It is really true!" There will be a *glorious* new you on a *glorious* New Earth with your *glorious* Savior and God. *Blessed are those who have not seen and yet believe!*

DAY 4 *inside and out*

THIS WEEK WE HAVE CELEBRATED Scripture's promise of a heavenly change of clothing. We've studied how Jesus was described following His resurrection and discovered that He was *not* a vaporous phantom. He was flesh and bone! His closest friends may have mistaken Him for *someone* else, but not for *something* else! I take comfort in knowing we won't become ghost-like, alien-like, or even angel-like. We will still be ourselves, yet new and improved in every way. I anxiously anticipate the instantaneous improvement that has been promised! Obviously, an indestructible, imperishable body that never ages, wearies, or gets the sniffles will be wonderful! A body fully empowered by the Spirit of God and capable of amazing feats is even more appealing. Today we will look again at Jesus as our example. But this time Jesus appears a bit different than He did on Earth. His appearance (and appearing!) caused an old friend quite a shock.

You'll find the surprising encounter in *Revelation 1:9–20.*

John was so stunned at the sight of Jesus that he "fell at his feet as though dead." **How do you respond to John's description of Jesus?**

Jesus made a surprise visit from Heaven to our friend John upon the isle of Patmos approximately sixty years after His ascension. John was worshipping "in the Spirit" when the object of his worship showed up! Wouldn't *that* change a church service! John knew Jesus as intimately as anyone. He had been with Jesus at His transfiguration and he had seen the Risen Christ. But *this* Jesus "floored" John! I'm encouraged by how Jesus touches John and dispels his fears. He is the awesome, omnipotent Son of God, yet He never wants us to be afraid of Him. So let's take a deep breath and try not to let this description of Jesus scare *us!*

Did you notice John's repeated use of the word "like"? His head and hair were *like*; His eyes were *like*; His feet were *like*; His voice was *like*; His face was *like*... etc. John could not find the words to adequately describe what his eyes were beholding! Perhaps the greatest revelation is John's first observation—Jesus was *like* a son of *man*. Heaven's Christ remains a man forever! What glory and honor God has ascribed to the human race.

Yet He is so much more than a man. Having ascended to Heaven, Jesus' divinity is no longer veiled as it was on Earth. The word "revelation" means "unveiling." Jesus' appearance represents *who He is*—His character and His position as the Son of God. Since *our* glorious body will be like His, let's spend a few moments considering each description of Jesus.

Listed in the left-hand column of the chart below is a title of Jesus along with additional insights into His character. Listed in the right-hand column is each description of Jesus in John's vision. **Decide which title best matches each description.** (I did the first one as an example.)

#	Who Jesus Is	How Jesus Appears
3	The Living One; the Holy One; splendor encircling His Head denotes a crown of glory.	1. Like a son of man
	The Word of God (John 1:1); the Word is sharper than a two-edge sword and it judges the thoughts and attitudes of the heart (Heb. 4:12).	2. Dressed in a robe with a golden sash
	Judge (John 5:27); He puts His enemies under His feet (1 Cor. 15:25).	3. Head and hair white like wool and snow
	The Messiah (Luke 19:10); God became man (Phil 2:8).	4. Eyes like blazing fire
	The Great High Priest and the King of Kings; robe is clothing of priest or king (Ex. 28); girdle is a symbol of power, righteousness, truth (Isa.11:5).	5. Feet like bronze glowing in a furnace
	Omniscient (John 1:48); all-penetrating nature of Divine knowledge.	6. In His mouth came a sharp double-edge sword
	The Light of the World (John 8:12); His glory is unveiled.	7. His face was like the sun

Jesus stands before John aglow in His holiness and uncompromising in His truth and judgment. His clothing resembles the robe and sash worn by the High Priest of Israel, symbolizing Jesus' position as the Great High Priest (Hebrews 4:14). Standing in the midst of the church (lampstands), Jesus establishes Himself as the Head of the Church. The seven letters to the churches recorded in Revelation 2–3 are a clear, sharp Word of both commendation and rebuke, symbolized by the double-edged sword coming from His mouth. (Answers: 3, 6, 5, 1, 2, 4, 7.)

I don't imagine that Jesus will forever appear as He does in this first encounter with John. (It would be difficult to get close to Jesus with a sword coming out of His mouth!) His appearance changes in the book of Revelation according to the task before Him. Perhaps *our* character and calling will impact our physical appearance in Heaven as well.

(☺) **Let's read a few scriptures describing our appearance in Heaven. Underline what you learn:**

Daniel 12:2–3 Multitudes who sleep in the dust of the earth will awake: some to everlasting life, others to shame and everlasting contempt. Those who are wise will shine like the brightness of the heavens, and those who lead many to righteousness, like the stars for ever and ever.

Matt 13:43 Then the righteous will shine like the sun in the kingdom of their Father.

Why will we shine in Heaven? I think Moses knows the reason. Read *Exodus 34:29–35.*

(☺) **Why did Moses' face shine?**

No wonder we will shine as the sun and stars—we will constantly be exposed to the Light of the World! Even in our earthly lives, love, joy, and peace have the power to change our appearance. Rest and health do as well. Imagine the face-lift that will result from the lifting of sin, sickness, stress, and aging! Concerning our physical appearance in Heaven, C. S. Lewis wrote: "Remember that the dullest and most uninteresting person you talk to may one day be a creature which, if you saw it now, you would be strongly tempted to worship . . ."[35]

Lewis considered the glorified body as being *inside the soul*, rather than the soul being inside the body.[36] Jesus' appearance in Revelation 1 may support his theory. If so, we need to know what our "insides" are going to look like! For the rest of today and tomorrow, we will study the transformation in store for our hearts, minds, and souls.

Let's begin by reading *1 John 3:2*.

🤔 **When do we become like Jesus?**

🤔 To determine how we will be like Jesus, scan the surrounding verses. Draw a line from the scripture reference to the quality we will possess.

2:20–21	• Pure
2:29	• Loving
3:3-	• Sinless
3:5	• Truthful
3:16	• Righteous

How do you like the "new you" so far? There's more…

🤔 **Read the scriptures below and circle how they describe our heavenly state:**

Colossians 1:22 But now he has reconciled you by Christ's physical body through death to present you holy in his sight, without blemish and free from accusation.

Ephesians 5:25b-27… Christ loved the church and gave himself up for her to make her holy, cleansing her by the washing with water through the word, and to present her to himself as a radiant church, without stain or wrinkle or any other blemish, but holy and blameless.

Jude 1:24 To him who is able to keep you from falling and to present you before his glorious presence without fault and with great joy.

Those of us over fifty years old are especially thrilled to read that we will be *"without wrinkle"* when we're presented to Christ. (Or if you are still young, you might be partial to the news that you will have no "blemish.") Seriously… the Greek word *rhutis*, translated "wrinkle" in Ephesians 5:27 means "a fold (as drawing together), i.e. a wrinkle (especially on the face)."[37] God's Word is full of Good News, isn't it?

Of course, these scriptures describe our new souls! Thankfully, God gives our "insides" a makeover as well as our "outsides." When we are presented before our Judge and King, we will be beautiful *inside and out!*

When I was only thirteen years old, I stood before a judge due to a traffic ticket. I had taken a premature stab at driving. (Bad, bad decision.) In an attempt to look innocent in court, I wore a pink linen dress my grandmother had made for me. (It had a longer hemline than anything else in my closet!) I pulled my hair back with a pink satin ribbon. I wore no make-up or jewelry. Get the picture? I'm sure my parents had a good chuckle when they saw my appearance. It seemed to work, however, because the judge ruled I only had to pay a minimal fine. Whew!

When I stand before my heavenly Judge, my outer appearance will *not* influence Him. He will see right through me! All He will look for is a heart possessed by Jesus Christ. Remarkably, on that day, I won't just *appear* innocent. In God's eyes, I will *be* innocent! Now *that's* what I call a miracle! We can be "transparent" in Heaven because no evil motives will dwell within us. We can "wear our emotions on our sleeve" because all of our feelings will be pure!

How do you respond to the idea of being faultless, undefiled and morally perfect?

Which description of our heavenly "insides" excites you the most?

❏	Holy	❏	Sinless
❏	Pure	❏	Faultless
❏	Joyful	❏	Radiant
❏	Loving	❏	Truthful

Who can choose? I'm glad we will receive all of the above! However, if Jesus had to choose just one word to describe those in Heaven, I think it would be *joyful*. Jesus spoke of Heaven and joy in the same breath. He used a wonderful word for joy, which according to the Greek means "to show one's joy by leaping and skipping, denoting excessive or ecstatic joy and delight."[38] Jesus wants the good news of Heaven to go to our heads *and* to our feet! How long has it been since you leapt and skipped about from pure joy?

My three-year-old joy was caught on film one Christmas morning. I was jumping up and down and spinning about at the sight of the toys around the tree when I abruptly ran out of the room. Moments later, I returned wearing my glasses! I either didn't believe what my eyes were seeing, or I wanted help taking it all in! I'm so glad that in Heaven we will have perfect vision to see the glory surrounding us. And don't you imagine we'll just have a fit of joy? I doubt anyone will act his or her "age" in Heaven. We'll all be like kids on Christmas morning! After all, the Kingdom of Heaven "belongs to such as these" (Matt. 19:14).

In Heaven, every dream, every longing, every measure of treasure will be ours. And imagine how joyful we will be over each other's joy! Paul speaks of it in 1 Thes. 2:19–20:

> For what is our hope, our joy, or the crown in which we will glory in the presence of our Lord Jesus when he comes? Is it not you? Indeed, you are our glory and joy.

Could you use a dose of excessive delight today? **Read the scriptures below and circle each reference to joy.** Allow them to set your feet to dancing!

Isaiah 35:5–6, 10 Then will the eyes of the blind be opened and the ears of the deaf unstopped. Then will the lame leap like a deer, and the mute tongue shout for joy… They will enter Zion with singing; everlasting joy will crown their heads. Gladness and joy will overtake them, and sorrow and sighing will flee away.

Psalm 16:11 (NAS)… in Thy presence is fulness of joy; in Thy right hand there are pleasures forever.

Matt 25:23 (NAS) His master said to him, "Well done, good and faithful slave; you were faithful with a few things, I will put you in charge of many things; enter into the joy of your master."

When we enter into Heaven, we enter into JOY. You could say that joy is the *climate* of Heaven! *And that's reason enough to start rejoicing right now!*

When we live for Jesus, He gives us *His* joy so that *our* joy is made "complete" (John 15:11). The Greek word *pleroo* means "to fill up; to cram." It depicts "a valley filled in; a house filled with perfume; a net crammed full of fish."[39] Let's apply these descriptions of joy to our lives. Christ's joy fills in the valleys of our lives and floods our souls with perfume. Then, as fragrant fishers of men, our nets become full—full of people to take to Heaven with us! Oh for a life crammed full of Jesus' joy!

So go ahead—jump up and down! The truth is, Jesus *expects* you to rejoice over your name being recorded in Heaven (Luke 10:20). Allow that news to lift your spirits and change your perspective! You've been promised an indestructible and immortal body, a perfect and pure heart, a beaming and blameless soul, a host of holy and happy friends, and a loving and lavish God. One day your eyes will behold the magnificent Jesus that John beheld on that island so long ago. And when you see Him as He is, *you will be like Him*—inside and out.

DAY 5 *if I only had...*

AS I CONTEMPLATE TODAY'S SCRIPTURES, I can't help but think of the motley crew from *The Wizard of Oz*. They endured hardships and overcame fears in route to the wizard, hoping that he could give them the one thing most lacking in their lives. Can you remember what each character desired? Their songs revealed their woes: Dorothy longed for a new home in *Somewhere Over the Rainbow;* Scarecrow sang *If I Only Had a Brain;* Tin Woodsman, *If I Only Had a Heart;* and Cowardly Lion, *If I Only Had the Nerve.*

How would your lament go? If I only had_____

_____.

Like the characters of Oz, many of us long for a great mind, a loving heart, or a courageous soul. We may long for a home, a family, or a special friend. All of these will be ours in Heaven. The moment we step out in faith and ask Jesus to be our Savior, God begins the process of making our hearts and minds new (Ezekiel 36:26–27). God transforms us into Christ's likeness "with ever-increasing glory" (2 Cor. 3:18). The Lord uses our yellow-brick-road journeys on Earth to refine our character until we arrive at the Shining City, when God's good work in us is complete (Phil. 1:6). Those presently in Heaven are described as "perfect" (Heb. 12:23). But does our transformation end there? Will we be so perfect in Heaven that we will cease to grow or learn?

Read *Ephesians 2:6–7.*

(?) **Where are you seated?** (v. 6)

(?) **What will God do for you in the coming ages?** (v. 7)

This scripture is good news for those who fear Heaven will be boring or stagnant! Ephesians 2:7 suggests that our hearts will *continue* to grow in love throughout the ages. God will nourish, nurture, and pamper us with an on-going display of His grace and kindness. Such an out-pouring will surely evoke a deeper and fuller measure of love within us. With every drop of His kindness, our heart's reservoir will expand and enlarge with ever increasing glory. After all, we love because He first loved us (1 John 4:19) and He will never tire of loving us!

Along with a new heart to love Him, God will give us a *new mind* to know Him.

Read *1 Corinthians 13:8–12.*

(?) **How is our *present* knowledge of God described?**

(?) **What will happen to our knowledge when "perfection" comes?**

Now read *Jeremiah 31:33–34.*

What will God do for His people?

Why will we need no teacher?

In this present age, God reveals Himself to us through His Word and His Spirit. Yet our lack of faith, our selective hearing, and our sinful nature muddles the message. As we read, "For now we see through a glass, darkly" (KJV). "Darkly" means a riddle, an enigma, or an obscure intimation. Doesn't that aptly describe our attempts to understand God? We now only know God dimly compared to how we will know Him in the perfect light of Heaven. In that day, God's truth will be clear and our present imperfect modes of obtaining knowledge will no longer be necessary.

Yet, I don't believe we will attain all the wisdom and knowledge we'll ever possess in the "twinkling of an eye." From the moment God breathed life into Adam's spirit, He purposely revealed Himself precept by precept. Since He is the same yesterday, today, and forever (Heb. 13:8), His manner of progressive revelation will undoubtedly continue in Heaven. As the created, we will never cease to be amazed by our Creator! God is too rich, too creative, and too generous to ever exhaust. We will not only never get bored, we will be thrilled by endless discovery.

Think expansively when you consider what it means to know God! He encompasses *all* subject matter. He invented math, science, and language. He authored history. He is a master artist and musician. His infinite and omniscient mind will open up the universe to us—no more dim mirrors or child-like reasoning. I hope field trips are part of God's plans to "show us" the riches of His grace. Can you imagine exploring the wonders of the world with the Creator of the world? Since God invented time, we may even be able to visit bygone ages! Wouldn't it be just awesome to witness our favorite historical events? We could attend Jesus' birth, or the original parting of the Red Sea! (I wonder if Charlton Heston truly resembles Moses?) I've no doubt that our Teacher has thousands of ways to *show* us His grace!

Good old-fashioned book learning may continue in Heaven as well. Psalm 119:89 declares, "Your word, O Lord, is eternal; it stands firm in the heavens."

What parts of God's Word are you anxious to understand?

Recently, I spoke with a man whose son suffers from cerebral palsy. At thirteen years old, his son is unable to read, but he is a worshipper! In church, he keeps his Bible open on his lap (although he sometimes holds it upside-down). During the sermon, he claps and raises his hands in response to God's Word. What a day it will be when his *mind* matches his vivacious *spirit*. Even the greatest theological minds will be astounded when face-to-face with the Word Incarnate. Glorious mysteries of God will be unveiled in Heaven—astonishing, delighting, and challenging our new minds.

> When the finger of God writes a truth on the human heart, it is a marvelous yet intensely personal moment.

Think about what it is like when the Spirit of God reveals a truth to you. A scripture you have known all of your life takes on a new depth of meaning. A verse you've never noticed before leaps off the page and into your present need. When God zings a new revelation my way, I can hardly wait to tell a friend or relate it to my class. Hours of digging into God's Word are worth one direct Word from Him! But somehow I'm never able to aptly articulate it—something powerful is lost in the translation. When the finger of God writes a truth on the human heart, it is a marvelous yet intensely personal moment. *Every day in Heaven will be like that, only better.* The more we learn of Him, the more we'll love Him; the more we love Him, the more we'll praise Him; the more we praise Him, the more we'll enjoy Him; the more we enjoy Him, the more we'll learn of Him. Round and round, up and up we'll go into fabulous heights of God.

Eternal life is all about knowing God and Jesus (John 17:3). But not only will we know God as never before, we will also know one another as never before. Consider the context of the verse, "Now I know in part; then I shall know fully, even as I am fully known" (1 Cor. 13:12). Set in the midst of the great love chapter of the Bible, it speaks to our relationships with each other in Heaven.

(?) **What will it be like to know others fully?**

(?) **What will it be like to be fully known by others?**

Even in our most intimate relationships on Earth, we only know each other "in part." Most of us keep a few thoughts to ourselves. We hide parts of ourselves we fear others would dislike or criticize. But masks and pretenses will fall away in Heaven. We will no longer suffer from shame or envy. We will be free of the self-sins that defile us and hinder our ability to love and be loved. We won't be looked down upon, taken advantage of, or misunderstood. There will be no need to protect our hearts from harm. We will be fully known and fully loved; we will know fully and love fully.

While we're on the subject of relationships, let's read *Luke 20:27–40.*

(?) **Will there be marriage in Heaven?**

(?) **What concerns does this create as well as alleviate?**

Jesus taught that in Heaven, we "will neither marry nor be given in marriage." Ephesians 5:31–32 helps us to understand why:

"For this reason a man will leave his father and mother and be united to his wife, and the two will become one flesh." This is a profound mystery—but I am talking about Christ and the church.

(?) **What is earthly marriage a picture of?**

There *will* be marriage in Heaven—to Christ! Earthly marriages are a shadow and a picture of the ultimate union and oneness that will culminate with God in Heaven. Don't think for one moment that there will be the *slightest* ache in your soul or any lack of love! Our heavenly Bridegroom will *fully* satisfy our longings for perfect love. It will be a Love Affair like no other. We will have eternity to know the absolute wonders of His Person. One thing is for sure—we'll never grow accustomed to *His* Face! Imagine dining with Him, asking Him endless questions, looking into His eyes…and He into yours. It's *not* a fairy tale—it's Heaven!

The love we will share with Jesus will outshine all other affairs of the heart; therefore, marriage *as we know it* will cease. But that does *not* mean married couples will cease to love each other! Far from it! In Heaven, our relationships with one another will always be *enhanced*, never *diminished*.

Charles Spurgeon said it well:

I have heard of a good woman, who asked her husband, when she was dying, "My dear, do you think you will know me when you and I get to heaven?" "Shall I know you?" he replied. "Why, I have always known you while I have been here, and do you think I shall be a greater fool when I get to heaven?" I think it was a very good answer. If we have known one another here, we shall know one another there.

Would not that be a dreary heaven for us to inhabit, where we should be alike unknowing and unknown? I would not care to go to such a heaven as that. I believe that heaven is a fellowship of the saints, and that we shall know one another there. I have often thought I should love to see Isaiah.…

O yes! We shall have choice company in heaven when we get there. There will be no distinction of learned and unlearned, clergy and laity, but we shall walk freely one among another; we shall feel that we are brethren; we shall "sit down with Abraham, and Isaac, and Jacob."[40]

🙂 **Who in Heaven would you like to sit down with and enjoy a good long chat?**

🙂 **Who are you looking forward to getting along with at long last?**

It comforts my heart to know that one day I will have all the *time* in the world for all the *people* in the world! Quality *and* quantity time—it can't get any better than that.

Are you curious as to how old we will be in Heaven? I wish the Sadduccees had asked Jesus *that* question! Theological opinion on the matter varies from our being "ageless" to "eternally youthful" to "thirty-something." Perhaps the best answer is that heavenly age is *no age and all ages.*[41] Isaiah's vision of God's Kingdom on Earth included children and infants (Isa. 11:6–9). King David, upon the death of his infant son, expressed his faith in a heavenly reunion (2 Sam. 12:22–23). Without question, God has something incredibly special in store for parents whose young children died or suffered from impairing diseases. Restoring the missed joys of parenthood surely befits God's loving, just, and redeeming heart.

In *Week Four* we set out to discover the "real want for Heaven" present in us. Mull over what we discovered this week and last. We have an amazingly beautiful Home being prepared just for us. We will share a Kingdom with our King. We will live in perfect harmony with creation, all of God's creatures, and all of God's children. We will receive glorious immortal bodies, fully equipped with new hearts and new minds. All our *If I Only Had...* tunes will cease. Whole and well-loved hearts will replace broken and lonely ones. We will possess the ability to know God and His universe in "mind-boggling" ways. We will never again be embarrassed by how we look or by how we act—there'll be no miss-matched shoes for the children of the King!

Let's end the week by declaring to God a few lines from Psalm 84:

How lovely is your dwelling place, O LORD Almighty!
My soul yearns, even faints, for the courts of the
LORD; my heart and my flesh cry out for the living
God. Blessed are those whose strength is in you, who
have set their hearts on pilgrimage. They go from
strength to strength, till each appears before God in
Zion. Better is one day in your courts than a thousand
elsewhere… O LORD Almighty, blessed is the man
who trusts in you.

Is your heart set on pilgrimage? I concur with the psalmist and with Dorothy:
There's no place like Home!

WEEK 6
Hell Week

hen I was outlining the lessons for this course, I kept moving "Hell Week" further to the end of the lineup. I didn't want it to be the final word, but I wanted to put it off as long as possible. Unfortunately, we've arrived at "as long as possible." I tried to find a transitional phrase to take us gracefully from the wonders of Heaven to the torments of Hell, but came up with nothing. I'm sorry. It's Jesus' fault. He never minced words concerning Hell or sugarcoated its reality. He gave it to us straight. I suppose that is the only way.

When I first shared with my pastor my desire to teach about Heaven, he responded, "I wish you'd teach about Hell." I balked! (And I was horribly tempted to answer, "That's *your* job!") Truly, who wants such a message? Would you? I feared being labeled the "Hell Lady." But I remembered a comment of Dr. Adrian Rogers concerning people who think kind preachers never mention Hell. He asked the question, "When people find themselves in Hell, will they still think those preachers are kind?" The greatest kindness is to warn; and Jesus warned of Hell repeatedly. So, please think kindly of me after this week's lesson!

It will be difficult reading. But before you shut your Bible and run, realize that Hell is a need-to-know subject if ever there was one. Too much is at stake for us to be uninformed, unconcerned, or unwilling to wrestle it through. Many of us have never really searched out the topic for ourselves. Few pastors preach on it and few Bible studies delve into it. Therefore, too few Christians understand it. Surveys indicate that a high percentage of people believe in Heaven, but comparatively few believe in Hell. Of those who *do* believe in Hell, I suspect most believe it only in their heads. If Hell's reality truly penetrated our heart, we would never hesitate to share Jesus Christ—any time, any place, with anyone, and at any cost. Therefore, we can't afford to stick our heads in the clouds and view only Heaven. We *must* allow our hearts to be stricken and sickened by Hell's reality, for there will be great gain for the pain. No other subject has the potential to spur us on to "earthly good" quite like this one.

Let's take *one week* to examine what God has to say on the subject. Deal? *One week*. It could prove to be the most powerful and life-changing part of your study. For our own sake, for the sake of the lost, and for the sake of the Savior's costly sacrifice, we must face these truths honestly and earnestly. And then act upon them. Next week, we will get back to Heaven and you will appreciate it all the more.

DAY 1 *hell by any name*

HELL IS ONE OF THOSE subjects that cause us to question the character of God. Most of us are steeped in the love and mercy of God, but our ears are less accustomed to the holiness, justice, and wrath of God. Did you know that Jesus spoke more on Hell than He did on Heaven? Was He ignorant of God's character? Would He make up such a place just to frighten us? As John Wesley would say, "Impute no such folly to the Most High!"

When I first began to seriously study the Bible, someone quipped, "If you don't like something the Bible says, just take your scissors and cut it out!" The image startled me. I committed myself to believing God's Word entirely, even the parts I could not or did not want to understand. My relationship with God took off at that point as His Word began to have power over my life. In retrospect I realize that until I fully surrendered to its truth, God's Word was little more than theory to me. In essence, I was telling God that I knew more than He did—that I had a better plan. No wonder I rarely (if ever) heard Him speak. Why should He bother to speak to me? I was smarter, after all. Hmm. Images of an empty soul, a selfish heart, and my college "Physics for Dummies" class flashed before my eyes. I laid down my scissors and I have rarely been tempted to pick them up again. Until this week, that is.

Although few of us would ever defile our Bibles with scissors, we often have cut God's authority out of our lives by picking and choosing which parts of His Word and His character we like. If we were to excise all that Jesus said about Hell, we'd have to cut out the beloved Sermon on the Mount and numerous parables. Actually, over one half of His parables deal with eternal judgment. Jesus evidently knew that we would be tempted to tune out such a message... so He turned up the volume.

I'll share my foolproof way of approaching subjects such as Hell and God's wrath. Repeat after me: "I am not wiser, fairer, more merciful, or more loving than God." Say it one or two more times, out loud if possible, and then begin.

What different ways do people try to cope with the idea of Hell?

What are your questions regarding the existence of Hell?

Many people cope with the idea of Hell by denying its reality. They reason that because God is good and loving, He would not condemn anyone to a place of eternal torment. They either believe that everyone will go to Heaven or that Hell isn't all that bad. Some believe that annihilation is Hell's eternal punishment—that evil persons will simply cease to exist. Others think that life on Earth *is* Hell.

If you're like me, you may have tried to spruce up Hell, making it bearable somehow. Over the next five days, let's allow Scripture to define our thinking. Try and reserve judgment on certain issues until the end of the week.

Just as there is a Present Heaven and an Eternal Heaven, there is also a Present Hell and an Eternal Hell. The words translated "Hell" in the various versions of the Bible are the Hebrew word *Sheol* and the Greek words *Hades* and *Gehenna*. The "lake of fire" is another name for Hell. There are differences.

The Hebrew word *Sheol* used in the Old Testament refers to the unseen abode of the dead. It can also refer to the grave. Sheol doesn't always suggest the domain of the wicked or a place of torment. It was believed to be a deep abyss beneath the center of the Earth. It corresponds to the Greek word *Hades*, yet Hades rarely denotes "the grave." Vine's Dictionary differentiates between Hades and Gehenna by their duration—Hades being the *intermediate* abode between death and Gehenna, and Gehenna being the *permanent* region of the lost.[42]

Let's begin with Sheol and Hades. In Psalm 16:9–10, David proclaims his faith in life beyond Sheol and prophesizes of Jesus (the Holy One) and His resurrection:

> Therefore my heart is glad, and my glory rejoices; My flesh also will dwell securely. For Thou wilt not abandon my soul to Sheol; neither wilt Thou allow Thy Holy One to undergo decay.
>
> (NAS)

Jesus helps our understanding of Sheol or Hades in His illustration of Lazarus and the rich man (Luke 16:19–31). Recall our study in *Day Two/Week Four*. The rich man went to *Hades* or *Hell* upon his death. An impassable chasm separated him from the abode of Abraham and Lazarus, known as *Abraham's Side* or *Paradise*. This visual image of Sheol being divided into two compartments, Hell and Paradise, was a popular belief of rabbis during the intertestamental era.[43]

Jesus visited Sheol between His death and resurrection. The Apostle's Creed declares Jesus was buried and descended into Hell. Jesus claimed:

> For as Jonah was three days and three nights in the belly of a huge fish, so the Son of Man will be three days and three nights in the heart of the earth.
>
> (MATT 12:40)

If by "the heart of the earth" Jesus meant Sheol, just think of all the rejoicing that would have taken place among those on Abraham's Side when Jesus appeared! The repentant thief on the cross would have just arrived (Luke 23:43). Can you imagine his thankfulness as he realized the implications of his "death-bed" confession? Those on the other side of the chasm may have heard Jesus preach during this time (1 Peter 3:19). Although it's difficult to discern from Scripture just exactly what took place when Jesus was "in the heart of the earth," we do know that following Jesus' ascension,

Abraham's Side was vacated and the saints followed Jesus to Heaven. (See *Day Three/Week Three.*) Their long-awaited Messiah had come and they "received what had been promised" (Heb. 11:39, 12:22–24).

Yet, in the midst of such Good News, there was bad news as well. Although Abraham's Side was relocated to the Present Heaven, Hades continued to be occupied by those who rejected God's provision for their salvation. Hades thereby becomes the *Present Hell,* with Jesus holding the keys (Rev. 1:18).

Recall that in Luke 16 we are privy to the thoughts, emotions, and sufferings of a desperate occupant of Hell. Being in "torment," the rich man *pled* with Abraham to send someone to warn his brothers. And though his request was denied, through the pages of Scripture his voice has warned untold millions. Oh may we believe his report!

Being "in agony in this fire," the rich man begged for relief. The "fire" does not consume him. He is able to see and talk in the midst of his suffering. Jesus describes him as having a physical form. If His description is *not* to be understood literally, then we must assume that a disembodied soul is visible and able to experience anguish. But a day is coming when those suffering in Hades will receive *eternal* bodies.

Let's look at a couple of scriptures that explain.

Daniel 12:2 Multitudes who sleep in the dust of the earth will awake: some to everlasting life, others to shame and everlasting contempt.

What are the two destinations we "awake" to? (Remember, "sleep" refers to the earthly *body.*)

John 5:28–29 Do not be amazed at this, for a time is coming when all who are in their graves will hear his voice and come out—those who have done good will rise to live, and those who have done evil will rise to be condemned.

What do those who have "done good" rise to?

(?) **What do those who have "done evil" rise to?**

All of those currently in Hades will one day experience resurrection. While multitudes rise to everlasting life, multitudes also rise to shame, contempt, and condemnation. They are released from death or Hades to appear before a Judge at the Great White Throne.

Let's take a deep breath and witness the scene in *Revelation 20:11–15*.

(?) **Where have those before the Throne come from?** (v. 13)

(?) **What happens to them after they are judged?** (v. 14)

(?) **What is the lake of fire also called?** (v. 14)

(?) **Why were they thrown into the lake of fire?** (v. 15)

No mention is made of the saved at the Great White Throne of Judgment. We'll discover next week that a Christian's deeds *are* judged, but only for the purpose of reward. We'll deal more with God's judgment then, but let's not pass up the opportunity to discover whose names are recorded in the "book of life."

Please read *Revelation 3:5*.

(?) **How are those "in the book" described?**

(?) What does Jesus do for those whose names are in His book?

(?) Keeping a hand in Revelation, flip to *Matthew 10:32* to discover who Jesus confesses before His Father.

Now turn to *Revelation 21:6–8.*

(?) How does Jesus describe those who enter into eternal life?

(?) How does He describe those who enter the lake of fire, or the second death?

The names of those written in the book of life have confessed Jesus as their Lord. Therefore, their sins—no matter how vile—are forgiven by His death on the cross. They are called "overcomers" because they have held fast to their confession of faith. True salvation is evidenced by a *continuance* in the faith (Matt. 24:13).

Those who *do not* drink of the water of life—provided freely through faith in Jesus Christ—will join the rich man and plead for a drop of water in Hades. There they will remain until the day Jesus unlocks the doors. At that time their bodies—whether buried in the sea or in the ground—will be resurrected. They are resurrected for the purpose of standing before God to be judged for their deeds. Since they have no Advocate, no Substitute, no Savior to forgive their sins, they are declared guilty and cast into the lake of fire. Although their deeds are judged, *it is their refusal to believe upon the Son of God* that keeps their names out of the book of life and seals their fate in the lake of fire.

Let's conclude for today with one last scripture: *Revelation 20:10.*

(💬) Who is in the lake of burning sulfur (or lake of fire)?

(💬) What will happen to them there and for how long?

Did you notice Satan is *tormented in* Hell, not the *tormentor of* Hell? So often he is depicted as being "in charge" of Hell. But he will suffer the worst punishment of all. In fact, Jesus reveals that "the eternal fire was *prepared* for the devil and his angels" (Matt. 25:41, emphasis mine). Oh that they were the sole occupants. But tragically (and needlessly), many for whom Christ died will join them there. If only they had called upon the name of the Lord, they would have been saved (Romans 10:13).

Tomorrow we will study Jesus' words regarding Gehenna. Defined as "identical in meaning with the 'lake of fire,'"[44] it has the same sense of permanence. But I must say, whether Hades or Gehenna, the lake of fire or the second death, Hell by any name is still hell. The Lord knows how "to hold the unrighteous for the day of judgment, while continuing their punishment" (2 Peter 2:9).

I want to challenge you to one last exercise. **Review the descriptions from Rev. 21:8 of those condemned to the lake of fire:**

- cowardly
- unbelieving
- vile
- murderer
- sorcerer
- idolater
- sexually immoral
- liar

Are you guilty of being any of the above? I confess I have been. And if it weren't for the Savior, one day I would stand guilty before God at the Great White Throne. So will everyone who has not been forgiven by the love and grace of Jesus Christ. If you are unsure of your salvation, please don't *hesitate* to ask Him to save you. It's what He came to Earth to do.

> *For God did not send his Son into the world to con-*
> *demn the world, but to save the world through him.*
> (JOHN 3:17)

DAY 2 *hell on earth*

"HELL ON EARTH." WHAT IMAGES come to your mind when you hear that expression? Those present at the collapse of the Twin Towers or the Oklahoma City bombing woefully described it as such. The Nazi concentration camps of World War II would certainly fit such a description. Human history has far too many examples. The Jews in Jesus' day had their own "Hell on Earth." It was called "Gehenna."

Gehenna was a deep and narrow valley located to the south of Jerusalem. Called the "Valley of Hinnom" in the Old Testament, it was the sight of hideous crimes.

Read *Jeremiah 7:30–34* and **note what atrocities occurred there.**

Topheth was located in the Valley of Hinnom. There the ancient Canaanites offered sacrifices to the gods Baal and Molech. Horribly, children were sacrificed to Molech. God had specifically commanded the Israelites *not* to follow the detestable rites of child sacrifice, declaring that anyone who does such evil shall be put to death (Lev. 20:2). But King Solomon set up an altar to Molech at the bidding of his foreign wives. God responded by tearing the kingdom from Solomon's line and dividing the kingdom (1 Kings 11:4–13). Years later, the idolatrous kings Ahaz and Manasseh made their children "pass through the fire" in Topheth (2 Chron. 28:3, 33:6). The custom of infant sacrifice continued for many years.

The name "Topheth" comes from the Hebrew word for "drum." Tragically, drums were used in order that the cries of the children might not be heard.[45] But God heard their cries! And He promised to judge the Israelites' abhorrent sin.

The good King Josiah attempted to put an end to such practices. He tore down the altars and spread human bones upon the area to make it ceremonially unclean (2 Kings 23:10, 13–14). Yet judgment still came. Due to their worship of Molech and other gods, God sent Israel into exile in Babylon (Acts 7:43). The Babylonians besieged Jerusalem, destroyed the Temple and took the Jews into captivity. Years later, when the Jews were allowed to return to Jerusalem, the Valley of Hinnom was so abhorred that the bodies of criminals, carcasses of animals, and all sorts of filth were cast into it. Worms bred continuously and fires were constantly smoldering, incinerating the corpses and garbage. It not only was a repugnant and despicable place, it was a visual reminder of the human capacity for depravity and evil.

"It became, therefore, extremely offensive; the sight was terrific; the air was polluted and pestilential; and to preserve it in any manner pure, it was necessary to keep fires continually burning there. The extreme loathsomeness of the place; the filth and putrefaction; the corruption of the atmosphere, and the lurid fires blazing by day and night, made it one of the most appalling and terrific objects with which a Jew was acquainted."[46] Therefore, *Gehenna* (the Greek name for the Valley of Hinnom) became a common term used by the Jews to denote the place of eternal torment.

With that gruesome bit of background material, let's read Jesus' words of warning concerning Hell. Keep in mind, Jesus is using the word "Gehenna" when your text reads "Hell."

Let's begin with *Mark 9:42–49*.

(⳽) **What is Jesus' warning?**

(⳽) **Does "Hell" seem to be a real place? Explain.**

(◡) Which descriptions of Hell pertain to what you have learned about Gehenna?

(◡) Is Jesus teaching self-mutilation as a means of dealing with sin? If not, what is He telling us to do?

(◡) Jesus concluded his remarks on Hell with the declaration, "Everyone will be salted with fire." **Looking back at the context of the passage, what might this statement mean?** (I'll give you a hint: salt preserves food from decay.)

Jesus presents two destinations: Life or Gehenna. The decision is ours, but Jesus does all He can to scare us off of the pathway to Hell. Jesus describes Hell as a real place in which a person goes "into" or is thrown "into." It is *so* horrible that He entreats us to do all in our power to escape its pull. Sin pulls us toward Hell. Since one could pluck out an eye and cut off a foot and keep right on sinning, it's improbable that Jesus was instructing us to actually "cut off" the part of the body that committed the sin. It's the heart that's deceitful and leads us into sin (Jer. 17:9; James 1:15). So what could He mean?

I recently read a newspaper article about Aramaic idioms in the Bible. (Aramaic was the every day language of the Jews in Jesus' day.) There is a saying in Aramaic, "If your hand offends you, cut it off." It would be the equivalent of you or I saying, "If you have a habit of stealing, cut it out."

But Jesus' solemn warning seems more emphatic than that, doesn't it? Jesus uses *startling* language to shock us out of our complacency toward sin! Nothing could be more radical than plucking out an eye or cutting off a limb. Yet that is exactly His point—*be radical* in removing sin from your life and *be vigilant* not to lead others into sin.

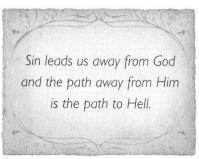

Sin leads us away from God and the path away from Him is the path to Hell.

Often it's necessary to amputate a limb to save a life. Even seemingly small or unimportant organs like the tonsils or the appendix, when diseased, must be "cut out" or the entire body is in danger of death. In a similar fashion, we must cut out the sin and the things that tempt us to sin from our lives. A seemingly small or unimportant sin can give way to greater ones, causing a deadly infection in the soul. Sin leads us away from God and the path away from Him is the path to Hell.

What are some things that lead to sin that need to be cut out of our lives?

Jesus' hyperbole is intended to spur us to action—to not dismiss sin, excuse it, entertain it, laugh at it, or be deceived about it. Sin's temporal pleasure leads to eternal misery. The things we do, the places we go, what we watch and read, who we hang out with... anything (and with a few exceptions, anyone) that leads us to sin should be avoided at all costs. Hell is so horrible, so excruciating, and so permanent that it is *far better* to lose some things in this life—no matter how valuable or useful—than to lose life eternally. Heaven will more than make up for anything we have "sacrificed" in this life. The greatest earthly treasure or pleasure cannot compare to life with God in Heaven. Why steal a bracelet of gold when Heaven offers streets of gold? Why lie or cheat for earthly power when Heaven offers an eternal crown and throne? Jesus encourages us to think beyond the day, beyond the hour, and beyond the Earth. Eternity comes quickly. Be wholly heavenly-minded!

If Jesus' enticement to "enter life" doesn't grab our attention, surely His description of Hell will. He likens Hell's horror to Gehenna where "their worm does not die and the fire is not quenched." Jesus isn't the first to use such a frightful expression. He was quoting a scripture from Isaiah on the eternal state of the wicked (Isaiah 66:24). Are we to believe that real fires and real worms will torment those in Hell? We'll deal with that question tomorrow. But truly, does it matter? If it is not to be taken literally, what must the reality be like? Jesus could not have painted a more dreadful portrait of internal and external pain: worms and fire.

It's difficult to know exactly what Jesus meant when He said, "Everyone will be salted with fire." *Several ideas come to mind:*

1. Just as salt preserves, so the "fire" of Hell will preserve the tormented body for eternity. What horror—those in Hell are kept alive by *pain!*

2. "Fiery" trials burn away the sin in our lives and "preserve" us for Heaven. (See 1 Peter 4:12–18 for a further explanation.)

3. The *threat* of hell-fire and damnation will "preserve" us for Heaven. The message of Hell is hard to give, yet I wonder how many people are now enjoying the glories of Heaven because such a message "scared the Hell" right out of them! Surely believing in the "fire" of Hell has saved many from such a destiny. It certainly kept me from a few sins in my youth and I rarely heard it preached.

Let's end with two passages from Jesus' Sermon on the Mount in which Jesus uses the term "Gehenna." First read *Matthew 5:21–24.*

(✏️) **What is Jesus' main point?**

Jesus makes it clear that there is no such thing as a "harmless" sin. In C. S. Lewis' *Screwtape Letters*, a demon advises another demon concerning his work against humankind. As you read the following excerpt, realize that God is called "the Enemy" because the letter is written by a comrade of Satan:

> You will say that these are very small sins; and doubtless, like all young tempters, you are anxious to be able to report spectacular wickedness. But do remember, the only thing that matters is the extent to which

you separate the man from the Enemy. It does not matter how small the sins are provided that their cumulative effect is to edge the man away from the Light and out into the Nothing. Murder is no better than cards if cards can do the trick. Indeed the safest road to Hell is the gradual one—the gentle slope, soft underfoot, without sudden turnings, without milestones, without signposts.[47]

Jesus warns us against anger's insidious effect and likens it to murder. "Raca" means empty-headed or worthless. It was an expression of contempt aimed at a person's intelligence. "Fool" expressed a much greater contempt. It criticized the heart and character of a person. (To understand how derogatory the term "fool" was to the Jew, you might want to read Isa. 32:6.) When we give in to hateful thoughts, we give them an opportunity to grow stronger and gain control over our life. James 3:6 makes a powerful point concerning our speech, underscoring the seriousness of allowing our mouths to run amuck. James used the word "Gehenna" (translated hell):

> "The tongue also is a fire, a world of evil among the parts of the body. It corrupts the whole person, sets the whole course of his life on fire, and is itself set on fire by hell."

How we kill people's spirits with our hurtful words! In Matthew 5, Jesus commands us to go to a person who harbors something against us and reconcile.

(꒰) **Why would He ask us to do such a humbling thing?**

I think Jesus not only wants you and me to keep *our* hearts free of anger and hate, He also wants us to help *others* get free. If someone acts as though you have offended them—even if you consider yourself innocent—Jesus instructs *you* to apologize. That's hard! But the grace you extend could be the lifeline someone needs to climb up the slippery slope that leads to Hell. (And it's always beneficial to scrape a little pride off of our own heart.) *P.S. Beware of worshipping God! He may require something noble from you!*

One last scripture: *Matthew 5:27–30.* When Jesus repeats an expression, it's because He wants it to be heard and heeded. So let's give it the attention He intended.

(◡) **What is Jesus' specific warning and what are we to do in response?**

Interestingly, when we are in the throws of temptation, the Bible often instructs us to *flee!* To "flee" means to "run away; to shun; to escape." We may think it is cowardly to run or shun, but it is actually being obedient (and very wise). Below are scriptures that teach us when to "*flee!*" **Take a moment with each one, asking God for insight into any weak areas in your life. Check which ones you are convicted to work on.**

(◡) **Flee from:**
- ☐ anyone leading you away from following Jesus (John 10:5)
- ☐ sexual immorality (1 Cor. 6:1)
- ☐ idolatry—loving anything or anyone above God (1 Cor. 10:14)
- ☐ the lust of youth (2 Tim. 2:22)
- ☐ false doctrines;
- ☐ quarrels and strife;
- ☐ envy and malicious talk;
- ☐ evil suspicions;
- ☐ godliness for financial gain;
- ☐ the love of money (1 Tim. 6:3–11)

OK. Break time. Two days down, three to go. Are you starting to see the benefit of going to Hell for a week? It should make each one of us run from sin's dangerous grip to the protective arms of Jesus. He loved us enough to suffer a horrible death to save us from Hell and for Heaven. Will you heed His warnings?

When Jesus uttered the word *Gehenna,* the Jews had a visual image before their eyes and under their noses. They were familiar with its abhorrent past, its repulsive present, and its desolate future. No one missed Jesus' message—I doubt anyone joked of the good company or wild parties happening there. There was no "sprucing up" Gehenna. The picture was worth a thousand unutterable words. It *was* Hell on Earth.

Gehenna. We are to fear it, for it's a fearful place.

DAY 3 *scary as hell*

AS WE BEGIN TODAY, I have a wise word (although a hard word) to share with you from a chapter on Hell in C. S. Lewis' book, *The Problem of Pain*:

> In all discussions of Hell we should keep steadily before our eyes the possible damnation, not of our enemies nor our friends... but of ourselves. This... is not about your wife or son, nor about Nero or Judas Iscariot; it is about you and me.[48]

Jesus' warnings about Hell are directed to an audience that knew something about God, whether the religious Jews of the day, His disciples, or the masses of people who flocked to hear Him speak. Jesus didn't preface His sermons on Hell with, "Listen closely so that you can warn others." He wanted you and I to listen closely so that *we* would not be deceived. So even if you are 100% sure of your salvation, the message of Hell is for *your* ears too!

Today we will continue to read Jesus' warnings about the Eternal Hell, paying special attention to how He describes Hell's sufferings. I'll add my own warning: Today's lesson brings new meaning to the expression, "Scary as Hell!" But hang in there! Remember that *all* of Scripture is profitable, equipping us for good works (2 Tim. 3:16–17). Our study of Hell *will* be to our benefit. We have God's Word on it!

Today we will study four passages in the Gospel of Matthew.

1. Matthew 8:10–12

How would you describe Heaven based on this passage?

How does Hell contrast?

Who are the "subjects of the kingdom"? Would they have known about God and Heaven?

2. *Matthew 13:24–30 and 36–43*
Who are the "harvesters" and when do they gather the harvest? (vs. 39, 41–42)

Who do the "weeds" or "tares" belong to and what are they guilty of? (vs. 38, 41)

What happens to the "weeds" at the end of the age? (vs. 40–42)

3. *Matthew 25:31–46*
We studied this passage in a previous lesson discussing how heavenly-mindedness results in earthly good. Now let's read it in regard to its message on Hell.
How is Hell described? (vs. 41, 46)

How are those in Hell described? (vs. 41–43)

(?) Below are Jesus' words to the "sheep" (on the right, of course) and to the "goats" (on the left). **Draw a line to the matching contrast. Then circle which group you want to be in!**

Goats	Sheep
the eternal fire prepared for the devil/angels	eternal life
depart	come
cursed	you did for Me
you did not do for Me	the Kingdom prepared for you
eternal punishment	blessed

4. Matthew 10:28–33

We studied this scripture in our lesson on the proper fear of God. Surely now we can better appreciate why God puts a little "holy fear" into our souls!

(?) **What is destroyed in Hell?** (v. 28)

According to Matt. 10:1, Jesus is sending His disciples out to proclaim the gospel. He warns them that some people would reject their message so vehemently that they would hate and betray the messenger. Jesus fortifies their resolve with eternal perspective. Although people may be able to kill the *body*, the disciple's *souls* were safe in the hands of their always-watchful Father.

We learn from this passage that no one is able to "kill the soul." Whether a person is righteous or evil, saved or unsaved, *the soul will survive death*. We also learn that *both* the soul and the body will be in Hell. Those bound for Hell will receive an eternal body, yet that body will be *destroyed* in Hell, as will the soul.

Does the word "destroy" indicate that those in Hell will be annihilated? I think it would be far better (or at least easier) to "cease to be" than to suffer for ever and ever! Does Scripture give us permission to believe that?

Let's look at a few scriptures that seem to support annihilation. I italicized the words that might cause us to believe that those in Hell come to a complete end:

John 3:16 For God so loved the world that he gave his one and only Son, that whoever believes in him shall not *perish* but have eternal life.

Mark 8:35 For whoever wants to save his life will *lose* it, but whoever loses his life for me and for the gospel will save it.

John 8:51 I tell you the truth, if anyone keeps my word, he will never see *death.*

In the first two scriptures, the words "perish" and "lose" are actually the same Greek word that is translated "destroy" in Matthew 10:28. *Apollumi* does not mean extinction, "but ruin, loss, not of being, but of well-being."[49] It means to "waste" or to "mar." Similarly, the word "death" in John 8:51 is defined as "the opposite of life; it never denotes nonexistence."[50] Keep in mind that Hell is *never* characterized as "life." In Heaven, *life* continues. In Hell, life is over and an eternal *death* begins.

How can something be "destroyed" or "dead" yet continue to exist? In the natural realm, the destruction of one thing can mean the emergence of something else—such as the resulting gases, heat and ash when a log is burned.[51] Perhaps that is how we should view the fate of those in Hell. C. S. Lewis considered the damned soul as "nearly nothing: it is shrunk, shut up in itself."[52] The *life* that once was is wasted, ruined, lost, and marred beyond recognition... *destroyed.*

Let's consider Jesus' descriptions of Hell. Write down what each communicates to you:

1. "fiery furnace"; "unquenchable fire"; "lake of fire"

2. "their worm never dies"

3. "weeping and gnashing of teeth"

4. "outer darkness"

5. "prepared for the devil and his angels"

6. "eternal punishment"

(👁) The following are insights concerning the expressions that Jesus used to describe Hell. **Underline what is as "scary as hell" to you!**

1. The "eternal fire" communicates both destruction and unspeakable suffering. The purpose for which a person was given life is destroyed in the fire and an entirely different being remains in the ashes. Some have envisioned Hell as an island surrounded by a lake of fire, explaining how one could eternally exist in a fiery furnace. The burning of Sodom and Gomorrah was "an example of what is going to happen to the ungodly" (2 Peter 2:6).

2. The phrase "their worm does not die" is often interpreted to indicate an agonizing and never-ending regret. Remorse "gnaws" upon the mind of the accursed in the same way a worm "gnaws" on a dead body. The use of the pronoun "their" regarding each "worm" underscores the individual nature of Hell's torment as opposed to a one-punishment-fits-all image.

3. The image of the "gnashing of teeth" worried me horribly as a child. I envisioned those in Hell beating themselves up for their stupid, irreversible rejection of salvation. Although this expression could indicate great sorrow over being excluded, it could also indicate the rage of the proud over God's judgment against them. "Gnashing" means to grate or grind the teeth in either pain *or* rage. The mental torment of Hell results in *self-inflicted* physical suffering.

4. The "outer darkness" contrasts to the light of Heaven and carries the idea of being separated from God. Banished from the joy of a festive gathering, the one cast "outside" is deprived of human companionship and camaraderie. Mark Twain's saying, "Heaven for atmosphere and Hell for company" simply ain't so. Strangely, complete darkness is found in the base of a flame. "Blackest darkness is reserved" for the opponents of Christ (2 Peter 2:17).

5. Hell was "prepared for the devil," not for human beings. Heaven was prepared as our inheritance from the beginning (Matt 25:34). We were created *for God!* (Col. 1:16). He therefore does *not* predestine any man or woman to Hell.

6. No combination of words could be more foreboding than "eternal punishment." "Eternal" inarguably means "never-ending." The word for "punishment" means torment. As one commentator stated, "It does not

mean simply a 'state or condition,' but absolute, positive suffering; and if this word does not teach it, no word could express the idea that the wicked would suffer."[53] John Wesley wrote of this scripture: "It is not only particularly observable here, that the punishment lasts as long as the reward; but, that this punishment is so far from ceasing at the end of the world, that it does not begin till then."[54]

Each of Jesus' descriptions of the Eternal Hell, whether understood literally or figuratively, reflect the chilling words Dante envisioned etched above Hell's gate: "Abandon every hope, you who enter."[55]

We've trudged through some harsh realities today. Jesus certainly didn't speak about Hell for the fun of it, did He? So let's conclude with one last question:

How has the reality of Hell challenged you to live?

Long ago, theologian Jonathan Edwards made a resolution to endeavor to his "utmost" to live as if he had already seen the happiness of Heaven and the torments of Hell. Today we've seen Hell's torments. In response, let's never quit believing or proclaiming—

> The LORD is near to **all** who call on him, to all who
> call on him in **truth**. He fulfills the desires of those
> who **fear** him; he hears their cry and **saves** them.
>
> (Ps. 145:18–19, EMPHASIS MINE)

DAY 4 *hell prevention*

TODAY WE ARE GOING TO shift our focus. Aren't you glad? We've had a good look at *what* Hell is like. Now we want to discover *why* Hell has to be. In attempting to answer the "why" of Hell, we often look into the character of God. We will do that today. But the answers to the "why" of Hell lie more within *our* character rather than in God's. Our scriptures today will underscore that reality.

To help us see the necessity of Hell, we are going to compare what God does to get us into Heaven (Hell Prevention) to what people do to get themselves into Hell (Hell Promotion). I think it will prove to be an eye-opener. Find the chart provided in today's homework. We will add to it as we go along.

Let's begin by reading *Matthew 22:1–14.* In the parable, Jesus is speaking to the religious leaders (Matt. 21:45). His message directly concerns their history as a nation. However, it also teaches us about the "why" of Hell.

(?) **What was the servants' job?** (v. 3)

(?) **Describe who was invited to the banquet after the first group refused to come.** (vs. 9–10)

(?) **Both "bad" and "good" people were invited to the banquet. What does that truth tell us about God and His salvation?**

(?) **What happened to the one without the proper wedding garments?** (v. 13)

(?) **List on the chart (page 196) under *Hell Prevention* what the parable teaches concerning God's part in offering Heaven.**

(?) **Under *Hell Promotion,* list the reasons why people refuse God's invitation.**

Hell Prevention:	Hell Promotion:
What God does to get people into Heaven	What people do to get themselves into Hell
MATTHEW 22	MATTHEW 22
LUKE 14	LUKE 14
JOHN 3	JOHN 3

Let's start with the good news! I love how Heaven is described as a wedding. Christ is our heavenly Bridegroom and one day the Father will host a *huge* and extravagant Wedding. He has sent out many invitations in hopes of having a great reception.

I can relate to God's desire for many to come to His Son's Wedding. In the weeks preceding my daughter's wedding, I was caught by surprise by just how badly I wanted all of my friends and family present. As each RSVP card arrived in the mail, I celebrated every response checked "Accept with joy" and lamented over those checked "Decline with regret." I even called a few people that I hadn't heard from to encourage them to come! My husband and I wanted *everyone* to share in our joy and help us celebrate a very meaningful day in our lives.

My heart aches over the response the King received. Did you notice that He sent out a second set of invitations to the group who refused the first time? But it was to no avail. The people were either indifferent or openly rebellious. He then sent His servants out to round up "anyone you find." Wow! God doesn't seem very discriminating, does He? And I'm *so* glad. I certainly don't mind being on His "B" list! I'm just thankful I don't have to have a pedigree or a PhD to be invited.

Jesus wants us to realize that His Father has invited *everyone* to His Heaven. He goes to extreme lengths and great expense to get the word out concerning eternal life. So many stories could be told of the sacrifice of *one* servant of God for the salvation of another. God never ceases to employ and equip His messengers until all the invitations to the Party have arrived in every corner of the world (Matthew 24:14).

According to this parable, the only ones excluded from the feast excluded themselves. They were unwilling to come, too occupied to come, or too rebellious to come. They "refused." They "paid no attention."

(😊) **Have you ever been (or are you still) guilty of any of those excuses? Explain.**

I'm afraid I've been guilty of them all. I marvel at how God *continued* to invite me to come—time and again—through friends, strangers, church, nature, music, failures, joys, births, deaths…I could go on and on. The invitations kept coming until I finally got the message. I learned that we have a determined and tireless Host who for some crazy reason so desires our fellowship that He uses every available means to entice us to His Party.

But there is grave danger in ignoring God's invitation. If we put off mailing our "Accept with joy" cards, we might find ourselves in the same predicament as the one improperly dressed in Jesus' parable. In Jesus' day, it was the custom for the host of a wedding to provide special garments for the guests to wear. All of the guests were rightly attired but one. Can you imagine how he must have stood out? I wonder if he realized he looked different—or did he not notice? We are not told *why* he didn't put on the wedding garments. Did he refuse? Did he think they weren't necessary? Did he fail to RSVP and therefore his name did not appear on the list for clothing?

(?) **Read the scriptures and underline the clues as to what the "wedding clothes" represent:**

Isaiah 61:10 For he (God) has clothed me with garments of salvation and arrayed me in a robe of righteousness, as a bridegroom adorns his head like a priest, and as a bride adorns herself with her jewels.

Zech. 3:3–4 Now Joshua was dressed in filthy clothes as he stood before the angel. The angel said to those who were standing before him, "Take off his filthy clothes." Then he said to Joshua, "See, I have taken away your sin, and I will put rich garments on you."

Revelation 7:14 These (in Heaven)…have washed their robes and made them white in the blood of the Lamb.

The one without the garments had nothing to say in his defense. I imagine he was silent because he was without an excuse (Rom. 1:20). Perhaps he didn't like the look of the garments. Maybe he thought he looked good enough in his own clothes. Or perhaps he was too proud to admit he needed a change of clothes. But we all must enter Heaven on God's terms, not our own. And no one sneaks in undetected.

Have you ever been afraid of how following God might make you look? Have you ever been too proud to admit that you didn't have it all together and you needed God? Have you ever thought that you were too nice, too smart, or too superior to others to find yourself in Hell? Or have you ever thought that you had to look good and "get it together" *before* committing your life to God? Scripture teaches:

1. *Our goodness* can *never* warrant admission into Heaven. We are never clean enough. Even our most righteous acts are like filthy garments without Christ (Isaiah 64:6).

2. *No one* is so *bad* that God doesn't offer him or her the robe of Christ's righteousness. It was for the *sinner* that Jesus died, for "His blood can make the foulest clean . . ."[56]

We can conclude that the man who had not "put on Christ" is thrown into Hell. (We are certainly familiar with the descriptive phrases!) Jesus leaves no room for discussion: *there are consequences* to refusing God's prescribed means to Heaven. Sometimes God's judgment comes upon this Earth (v. 7). Other times it doesn't come until we see Him face-to-face. But if we refuse His invitation to Heaven, *it comes*. And if it surprises you that God gets angry when people reject Him, just think of what it would indicate about His character if He did not. I think we have no idea how desperately God wants us eternally safe with Him and out of the grip of Satan.

📖 Let's take a close look at *Matt. 22:14*. **Based on what Jesus has just taught us, how would you explain the comment, "For many are invited, but few are chosen"?**

At first glance Jesus' comment (most likely an ancient proverb) seems to contradict the parable. It would be easier to understand if Jesus said, "For many are invited, but few choose to come." After all, that is *the point* of His parable. Yet the expression seems to indicate that although God invites everyone to Heaven, in reality, only a few pre-selected ones get in.

The definition of the Greek word *eklektos* translated "chosen" sheds some light for us. The closely related word, *eklego,* means "to choose for oneself, not necessarily implying the rejection of what is not chosen." God's sovereignty in salvation and man's responsibility to respond work together. We cannot understand all of God's complexities. Jesus doesn't try to explain it to us. But He *does* state two very clear truths:

1. God wants everyone at His Son's wedding. You and I might invite some people to our wedding for propriety's sake and hope they won't come. But not God. He is unwilling for ANY to perish (2 Peter 3:9).
2. Compared to the huge mailing list, few "Accept with joy." *Why?* For a multitude of reasons, all of which lead to Hell.

More reasons why people refuse God's Heaven are found in a similar parable recorded in *Luke 14:15–23*. Please read it.

(☺) **Add any additional insights into God's anti-Hell campaign to the chart.**

(☺) **Add the reasons why the people refused God's invitation under *Hell Promotion*.**

Are you getting a feel for what God is up against? He has done *everything possible* to compel *all* to come, sending out His servants to every highway and byway. In earlier times He sent out prophet after prophet after prophet, and finally, His own Son. Yet mankind killed and mistreated the very messengers who brought the greatest invitation to the greatest event of all—Heaven. And we are no better today. We drown out the messengers' voices. We go about our business. We deem other relationships more important. We invent excuses.

Will God listen to our excuses when the Day of Judgment comes? Can any of us claim we never knew there was a God, or that our invitation to His Party was never received? *Romans 1:18–2:11* clearly says no. Read it if you have the time. You will be appalled at mankind's response to the love of God. This passage makes it perfectly clear that God has made Himself known to all people. The testimony of His power and His character is "clearly seen" in creation. The testimony of His existence and His goodness resounds within the human spirit. Those who refuse to believe in God "suppress the truth," claim to be wiser than God, and do not think it "worthwhile to retain the knowledge of God." Therefore, all such persons "are without excuse."

You simply must read Paul's conclusion in *Romans 2:5–11*.

(☺) **Check which descriptions fit the person who will incur God's wrath:**

❑	Stubborn	❑	Self-seeking
❑	Unrepentant	❑	Rejects truth
❑	Innocent	❑	Follows evil
❑	Predestined	❑	Never heard of God

"... God's judgment against those who do such things is based on truth."

(Rom. 2:2)

(꙳) **On the other hand, how are those who inherit eternal life described? (v. 7)**

We'll finish with one last very revealing passage. Read *John 3:16–20.*

(꙳) Record God's actions for *Hell Prevention* on the chart.

(꙳) Record what some people choose over Jesus in the *Hell Promotion* column.

(꙳) According to this passage, does every person have an opportunity to believe?

(꙳) **In light of all the scriptures you have read today, why is there a Hell?**

Job 21:14–15 says it all too well:

> Yet they say to God, "Leave us alone! We have no desire to know your ways. Who is the Almighty, that we should serve him? What would we gain by praying to him?"

Our scriptures today present overwhelming evidence that God makes Himself known to some degree to every man and woman He creates. He does not force Himself upon us; neither does He show favoritism (Rom. 2:11). He presents each of us with a choice as to whether or not we want His companionship—for now and for eternity. *A "no" to God is a "yes" to Hell.* There is no place else to go; there is no in-between.

We will continue to explore the Bible for more answers on this issue tomorrow. But we've seen today that some people refuse to surrender to God's Lordship, no matter how many chances they are given... no matter how magnanimous the demonstration of love... no matter how horrendous the threat of wrath. Even during the Tribulation days on Earth, many curse God and refuse to repent (Rev. 16:9). I suppose that is why there must be a Hell. *We insist upon it.*

I'll give C. S. Lewis the last word:

> In the long run the answer to all those who object to the doctrine of hell, is itself a question: "What are you asking God to do?" To wipe out their past sins and, at all costs, to give them a fresh start, smoothing every difficulty and offering every miraculous help? But He has done so, on Calvary. To forgive them? They will not be forgiven. To leave them alone? Alas, I am afraid that is what He does.

And here is the real problem: so much mercy, yet still there is Hell.[57]

DAY 5 *turning up the heat*

I HAVE A STORY TO share with you. The night before I began to write this week's lessons, I asked God to make Hell's reality move from my head to my heart. Less than 24 hours later, I stepped out of my door to the unmistakable smell of fire. I frantically tried to locate the flames but could not. To the west, a thin line of black clouds stretched across the horizon, just above the setting sun. A strong wind began to blow and in a matter of *seconds* the sky above me turned black with smoke. I watched as it covered the moon, turning it an eerie red. Talk about terrifying! I had been writing about Hell all day, but this was no intellectual exercise. I fervently pled with the Lord for protection.

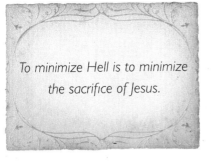

To minimize Hell is to minimize the sacrifice of Jesus.

I ran inside to get what information I could. Fires were raging on land to the west and to the north. The 50 mile-per-hour wind was making the grassfires seem closer than they were. Attempts to contain them were not succeeding. Fire tornadoes were popping up, and towns were being evacuated. It proved to be a *long* night. Praise God no human lives were lost.

Now I don't believe that God set the fires to prove a point to me. (Although He surely could have commanded the wind to blow the smoke my way!) But God surely used the event to respond to my request. The reality of Hell moved from my head to my heart with the power and speed of a lightning bolt. I hope I never need such a visual aid again.

Perhaps God's Word has made a similar impact upon your heart this week. Staring intently into Hell is difficult and distressing. But to overlook Hell is to overlook redemption. To minimize Hell is to minimize the sacrifice of Jesus. To downplay its reality is to downplay the urgency and ramifications of the gospel message.

> Behold then the kindness and severity of God.
>
> (ROMANS 11:22, NAS)

When we reject God, we reject His Heaven. When we reject His Heaven, we choose Hell. God's great gift of love has an undesirable and unavoidable side effect—the possibility of refusal.

Look up the following scriptures and record what choices we have been given.
Deut. 30:19–20

1 Chronicles 28:9

God sent the Light to enlighten *every* man and woman (John 1:9). Yet, "This is the verdict: Light has come into the world, but men loved darkness instead of light because their deeds were evil" (John 3:19).

Today we are going to deal with the "fairness" issue of Hell and answer the following questions:

- Do *all* people truly have a choice to make concerning their eternal destiny?
- Of those who go to Hell, do all suffer to the same degree?
- Is the unsaved "nice person" punished the same as the vile sinner?
- What crimes receive the severest punishment?

Let's start by reading *Romans 10:11–21*.

Who will be saved? (vs. 11, 13)

(question) How does faith come? (v. 17)

(question) How will "all" hear the message? (vs. 18–21)

While in *Romans*, flip over to *9:14–16*.
(question) Is there any injustice with God? (v. 14)

(question) What does salvation depend upon? (v. 16)

(question) Now turn to *Colossians 1:23*. Who is the gospel proclaimed to?

Salvation belongs to God. It is dependent upon *His mercy* and free of *any* injustice. The gospel is "proclaimed to every creature under heaven." So often we struggle with the doctrine of Hell because we fear that people who have never heard of Christ are unfairly assigned a place in Hell. We fear that some don't have enough information to know the severe consequences of rejecting or ignoring the voice of God. We fear that God may indiscriminately choose who goes to Heaven and who goes to Hell.

The doctrine of Hell is understandable only in the light of self-choice. To believe that God would send an innocent man, woman, or child to an eternal Hell undermines all that Scripture reveals about His character. Our legal system sometimes condemns the innocent. Not our God.

(question) Read *Psalm 145:8–21* and **record what you learn about God.**

God is more concerned about getting His creation *into* Heaven than in keeping anyone out. As we learned yesterday, Scripture insists that *a degree of light* is given to every person to point them to the one true God. Granted, more light is given to some than to others. But even that incongruity is dealt with in the end.

Read *Matthew 10:7–15 and 11:20-24.*

(⊙) **Why will judgment be less tolerable for some than for others?**

Luke 12:42–48 explains this principle further.

(⊙) **What are the different degrees of punishment based upon?** (vs. 47–48)

In this passage, Jesus promises to reward those who live righteously and faithfully serve His people. He promises punishment to those who don't. Judgment will be harshest for those who have been graced with much truth, yet turn against God and the people entrusted to their care. To cut someone "to pieces" was practiced in ancient times. Such a wretched and shameful demise certainly punctuates Jesus' point!

Those who *intentionally* defy God are punished more severely than those who do not know God to the same degree. The Law made a distinction between sins committed in ignorance and those committed defiantly (Numbers 15:29–30). So will God on Judgment Day.

Those given the greatest opportunities for faith—through the exposure to the gospel, the working of miracles, and the convicting power of the Holy Spirit (Hebrews 10:26–31)—yet ignore them or reject them, will suffer more in Hell than those who had a lesser revelation of God's truth.

It would have been better for them not to have known the way of righteousness, than to have known it and then to turn their backs on the sacred command that was passed on to them.

(2 PETER 2:21)

Although Hell is *hell* for each and every one who rejects God, He will "turn up the heat" on those who deserve it the most. Their punishment will fit their deeds.

2 Thessalonians 1:6–10 explains why non-believers must be in Hell.

How is God described? (v. 6)

Who is punished and what is their punishment? (vs. 8–9)

Those who say "no" to God's love get what they desire—eternity apart from God's presence. In C. S. Lewis' fantasy, *The Great Divorce,* those in Hell are given a chance to visit the outskirts of Heaven. Incredibly, all but one decide to return to Hell. Their misery and sin have such a hold on them that they cannot bear to surrender to God's love and be made whole. Their attitude illustrates Jesus' declaration, "You are *unwilling* to come to Me, that you may have life" (John 5:40, NAS, emphasis mine). Yet, contrary to Lewis' novel, Jesus warns that many will "seek to enter and will not be able"—pounding on the door of Heaven, desperately wanting in and realizing too late that they should have believed Him (Luke 13:24–25).

Let's review what we've learned about those headed for Hell:

- *The rebel*: knows God yet refuses to worship Him, preferring to be his own god.
- *The unrepentant sinner*: prefers his sin to God's salvation.
- *The self-righteous*: believes he will go to Heaven because of his own goodness.
- *The unbeliever*: denies or explains away the testimony of God in creation and within his own soul.
- *The procrastinator*: keeps saying "some day" to God.
- *The deceived*: trusts in another means of salvation rather than in Jesus Christ.

Now let's review what we've learned about God. Fill in the blank with the truth concerning salvation that the following scriptures reveal:

Yet your countrymen say, "The way of the Lord is not just." But it is their way that is not just. I will judge each of you according to his own way.

(EZEK. 33:17, 20)

- God is perfectly_____in salvation.

When the disciples asked, "Who then can be saved?" Jesus replied: "What is impossible with men is possible with God."

(LUKE 18:27)

- God is perfectly_____to save.

As surely as I live, declares the Sovereign LORD, I take no pleasure in the death of the wicked, but rather that they turn from their ways and live. Turn! Turn from your evil ways! Why will you die?

(EZEK. 33:11)

- God is always_____ to save.

… choose for yourselves this day whom you will serve…

(JOSH. 24:15)

- God presents every person with a _____ .

Jesus said, "Let the little children come to me, and do not hinder them, for the kingdom of heaven belongs to such as these."

(MATT. 19:14)

- If one dies too _____ or is too handicapped to be able to make such a choice, they will inherit Heaven.

When I say to the wicked, "O wicked man, you will surely die," and you do not speak out to dissuade him from his ways, that wicked man will die for his sin, and I will hold you accountable for his blood.

(EZEKIEL 33:8)

- God expects _____ to take His message to people.

Woe to you... you hypocrites! You shut the kingdom of heaven in men's faces. You yourselves do not enter, nor will you let those enter who are trying to.

(MATTHEW 23:13)

- We are called not only to preach but to _____ what we preach.

Some scriptures stress our role in salvation while others emphasize God's role. It's fortunate that salvation does not rest *solely* on our shoulders. But God expects us to open our mouths and move our beautiful feet! (Possible answers to the above blanks: 1. just; 2. able; 3. willing; 4. choice; 5. young; 6. people; 7. live.)

I've never forgotten the testimony of a woman who was angry at God, believing that her husband had died unsaved. She had prayed for his salvation for years and believed God would save him. But then he died in a car accident. Five years later, the wife learned that on the day of his death, her husband had given a young soldier a ride. Prompted by the Holy Spirit, the soldier had led her husband in a prayer to receive Christ.[58]

Pray for those you love to know Christ! Share and live out your faith before them! Do your part... and trust God to do His. God wants your loved ones in His Heaven even more than you do!

When considering the millions of people who worship other gods—such as the Muslim, the Hindu, or the Buddhist—remember that Scripture has promised *all* who seek to know God will find Him. Just this morning I read a testimony of a Christian teacher in South Asia who offered the father of one of his Hindu students a wall calendar. He carefully explained to him that the calendar had a scripture on it. Aware of this, the Hindu man took the gift and hung it on his wall. This small step towards the Light invited in more Light. The Holy Spirit went to work through that one scripture. After a period of time, the father received Jesus and even opened his home as a gathering place for believers. God used *one verse* of His Word, given by *one messenger*, to penetrate the darkness of a false religion.[59] When a bit of truth is received, God sends more truth... and more truth... until the door is opened wide or shut entirely.

Scripture is clear. God is a *holy* God—too pure to look upon evil or tolerate wickedness (Hab. 1:13). God is a *jealous* God—He will not force anyone to love or serve Him against their will and will give them over to their own desires (Joshua 24:19). Yet God is a *forgiving* God—even of those who nailed His Son to a cross: "Father, forgive them, for they do not know what they are doing" (Luke 23:34). He is good to *all*, compassionate to *all*, loving to *all*; but the wicked He will destroy (Psalm 145). God created us with free will so that we could *choose* to love Him. He did not create robots or puppets. Instead, God did *everything* necessary and *everything* possible to keep *everyone* from going to Hell. As one preacher put it, "God has an 'anti-hell' vaccine, the blood of Christ, available to all who trust Christ alone for their eternal salvation."[60]

It's time to declare "Hell Week" officially over. If questions still linger in your mind about Hell, I encourage you to get alone with God and hash them out. Just a piece of His mind can bring peace to your mind! (Just ask Job!)

This week of study has been a sobering and humbling reminder of where I would be if not for the grace of God Almighty, the sacrifice of Jesus Christ, and the conviction of the Holy Spirit. I'm uncomfortably comforted to know that those who are in Hell chose to be. I'm also painfully aware that many people in our world today may need *just a bit more light* to open their hearts to the Eternal Light. God has turned up the heat of my desire to get His message of redemption to everyone I possibly can. I pray it has done the same for you.

I've never forgotten the scene in the movie *Schindler's List* when Oskar Schindler berates himself for not selling *anything* and *everything* in his power and possession to help one more person escape the Nazi concentration camps. His heroic and courageous efforts kept 1100 people from certain death. Yet to him it wasn't enough. He anguished over what he else he might have done, over what else he might have sold to obtain freedom for *one more.* If he'd made more money… wasted less money… sold his car… bartered his lapel pin… then maybe ten more persons… two more persons… even *one more* person might have been saved. Sobbing, his words are haunting: "I could have gotten one more person… and I didn't! And I… I didn't!"[61]

Oh that our hearts would ache with such intensity for the sake of *one* soul. To save one soul from Hell… from *Gehenna*… where are you willing to go? What are you willing to give? What are you willing to do?

Turn up the heat in our hearts, Lord. Turn up the heat.

WEEK 7
The Crowning Moment

As a child, I loved watching a TV show called *Queen for a Day*. During the show, a few women told the studio audience about recent heartaches and hard times. Whoever received the most "sympathy applause" would become Queen. The tearful winner was crowned to "Pomp and Circumstance," draped in a red velvet robe, and showered with prizes—most often household items like a new washer and dryer. (Some prize for a queen, huh?) The show, although sappy, was wildly popular and aired for nearly twenty years. After all, what is more heartwarming than to witness a humble soul being honored, a suffering saint being cheered, or an underdog winning top prize? Most folks would love to get the royal treatment and be recognized for their hard work and sacrifice at least once in their life.

Scripture promises that a day is coming when every believer in Jesus Christ will have his or her own "crowning moment." In some ways it will resemble *Queen for a Day*. The least will be the greatest and the last will be first, the poor will be made rich and the downcast will be raised up. But it won't have a thing to do with "sob stories" or "applause-o-meters." It will have everything to do with how we lived this life, how we loved God and others, and how we used the gifts and grace entrusted into our care.

You may be surprised at how frequently Scripture refers to the rewards we will receive in Heaven. Like the subject of Hell, the doctrine of rewards is rarely preached in churches or taught in Bible classes. The proud and the humble, the complacent and the committed often resist its message. But rightly understood, it has the potential to catapult us all into victorious

Christian living. If you could use some extra incentive to live life God's way (and Jesus apparently believes we all could), this week is for you.

Heaven won't have a "queen for a day," but it *will have* princes and princesses for an eternity! What might your crowning moment be like? Let's jump into Scripture and find out.

DAY 1 *the final word*

THOSE OF US WHO LISTENED to the news coverage of the last conversations between husband and wife, parent and child on September 11, 2001, will never forget them. Precious parting words sent from hijacked planes and burning buildings pierced the heart of America. In the midst of devastating and frantic circumstances, heroic people searched to find just the right words to say… to leave behind hope, to muster up courage, and to say "I love you."

I have often thought of what it must have been like to be in their position. What would I say if I had to make such a call, or receive one? Perhaps you have had the sacred experience of saying goodbye to a loved one who was dying. If you have, you know that final words matter deeply. They are carried in the heart, mulled over and over, reviewed (and sometimes rewritten), and always and forever *remembered.*

Have you ever considered Jesus' last words? True, He speaks to us daily through His Word and His Spirit. Yet don't you imagine that He carefully chose what His last *recorded* words would be? Of all the things that Jesus would like for us to remember, what did He consider the most important? What did He want us to carry in our hearts, to mull over and over? What word of hope, what word of courage did He give us?

Without peeking, what do you think His parting words were? (Think beyond His ascension to His last recorded visit to Earth!)

Now let's peek! Turn to *Revelation 22* and discover His words recorded in *verses 7, 12–16 and 20.*

(☺) Summarize what Jesus had on His mind.

(☺) Jesus repeated Himself, didn't He? Why would He do that?

(☺) What will He bring when He returns and what will it be for? (v. 12)

(☺) How does Jesus identify Himself? (vs. 13, 16)

Talk about a "heavenly-minded for earthly good" pep talk! Jesus *is* coming back! Just as surely as He came the first time, He is returning—this time to *stay*. And how we live *now* will determine how we will be rewarded *then*. If we pondered this truth each and every morning, our lives would take on a new purpose and focus. Worldly things would take a backseat to eternal opportunities. We would live holy, faithful, and generous lives. We'd leave nothing in the bag!

Three times in ten short sentences Jesus declares His imminent return. Yet 2000 years later, He still hasn't come! Was He misinformed? Did He "fib" so all generations would be on the alert? Or was He talking like a God whose watch ticks to a different meter than ours? Surely, "With the Lord a day is like a thousand years, and a thousand years are like a day" (2 Pet. 3:8). But it's also helpful to know that the Greek word translated "soon" or "quickly" can mean suddenly, or by surprise. Jesus most likely is saying that His coming is *inevitable* and may occur at *any moment*. He frequently warned that His return for His church (the Rapture) would catch people off guard. Sometimes we act like rebellious teenagers whose parents are out of town—either "living it up," "playing hooky," or "trashing the house." Jesus knows our self-destructive and faithless tendencies. His words are intended to help us overcome temptations and live lives pleasing to God.

Surprisingly important to Him is the matter of what He will bring to us when He returns. He will bring *reward*. The Greek word for "reward" used in this scripture, (*misthos*), means wages or hire. It can refer to a good reward or an evil one. Jesus will "pay" every man for deeds done on the Earth, whether good or bad. This was not a new concept. Isaiah and others had long ago declared it:

> The LORD has made proclamation to the ends of the earth:"Say to the Daughter of Zion, 'See, your Savior comes! See, his reward is with him, and his recompense accompanies him.'"
>
> (ISA. 62:11)

Yet the fact that it is Jesus' *final word* to us should cause us to give it special attention. It must be crucially important.

Last week we studied Jesus' *misthos* for the unsaved. Their deeds are examined at the Great White Throne, resulting in a varying degree of punishment in Hell. The *wages* of sin is death (Rom. 6:23) and they did not accept Jesus' offer to pay the debt for them.

This week we will study Jesus' *misthos* for the saved. Their deeds are examined at what the Apostle Paul called the "Judgment Seat of Christ." The Judgment Seat is our focus this week.

Let's begin with *John 5:22–24*.

Who is the Judge? (v. 22)

Do believers in Jesus Christ come into judgment? (v. 24)

When does the believer pass out of death and into life? (v. 24)

Christians are not judged *with regard to their sin*. Just as those in Hades are raised to stand before God with no chance of being acquitted, so Christians who stand before Christ have no chance of being condemned.

> He who believes in Him is not judged; he who does not believe has been judged already, because he has not believed in the name of the only begotten Son of God.
>
> (JOHN 3:18)

Why are Christians not judged? The sacrifice of Jesus Christ cancelled their "debt" when sin was judged at the cross. Therefore, God no longer "remembers" the sins of those in Christ! (See Col. 2:13–14, Heb. 8:12.) Does that mean the Christian's sins won't be a factor at the Judgment Seat of Christ? Good question! We'll discover the answer this week. But when Scripture states that God "remembers" it doesn't mean He has temporarily forgotten someone or something. It means that He is about to *act on the behalf* of the thing or the one He has "remembered." So when God does *not* remember our sins, it means He will *not* act upon those sins. That's *good news*.

Now, for the not-quite-as-good news... read *Hebrews 4:13*. **What do you learn?**

Such news is a bit unsettling if we have tendencies to be complacent and get by with the "minimum." In fact, it's unsettling for *anyone* to know that they will give an account of their lives. Particularly when you are accountable to the One from whom *nothing* is hidden! No bluff or fluff makes it tough!

We may think that because we are saved by grace, God will not hold us accountable for the way we live. Not true. It is our *works* that are rewarded at Jesus' return. However, Jesus' reward of our works does *not* imply that our salvation is *earned*. Let's examine a few scriptures that beautifully illustrate the relationship between faith and works.

1. *Titus 3:3–8*

Who are we before salvation? (v. 3)

How are we saved? (vs. 4–6)

What are we *not* saved by? (v. 5)

Who are we after salvation? (v. 7)

What do we do as a result of our salvation? (v. 8)

How are the works described? (v. 8)

2. *Ephesians 2:1–10*

Who are we before salvation? (vs. 1–3)

How are we saved? (vs. 4, 8)

What are we NOT saved by? (v. 9)

Who are we after salvation, and what do we do as a result? (v. 10)

How are the works described? (v. 10)

From what was revealed in these scriptures, how would you summarize the relationship between faith and works?

Our deeds could never warrant entry into Heaven. It is not what *I do* for Jesus that gets me to Heaven; it is what *He has done* on the cross. Yet the evidence of *true* salvation is a *transformed life*. Good works come with the package of salvation.

Have you ever opened a gift to find another wrapped gift inside? You unwrap it only to find another and then another? I used to have fun wrapping small packages in big boxes to delight my children! I think the Lord does the same with His children. Salvation is God's *gift* to all who will accept it. But wrapped inside salvation's package are smaller gifts of great works "prepared in advance for us to do." Just as we must choose to open the gift of salvation, we must choose to open the gift of God's good works. When we do, we discover *another* gift tucked inside—our works enrich our lives and bless other lives! But the giving doesn't end there. One last gift remains: "*To be opened in Heaven.*"

What a wonder. Our Lord dies for us, forgives our sin, gives us His Holy Spirit to empower us to serve Him, and then He rewards *us* for the work *He* does through us! It causes us to want to say "No! I don't need a reward! Your love is enough! *You* are enough!" But God plans to reward us anyway, no matter our protests. It's just a further demonstration of His *amazing* grace.

When will we open our gifts in Heaven? Jesus' final words indicate that the time of rewards occurs when He returns for the church and all believers are assembled in Heaven. It most likely will occur *after* the Rapture and *before* the earthly Kingdom of Christ begins:

> The kingdom of the world has become the kingdom of our Lord and of his Christ, and he will reign for ever and ever.... The time has come for judging the dead, and for rewarding your servants the prophets and your saints and those who reverence your name, both small and great.
>
> (REV. 11:15, 18B)

☺ **Can you think of a reason why Jesus would wait to judge our works until all believers of all time are assembled in Heaven?**

There may be many reasons. For one, our lives affect generations to come. Sometimes we don't live to see the answers to our prayers or the fruit of our labor. But that doesn't mean that God won't reward them! For example: The prayers of a grandmother for her grandchild go unanswered in her lifetime. After the grandmother has died, the grown grandchild receives Christ. The grandchild leads others to Christ, and on and on God works—generation after generation, the ripple of one grandmother's prayer continuing until the end of the age! Similarly, a Bible study may start out very small. Yet thirty years later, revival may break out due to the Word of God being taught. Countless lives in the community are impacted and one seemingly small deed grows to unimagined heights. If heavenly rewards are given when all the results are in, then we can enjoy the full impact (and astonishment) of obeying God.

Also, think about how marvelous it will be to witness your loved ones receiving their reward! Not to mention the joy of seeing Mary, Peter, Mother Teresa and other sold-out Christians stand before Jesus! How wonderful to gather as *one* body and be able to understand how each part and each gift contributed to the whole work of God. Part of the proceedings at Christ's Judgment Seat may well be private. But I hope the reward ceremony is for all to see!

Let's conclude with *Hebrews 11:6*. **Fill in the blank:**

"And without faith it is impossible to please God, because anyone who comes to him must believe that he exists and that he_____ those who earnestly seek him."

It doesn't sound like God gives us a choice as to whether to buy into this reward business or not, does it? God *is* a rewarder! He desires to lavish His riches upon us and we *please Him* as we believe in the blessings of the world to come. Jesus' final words were chosen to strengthen our resolve and encourage our selfless efforts. But He leaves it up to us to accept the challenge. He doesn't force His will upon us *or* magically do the work for us without our participation. *God-works* may require *hard work*. And they always require faith!

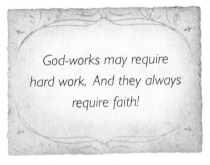

God-works may require hard work. And they always require faith!

I heard a story about a father, son, and daughter who were swimming in the ocean. A storm rose quickly. Before the father could react, the current swept them away from the shore. The father realized he could not swim back with both children. So he had to make a hard decision to take his three-year-old son and leave his six-year-old daughter to fend for herself. He told her that she could float all day if she would not get scared and fight it—"Just float and swim, float and swim," he told her, "and Daddy will come back for you."

He swam back to the shore with his son and immediately enlisted help. Boats searched the area for four hours. Miraculously, his daughter was found—miles from shore—but safe. After the rescuers pulled the little girl into the boat, they asked her, "Were you scared?" Surprisingly, she said no! She explained: "My Daddy said I could float all day. He said that he would come back for me. I was just doing what he told me to do until he came back for me."

The life of faith can seem scary and rough at times. We may feel like we're treading water and about to go under. We may grow weary of doing good. But Jesus *is* coming back for us. *We have His final word on it.* He could show up at any moment, with an amazing reward in tow! He has told us what to do and has given us the power to do it. We just need to do what He told us to do until He comes back for us!

DAY 2 *beaming at the bema*

I CAN'T BEGIN THIS SEGMENT without grinning. A few years ago, I taught a series on Heaven at a church in another city. On my fourth visit, I had planned to teach on the Judgment Seat of Christ and heavenly rewards. Large screens in the sanctuary flashed the title of the lesson, "Then Comes the Judgment." (Not the most inviting title I've ever come up with!) The pastor in charge pulled me aside and told me that his congregation rarely heard messages on sin and never on God's judgment. He then asked me, "When you teach this lesson today, would you do so with a big smile on your face?"

Fortunately, he had a smile on *his* face! And I understood his concern. Our churches are full of people who would rather not know about God's judgment of their lives. You may be one of them. Trust me, I can relate! But actually the topic of judgment for Christians is an *encouraging* word with eternal and beneficial ramifications. *Yes* it is challenging... but the challenge is for a fuller and more abundant life. Sticking our heads in the sand regarding what awaits us after death not only costs us in eternity, *it steals joy from our lives today.* God revealed the truth concerning the coming judgment so we would *act* upon it, not be threatened by it!

As we learned yesterday, upon His return, Christ will reward every person for his or her deeds. The reward Christ brings has nothing to do with whether one goes to Heaven or Hell. That is determined solely by faith in Christ. Therefore, as a Christian, when you stand at the Judgment Seat of Christ, you are already *in* Heaven! The riches of eternal life have already been granted to you! Nothing that happens at the Judgment Seat could *ever* change that. The Christian *passes out of judgment* when he or she trusts in Jesus Christ. There is *no condemnation* for those in Christ Jesus (Romans 8:1). Yet, we *do* give an account of our lives to God and our earthly works are examined.

The word "judgment seat" used in the scriptures we'll read today is the Greek word *bema*. The bema was a raised place or platform, reached by steps, originally used in Athens for orations or to present rewards at the athletic games. The bema was also used in the law courts of Greece, one for the accuser and one for the defendant. It was later applied to the tribunal of a Roman magistrate or ruler.[62] Jesus appeared before Pilate at the bema (John 19:13) and Paul appeared before the bema in Corinth (Acts 18:12). Herod built a bema in the theater of Caesarea from which he viewed the games and made speeches. Thus the word *bema* is representative of a place of authority, justice, and reward.

In *Day Four/Week Five,* we examined scriptures that revealed the condition of our "insides" when we are presented to Christ in Heaven. **Let's take another look, paying special attention to the word "present."**

> *Colossians 1:22* But now he has reconciled you by Christ's physical body through death to *present* you holy in his sight, without blemish and free from accusation...
>
> *Ephesians 5:25–27*...Christ loved the church and gave himself up for her to make her holy... and to *present* her to himself as a radiant church, without stain or wrinkle or any other blemish, but holy and blameless.

The word "present" *(paristemi)* means "to stand beside, to be at hand, to aid, to recommend." Isn't that a courage-booster? Our Judge is on our side *and* by our side! The Greek word translated "free of accusation" *(anegkletos)* means "one who gives no occasion for his being brought to a court of law." [63] At this judgment scene, there *will not* be a bema for an accuser! Fortunately, the accuser, Satan, will be bound-up in a deep abyss far, far away (Rev. 20:2–3).

For our lesson today, we are going to examine four passages that describe what will occur at the Judgment Seat of Christ.

1. 2 Corinthians 5:8–10

(⋮⟩) **Why does Paul want to be pleasing to God?**

Continue reading *verses 11–15.*

(☺) How would you describe Paul's attitude towards this life in light of the coming Judgment Seat?

(☺) What two factors drove Paul to persuade all men of the truth? (vs. 11, 14)

2. Romans 14:10–12

(☺) What will we do at the Judgment Seat? (v. 12)

(☺) What should the knowledge that all people will be accountable to God keep us from doing? (v. 10)

(☺) Why?

Now read the preceding verses, *7–9.*

(☺) What is our attitude toward life to be in light of the coming Judgment Seat?

3. 1 Corinthians 4:3–5

(?) What about our lives will Jesus examine? (v. 5)

(?) How should this knowledge affect how I live?

(?) What will we receive from God? (v. 5b)

4. 1 Corinthians 9:24–27

(?) How are we encouraged to run this race of faith? (v. 24)

(?) What kind of reward will we receive and how long will it last? (v. 25)

(?) What does an athlete do to win a prize that we should do to win an eternal prize?

(?) Is it possible to be disqualified from receiving a reward?

(?) Thinking upon the scriptures that you have just read, **check which one(s)** describe your feelings toward your future appearance at the Bema of Christ:

❑ I'm fearful of it.
❑ I'm looking forward to it.
❑ I want to live more fully for God!

❏ I wish I'd never heard of it!

❏ Accountability motivates me.

❏ I need God to work on my motives.

❏ I can't even imagine standing before God and being rewarded by Christ.

I think that the scriptures we have studied today give us permission to have a bit of holy fear about this day, don't you? Both fear and love compelled Paul, and he is a good example for us to follow.

(☺) **After reading today's scriptures, what change is the Holy Spirit encouraging in you?**

Let's consider two major points in today's scriptures:

First, the knowledge of the coming Judgment should cause us to live wholly devoted to God. The fact that we will give an account of our lives proves that what we do on Earth matters to God. Therefore we should give our very best effort. When Paul said that he beat or buffeted his body, he was saying he "knocked himself out" so that he would not lose his eternal reward.

(☺) **Has there been something or someone you could say you knocked *yourself out for?* Explain.**

I can relate to the life of faith being a race and the bema as a platform for reward. Some people are born with a silver spoon in their mouth; I was born with a rubber flipper on my foot! My size 10s gave me a great advantage in the swimming pool. I also came to Earth equipped with a competitive spirit. (Thanks Mom and Dad.) Even at a young age, something about the sport made me willing to get up at 5:00 AM to work out before school and return again after school. The practices were hard work! There was no horsing around or goofing off. The coach's whistle blew relentlessly and the stopwatch revealed any slackers. My weekends consisted of swim meets with long stretches of time spent waiting on hard bleachers. My hair shone and smelled of chlorine and my swimmer's build looked silly in dresses. Yet for some crazy reason, it didn't matter! I loved to swim, I loved to compete, and I loved to win!

At the state level meets, awards were ceremoniously presented to the first, second, and third-place winners. It was quite a moment to step up on the bema-like platform and have the medal hung around your neck. Somehow it made all the hours of hard work worthwhile. My Mom always told me that the bigger the medal, the faster I swam! And if there were trophies, I would grow gills!

But even though I had an eye for the rewards, I only wanted them because I passionately loved the sport! Surely there would have to be an easier way to collect ribbons! I swam for the cheers of my family. I swam for my teammates. I swam for my coach's approval and attention. The reward represented the dedication and priority of my life. It represented success—a job well done. *It represented my best.*

Paul likens our journey of faith to an athletic race because it vividly illustrates what we are willing to do in order to excel and reach a goal. Athletes are determined, dedicated, disciplined, single-minded, and willing to make great sacrifices… all for a perishable wreath! A tin medal! *Temporal, fleeting glory!* Paul's point? How much more willing we should be for eternal glory! The reward that awaits Christians represents our love for Jesus. Therefore, we should give our Heavenly Coach our absolute best—100 percent of ourselves every day, in every endeavor. And the crazy thing is, when we do, the sacrifice doesn't matter! For God rewards such devotion with His presence, power, and approval, with which nothing in life can compete. Exercising our spiritual muscles in God's Living Water gives us a peculiar shape, sheen, and even smell—the sweet aroma of Jesus Christ.

Secondly, the knowledge of the Judgment Seat of Christ should cause us to stop judging and comparing ourselves to others. Christ will judge all lives. Such knowledge should stop us from focusing on our brother's faults and weaknesses and keep us concentrating on our own. When we stand before God, our life alone will be up for review. The blame-game will not be played. Can you imagine looking into Jesus' eyes and giving excuses?

When I'm tempted to compare myself to someone else, I remember Jesus' words to Peter in John 21:22. In the scene, Peter is face-to-face with the Risen Lord. He has been forgiven for his denials of Christ and commissioned to shepherd the church. But upon hearing that he would die for Christ's sake, he points to his friend John and says, "Lord, what about him?" Oh my! Isn't that just like us? Peter would feel better about dying for Christ if it was required of his friend as well! But Jesus rebuked his question and said, "If I want him to remain alive until I return, what is that to you? You must follow me."

Have you ever felt that God was requiring more of you than of someone else? To give more, do more, say more, or risk more? If so, what was the ultimate outcome?

We cannot, and therefore should not, judge the call of God upon another life. All that will do is make us feel superior, inferior, or give us an excuse to back down. We must be true to God's call upon our own life, or we will miss the purpose for which we were created! *Heed God's still small voice.* Follow His plan for *your* life. That's all He will hold you accountable for when you stand before Him. Err on the side of loving Jesus *too* much—if there even is such a thing!

Let me end with one last swimming story. (I'm so glad Paul brought up the subject of racing...) I was ten years old. It was the last big meet of the summer and I had one final chance to beat my toughest competitor. She had qualified first and I had qualified second. The race was a short sprint; just one lap of the pool and it was over! On the first length we were neck-and-neck, but coming out of the turn she was nowhere in sight. I couldn't fathom making that good of a turn! What had happened? Did the official blow the whistle due to a false start? Was I swimming by myself, looking stupid? I then did the unpardonable... I pulled my head out of the water to see. The race was still on! And while I cranked my neck around to look for the others, my competitor caught up. The finish was so close that the officials called for a judge's decision.

She won; I lost. She got cheered; I got chewed out by my coach. And there was more at stake than the color of the medal. We had broken the state record! Her name went into the books; mine did not. It was a hard lesson for a ten-year-old. I obviously have not forgotten it.

You know what? Our earthly lives are just a couple of lengths of the pool compared to eternity. Don't slow down to look at others! Don't worry about looking foolish! Don't risk being disqualified! *You have no idea what reward you may forfeit.* Keep your eyes on the goal! Knock yourself out! Hold nothing back! Such effort will please your Coach, benefit your team, and result in reward for you. And the reward you receive won't be a tin medal around your neck—*it will be a crown that will last forever.*

The Judgment Seat of Christ will be your time of accountability and reward. Get a good picture of yourself beaming at the *Bema!* It is worth your all!

DAY 3 *inspection day*

YESTERDAY WE STEPPED UP TO the Bema of Christ to imagine what it will be like when we give an account of our lives before God. Such imagining caused Paul to live his life with one goal in mind: pleasing God. He persuaded others to do the same, using the surety of eternal reward as a means of encouragement and warning. He exhorted us to race in such a way as to *win the prize*—to knock ourselves out for the love of Christ! I hope you were able to relate to Paul's athletic analogies and endure my reminiscing of swim days gone by. Today we'll exchange our swimming caps for hard hats and our flippers for steel-toed boots. Come along as we go to a rather awesome building site.

Our main focus will be 1 Corinthians 3:10–15, but please read *1 Corinthians 3* for context.

(☺) **What is the problem in the Corinthian church?**

What is Paul's solution for them?

Now let's zero in on *verses 10–15.*

What do the materials listed in verse 12 represent? (v. 13)

What will the fire reveal and test? (v. 13)

What will be the result of our works being tested by fire? (vs. 14–15)

Based upon this passage, will some receive more reward than others? If so, how do you feel about such a variance?

What does this passage teach you about how to live your life?

Have you ever found yourself in a squabble like that of the Corinthians? Arguing over which ministry is more important, which pastor is more effective, or which denomination is superior? Unfortunately, I imagine we all can relate. The Corinthian church was quarrelling over loyalties to different teachers, proving themselves immature and worldly. Paul rebukes their jealousies, reminding them that he and Apollo are fellow workers in God's field—assigned to different, yet necessary works. Neither was worthy of any credit, for God alone was responsible for the effect of their labors. Paul hushed their divisive and senseless judgments with the reminder that a Day is coming in which everyone's works will be rightly judged and rewarded by the Lord Himself. Oh how a little heavenly thinking exposes our petty and prideful thinking! Zephaniah 1:7 says, "Be silent before the Sovereign LORD, for the day of the LORD is near."

Let's pull some truths from this passage that will help us understand this time of examination. **Underline the points that speak to you.**

1. This judgment does not concern salvation; only works done after a believer's salvation are judged by the fire. All who stand at this judgment stand upon the foundation of Jesus Christ. They are beloved children of God and will dwell with Him in His Heaven forever! I know I've said this before... but it is *vital* to our understanding of this time of accountability. Even when an entire structure burns, the foundation remains. Praise God, the faithfulness of Jesus Christ will hold us up even if we are faithless (2 Timothy 2:13). Therefore, even those with earthly works that do not pass the test of God's inspection are saved, albeit "through the flames." However, who wants to escape through the flames? It's not the entrance into our eternal home that any of us want.

2. We are urged to be *careful* how we build. The Greek word translated "careful" means "to take heed, to beware." We are to be very particular in picking out the materials we use to build upon this great foundation laid by Jesus. We must resist the temptation to cut corners and do things our way. Quick fixes sacrifice long-term beauty and durability. Let's be extravagant and follow God's specifications to the tiniest detail! If we use inferior materials, such as wood, hay and straw, they will not survive Inspection Day.

In my work as a home designer, a few builders would make changes in the plans without consulting me. The adjustments were almost always for the sake of expediency, in the name of "it's always done this way." They failed to see the vision I had for the completed structure. We too fail to see God's grand vision for our lives. We are His Temple! We must trust in His design ability and stick to the blueprints! It may require learning a new thing or two, but the result is the difference between gold and straw.

3. The quality of our work will be revealed at the Judgment Seat. Our "work will be shown for what it is." Were our works used to attract others to God, or to attract attention to ourselves? Were we diligent to do what God put on our hearts to do, or did we have our own agenda? Did we embrace our God-assignments with joy, or did we grumble and complain about the personal cost? Did we regard our work as a sacred privilege, or did we do as little as possible? Did we serve with love in our heart, or did we treat others poorly as we performed our "good deed"? This passage warns us against simply checking good deeds off our lists. It's not the *quantity* of the deeds but their *quality* that is addressed.

4. Gold, silver, and precious stones survive God's test of fire and receive His reward. They represent works of obedience from a heart that loves Jesus. Inspired and empowered by God's Spirit, such works follow us into eternity (Rev. 14:13).

5. Wood, hay, and straw are consumed by the fire and do not receive God's reward. They represent the works of a believer that are self-led and self-fed. Jesus warned us about "righteous deeds" done for show rather than for God. Our giving, praying, and fasting will receive no eternal reward when they are done to "look good" in front of others (Matthew 6:1–18). We must constantly ask God to reveal wrong motives, loveless attitudes, and hypocritical displays of righteousness. It is so much better to hear the truth now than on Inspection Day.

Let's pause for a second and think of the ways we spend our time, energy, and money. Think of how and why you serve God and others. Do any places of your service seem dead, void of God's Spirit and His joy? Do you need to do less with more excellence?

(☺) **Spend a few moments on this matter with the Lord, and then fill in the chart on the next page.**

My works of gold, silver, or costly stones	My works of wood, hay, or straw

6. It is possible to "suffer loss" upon entering Heaven. The Greek word *zemioo* means to "experience detriment; to receive damage."[64] We are always free to say no to the Lord, but we will lose out on something wonderful if we do—in the short and the long run. Jesus urged, "I am coming soon. Hold on to what you have, so that no one will take your crown" (Rev. 3:11). Jesus wants to reward you to the max!

7. Not everyone will receive the same eternal reward. Just as some in Hell will receive greater condemnation than others, so some in Heaven will receive greater reward than others. Our next two lessons will discuss this subject in greater detail.

8. With a foundation laid by Jesus Christ, we can build a mighty structure. Visualize yourself standing upon His foundation, spanning as far as your eye can see. Deep piers, massive beams, and steel reinforcement support the concrete slab beneath your feet. Reflect upon all that available power. What will you build upon it?

We are limited only by *John 14:12–14.*

What are we capable of doing? (v. 12)

(?) **List a few of the works Jesus did.**

The foundation Jesus has laid invites us to build amazing skyscrapers of marble and gold—works of life-saving and soul-saving proportions. Yet so often all we construct are shanties of thatch and wood—a prayer here and there, an occasional church service, a few coins in the plate, a good deed to get our name in the paper. Picture such small and lightweight structures sitting out on our imposing foundation. What a waste of God's power and provision! He has given us all we need to dream big, build big, and live big!

Are you investing the very best of yourself, believing that you can do the very works Jesus did? Are you stepping out in faith, confident of your foundation's ability to support you? Are you building to the extremities of the footprint of His foundation wall? Or are you only claiming a tiny bit of the real estate He has granted to you? One day our Building Inspector will judge what we have built. What about your structure will pass His test?

Let's learn from a couple of examples in Scripture. Turn to *Luke 10:38–42* and read about two believers in Jesus, sisters Mary and Martha.

(?) **How does Jesus describe Martha?**

(?) **How does Jesus describe Mary?**

Now flip over to *Revelation 2:1–5.*

(?) **What is Jesus pleased with?** (vs. 2–3)

(⋅·) **What is He not pleased with?** (v. 4)

(⋅·) **What do we learn about our pursuit of works in these two passages?**

I can relate to Martha. Many times have I been so busy serving that I have lost sight of the One I am serving! Think of it—*the Son of God* came to visit Martha—*He was sitting in her living room*—yet she couldn't quit scurrying around the kitchen! Similarly, day after day Jesus waits to meet with us, one-on-one! Yet we sacrifice our time with Him to get some work done. Martha, Martha.

Scripture describes Martha as "distracted." She was multitasking to the point of overload! The result? She threw a pity-party followed by a temper-tantrum. She accused her sister of not helping and Jesus of not caring. Isn't that what happens when our focus is our works? We start to think we are doing "all the work" and we get overcome with self-importance! If Martha had spent some time *with* Jesus, she would have known how much He cared for her.

Jesus gently, but firmly, corrected Martha's attitude and busyness. She was doing *many* things compared to Mary's *one* thing. Mary had chosen the *needful* thing... the *better* thing. She valued her time with the Lord above all and set aside whatever she was doing to listen to Him. Such action is always *chosen*. Lesser things will always compete for our attention. But the fruit born of Mary's encounter with Jesus would "not be taken away from her." It was gold, silver—an eternal gem. Martha's work on the other hand, burned on the stove that day!

Jesus drives home the same lesson to the hard-working folks in Ephesus. *The priority of our life is always to be our love for Him.* If we ever get the works ahead of the relationship, Jesus says, "Repent! Return! Put Me first!" If we don't heed His warning, He will remove His light. And we *burn out.*

There was a time when I taught second grade Sunday School solely for the purpose of getting myself and my children to church. It was all duty. I was doing a "good deed" that did little good. A year later, after a life-changing encounter with God through His Word, a new woman emerged. I couldn't *wait* to get to church. I couldn't *wait* to teach the kids. I even volunteered to participate in a new children's ministry! Each week, I dressed up in a crazy costume to illustrate a Bible verse and lead the kids in a game. I spent an enormous amount of time, effort, and prayer for a five minute sermon-ette! But for four years, serving those children was my *absolute* delight. People worried about my "burning out." On my own flame I would have. But the Lord ignited my heart with His love and kept me fueled through time with Him. Although I had much to learn (*and still do*), I believe that work will be revealed as gold when I stand before God. It was His idea, His love, His Word, and His energy. Therefore it had an eternal purpose!

In our emphasis on rewards this week, we need to write this truth across our brains in capital letters: MY FIRST WORK—MY BEST WORK—IS TO LOVE JESUS. *Only* from relationship with Him will eternal works flow. When we abide in Him, we bear much fruit. But apart from Him, we can do nothing (John 15:5). *Never seek the works.* Seek the heart of the One who will stir you towards love and good works. Then gold will come forth. The greatest deterrent to producing deeds of wood, hay, and straw is to love God with all your heart, mind, and soul!

It matters not whether you are an Apollo or a Paul, a mentor of one or a teacher of thousands, a bedfast intercessor or a door-to-door salesman. When you build according to God's Building Plan, your life will give Him glory. Trust your Foundation. Choose the most lavish materials. Build to please your Inspector! Only His opinion will matter.

> But whoever lives by the truth comes into the light,
> so that it may be seen plainly that what he has done
> has been done through God.
> (JOHN 3:21)

DAY 4 *bookkeeping for keeps*

MY ALL-TIME FAVORITE CLASS IN high school was Bookkeeping. Weird as it may sound, I just loved keeping a ledger! Debits, credits, accounts receivable, accounts payable—I marveled when they balanced. It was a bona fide miracle to me. So pardon me for my "ledgers" in this lesson. I couldn't resist.

This week we have stood at the Judgment Seat of Christ as an athlete and as a builder. Today we will stand as an entrepreneur! Sound intriguing? By definition, an entrepreneur is "a person who organizes and manages a business undertaking, assuming the risk for the sake of profit."[65] Even though it may not seem very "spiritual" to view our life as a business venture, that is exactly what Jesus challenges us to do in the Parable of the Talents and the Parable of the Minas. They are the focus of our study today.

These parables may be very familiar to you. If so, read them in light of what you have learned so far concerning the Judgment Seat of Christ, noting what will be judged, why we'll be praised, and what the reward will be. Do the math and fill in the ledgers! You'll discover that Jesus keeps the books a little differently than we do.

Let's begin by reading *Matthew 25:14–30*.

(?) Glance up at *verse 1*. **What is Jesus' subject?**

(?) **Fill in the chart below.**

servant	amount given	amount gained	How the servant is described by his master	The reward (good or bad)
1				
2				
3				

Bookmark Matthew 25; more questions are forthcoming! But first let's read *Luke 19:11–27.*

(?) Who does the "man of noble birth" who became the king represent?

(?) What did the king instruct his workers to do until he came back? (v. 13)

(?) Fill in the next chart where applicable.

servant	amount given	amount gained	How the servant is described by the king	The reward (good or bad)
1				
2				
3				

Now let's consider both parables. Talents are a measure of weight, usually silver. Minas are a much smaller measure of money. Notice that both are *given* to the servants. The talents are given in different amounts, according to the servant's ability.

(?) What could the "talents" represent? (What does God give His servants in varying amounts?)

The minas are given out in equal amounts, one to each servant. **What does God give His servants in equal amounts?**

What "earns" Jesus' praise and Heaven's reward?

What is the reward for the faithful servants? (Matt. 25:21; Luke 19:17)

Sometimes we may feel like a one-talent servant when we compare ourselves to others. What is Jesus' message to us at those times?

Let's first consider the faithful servants. Both of these parables emphasize the importance of what we do with our earthly lives. While Jesus is in the Present Heaven, we have a job to do. We are to put our Master and King's "money" to work and make a profit. Jesus clearly teaches us that we will be accountable for how we use His gifts and rewarded accordingly.

Although these parables have several similarities, the math lesson is different. The two servants in the Parable of the Talents have *equal devotion, yet unequal advantages.* Both servants doubled their money, which resulted in the *same* praise from Jesus and a jubilant entrance into the Eternal Heaven. Their *devotion* is measured and rewarded, not their numbers.

In the Parable of the Minas, the servants have *equal advantages, yet unequal devotion.* When the inequalities and variables are removed from the equation, the numbers matter. Greater devotion is rewarded and the reward is directly proportionate to the investment of heart and soul.

Both lessons teach the criteria for eternal rewards. *It's all about devotion.* The differences in our abilities are obvious. Not everyone has the same degree of intelligence, natural talent, money, spheres of influence, or even spiritual gifts. Yet God gives us each the *perfect measure of grace* to fulfill the unique call upon our lives (Romans 12:6). Some are given more because they have greater responsibilities to fulfill than others. Paul labored more than all the apostles, by the "grace of God" given to him (1 Cor. 15:10). At the same time, the fruitfulness of a believer's life can be a direct result of desire and obedience. Such will be rewarded in Heaven.

The servant who earned the most was given *even more.* Perhaps this servant did the work the one-talent/mina servant failed to do. No doubt the Lord has to "re-assign" tasks when we allow fears to bury our faith. Luke 12:48 gives us additional insight:

> From everyone who has been given much, much will be demanded; and from the one who has been entrusted with much, much more will be asked.

A ten-talent or ten-mina servant takes the most risk and bears the most responsibility, thus being worthy of additional reward. Ten-talent/mina persons sometimes must leave the comfort of home and family to minister. Others face persecution, imprisonment, or even death. We shouldn't think ten-talent/mina folks have it easy! People that are on the front lines of the faith often take the most hits from Satan and the most criticism from others.

What earns Jesus' praise is the servants' goodness and faithfulness. The Greek word for "good" (*agathos*) always carries the meaning of being "beneficial in its effect."[66] The Greek word for "faithful" (*pistos*) signifies one who is "believing, trusting, relying" in and upon God.[67] These servants believed God's Word and acted upon it, immediately and diligently doing the Master's bidding. They seemed thrilled to be included in divine dealings! The definition of the word "good" indicates that their works benefited others. Once again, we learn how heavenly-mindedness results in earthly good.

The manner in which the faithful servants approach Jesus should inspire and encourage us. They are obviously *excited* to present to Jesus the fruits of their labor. Because their service was joyful, their Judgment Day was as well.

The more faithfully we serve Christ, the more **authority** will be given to us in the Kingdom of Heaven.

These parables give us a clue as to what our reward will be. The more faithfully we serve Christ, the more *authority* will be given to us in the Kingdom of Heaven. Part of the reason our works are examined at the Judgment Seat is to *ascertain our capacity* to serve God in Heaven. Saints will rule and govern cities! Isn't that wild? Let's check this out with other scriptures.

(⚲) **Underline what you learn in the following scriptures concerning leadership in Heaven:**

Dan. 7:27 Then the sovereignty, power and greatness of the kingdoms under the whole heaven will be handed over to the saints, the people of the Most High. His kingdom will be an everlasting kingdom, and all rulers will worship and obey him.

1 Cor. 6:2a, 3 Do you not know that the saints will judge the world? Do you not know that we will judge angels?

Rev. 2:26 To him who overcomes and does my will to the end, I will give authority over the nations.

Rev. 3:21 To him who overcomes, I will give the right to sit with me on my throne…

Rev. 5:10 You have made them to be a kingdom and priests to serve our God, and they will reign on the earth.

(⚲) **Does the thought of being placed in a position of rule and authority in Heaven excite you, scare you, bore you, motivate you, or irritate you?**

Like it or not, Heaven will be run by redeemed people! Jesus will be the King of Kings, but He will employ our assistance in running His Kingdom. You may prefer to think of crowns and thrones and cities as symbolic of something less "earthy." But don't forget that the Eternal Heaven includes a New Earth! When Jesus returns, He will reinstate mankind to His original design—to rule over the Earth and all that is in it (Gen. 1:28). The authority we lost in the Garden of Eden will be regained. Those who prove themselves trustworthy with little during their tenure on Earth will be put in charge of much in the New Earth.

Personally, I don't care one hoot about ruling a city! But I *do* care about working face-to-face, side-by-side, and hand-in-hand with Jesus Christ! I *do* care about proving myself a good steward now to insure no regrets later. Let's not underestimate the glory that is at stake! Jesus is *not* making up fairy tales. He is graciously giving us a glimpse of the future and inviting us to prove ourselves faithful. A promotion of unimaginable proportions is promised in these parables. Unimaginable loss is also portrayed.

Let's shift our attention to the third servant and see what we can learn from him. In the Parable of the Minas, the wicked servant suffers great loss, but is not among those punished as enemies of Jesus. If he is a believer, we learn that *doing nothing is a serious offense* to God. In the Greek, the word "wicked" indicates "the active form of evil; bad in effect, malignant."[68] The wicked servant's life had the exact opposite effect from the good servant's life. No matter how the world judged him, his life produced nothing of eternal benefit.

In the Parable of the Talents, the description of the punishment of the third servant leads us to believe that he went to Hell. But Jesus' words *could* describe what it would be like to appear empty-handed at the Judgment Seat. As we learned yesterday, to be saved "through the flames" would have to be a painful experience. To be thrown "outside, into the darkness" could describe the exclusion from the celebration of reward. "Weeping and gnashing of teeth" could express the great remorse over a wasted life. Fortunately—and blessedly—the Lord will wipe away every tear. But He is perfect Truth. How could we ever enter into eternity without facing the truth of how we lived our life? *His truth will set us free,* even if it's painful.

But our judgment needn't be like that! The one-talent servant had the *same opportunity* to receive praise and honor as the five-talent and two-talent servants. Sometimes we tend to leave all the Jesus-work up to our preachers, thinking they have more knowledge and opportunity. This parable warns us against such thinking! We are to use every bit of grace given us to labor in God's field, no matter how small it may seem next to that of another.

The third servant *hid* what had been entrusted to him. He *buried* the witness of God in his soul. He put God out of mind and out of sight. Then on Judgment Day, he blamed God for his lack of effect! Jesus quickly exposed his true motives. He hadn't feared his master as he claimed! If he had, he would have at least given his money to the banker. In truth, he was lazy, worthless, and wicked.

I can recall using similar excuses as a teenager when my parents caught me doing what I was not supposed to be doing. I tried to shift the blame to them, hoping that would get me out of trouble. It never worked; they saw right through me. How much more so with God! If you have a list of excuses as to why you aren't whole-heartedly serving God, try them out on Him. See how they go over!

In fact, let's pause and do just that. (Better now than you-know-when!) As you pray, be sure and give God time to respond. He will give you all the love, all the forgiveness, and all the power you need to live for Him. *But He won't let you off the hook of living fully devoted to Him.* It's His number one goal for your life.

The idea of eternal reward may be brand new to you. If so, please give yourself some time to consider its validity. Jesus deemed it important. Therefore, we should as well.

John Wesley had a strong opinion on the variance of reward:

> There is an inconceivable variety in the degrees of reward in the other world. Let not any slothful one say, "If I get to heaven at all, I will be content:" such a one may let heaven go altogether. In worldly things, men are ambitious to get as high as they can. Christians have a far more noble ambition. The difference between the very highest and the lowest state in the world is nothing to the smallest difference between the degrees of glory. But who has time to think of this? Who is at all concerned about it?[69]

Jesus has me concerned—how about you? Hopefully we are both experiencing the type of conviction that results in transformation! After all, that is Jesus' goal in these parables. Let's praise Him for the "heads up"! Let's act upon His words! Every new day is an opportunity to trade our temporal earnings in for eternal stocks and bonds. My 89-year-old father-in-law still enjoys playing the stock market and increasing his portfolio. Oh to be so committed in the spiritual realm! We can all be heavenly-minded entrepreneurs when we're on God's payroll—at any age or stage—and our divine portfolio pays *sky-high* dividends!

Jesus' bookkeeping is for keeps. For those who employ His services, He keeps a lop-sided ledger. He fills in the debit column with disappearing ink. (Thank you, Jesus!) Yet He records in the credit column every expenditure of faith, every investment in His Father's business, and every deposit of service. Future rewards are calculated relative to present actions. The more we *spend* on His account, the more He *credits* to our account. And the final tally... well, that's up to you and me.

The time to invest is now! When we step into the Eternal Heaven, our fruitfulness from this lifetime will step in with us. Some will have little or nothing. Others will have a great reward—thirty, sixty, or even a hundred times what they sowed (Mark 4:20). Therefore, we are to be risk-taking, sold-out workers for the Kingdom, living to hear Jesus say, "Well done, good and faithful servant! Come and share your master's happiness!"

DAY 5 *the exceedingly great reward*

TODAY WE WILL CONCLUDE OUR study of the Judgment Seat of Christ. In order to wrap things up, we need to unwrap a few more scriptures. Even with all the scriptures we have explored this week, there are so many more! Amazing, isn't it? We rarely talk about eternal rewards or Judgment Day, yet God talks about it at length! I hope you have learned much. I know I have. Let's begin with a quick review.

From what you have learned so far, which of the following are true statements and which are false? Mark "T" for true and "F" for false. At the Judgment Seat of Christ...

_ our earthly works will be up for reward.

_ our sin will be replayed before us.

_ our faithfulness and devotion are measured.

_ we are judged to determine whether we go to Heaven or Hell.

_ our capacity to serve God in His Kingdom is determined.

_ we are compared to others.

Now that we know what is expected of us on Earth, we can hardly ignore it! Hopefully, our knowledge of the Judgment Seat will cause you and me to follow Jesus more closely and love Him more extravagantly. (The answers to the true-false questions alternate: True, False, etc.)

Since we have so many great scriptures left to read, I've printed many of them out for you. Therefore, today's lesson may look long, but it won't take long. I want to overwhelm your heart, not your fingers! We're going to look at specific actions and attitudes that God deems worthy of reward. His Word is specific. I like that! We can know what we are to do in order to lay up treasure in Heaven.

Scripture in fact emphasizes the importance of our *knowing* about rewards:

> Serve wholeheartedly, as if you were serving the Lord, not men, because you *know* that the Lord will reward everyone for whatever good he does…
>
> (EPH. 6:7–8, EMPHASIS MINE)

Our Father knows how to motivate His children to right thinking and right living. Desiring God's rewards is not selfish or prideful. It might be possible to start out with a wrong attitude, but it would be *impossible* to stay that way. (James and John will later prove my point!) If the promise of reward could in *any* way sully our motives, God would have surprised us when we reached Heaven instead of telling us in advance. He doesn't put stumbling blocks in our path to obedience!

It's odd that we resist being motivated by God's prizes. We certainly respond to worldly ones! We covet the Nobel Prize, the Heisman Trophy, and the Oscars. We build a Hall of Fame for every imaginable occupation. We applaud the Class Valedictorian, Employee of the Month, and Eagle Scout. We compete for year-end bonuses and gold-star stickers. We have filing cabinets stuffed with grade school award certificates. (What else can you do with those?) I'm sure you can think of lots more.

(?) **Has the promise of reward, or loss of reward, ever positively motivated you? Explain.**

My husband and I used the reward system at times to encourage our children. One such time was when our seven-year-old son participated in a second grade basketball league. Although he was a head taller than the other boys, he was timid on the court and let the other boys do the scoring. We wanted him to give sports a try! So we promised him a quarter every time he got his hands on the basketball. Mind you, he didn't have to make a goal or even take a shot—he just had to *touch* the ball! The incentive had a positive effect! He had some successes—even made a few goals—and a lasting love for sports was ignited.

Did we think less of our son when he responded to the promise of reward? Of course not—it was our idea! Actually, it was a *joy* to reward him at the end of a game, and the more quarters it cost us, the better! We loved to see him take a risk or two, gain confidence, and grow in his abilities.

Don't you know that it's the same with our Heavenly Father? He wants us on the ball! He loves to reward us—it was His idea! God delights in helping us over our fears and insecurities so we can live successful, *fully engaged* lives. We ignite our love for Jesus when we step up and put our faith on the line, thereby experiencing the faithfulness and reality of our God.

The following scriptures emphasize the positive effect of eternal rewards. **Read them and answer the question(s) that follow:**

> *Ps. 62:11–12*... two things have I heard: that you, O God, are strong, and that you, O Lord, are loving. Surely you will reward each person according to what he has done.

> *Jer. 17:10* I the LORD search the heart and examine the mind, to reward a man according to his conduct, according to what his deeds deserve.

> *Heb. 6:10* God is not unjust; he will not forget your work and the love you have shown him as you have helped his people and continue to help them.

Based upon these three scriptures, why is God qualified to be our Rewarder?

> *Colossians 3:23–24* Whatever you do, work at it with all your heart, as working for the Lord, not for men, since you know that you will receive an inheritance from the Lord as a reward. It is the Lord Christ you are serving.

What will we be rewarded for?

(?) What are we to "know"?

1 John 4:16b-18 Whoever lives in love lives in God, and God in him. In this way, love is made complete among us so that we will have confidence on the day of judgment, because in this world we are like him. There is no fear in love. But perfect love drives out fear, because fear has to do with punishment. The one who fears is not made perfect in love.

(?) **How can we have confidence at the Judgment Seat and not fear punishment?**

When I teach on the subject of heavenly reward, some people balk. They protest that we should serve and obey Jesus solely for love's sake. Yet it is impossible to desire heavenly rewards *without* love for Jesus; the scriptures above prove it true! *Abiding in His love* is the *only way* to reap eternal rewards! Scripture testifies that *the greater our love* for God and the more fully we surrender to His will, the more confidence we will have in the day of judgment. We need not fear standing before Him in the future when we *love* Him in the present!

Scripture negates the assumption that only immature Christians would need the encouragement of eternal rewards. *Paul* pressed on for the prize (Phil. 3:14), *Moses* looked to the reward (Hebrews 11:26), *Jesus* endured for the joy set before Him (Hebrews 12:2).

Please read *Hebrews 10:32–39*. It is a good illustration of our need for extra motivation.

(?) **What did these Christians "know" that enabled them to joyfully surrender earthly possessions?** (v. 34)

(◉) **In the midst of their trials, what did they have need of?** (vs. 35-36)

(◉) **What future event were they to live in the light of?** (v. 37)

(◉) **What pleases God and what does not?** (v. 38)

The Hebrew Christians were standing firm amidst great trials. They were letting go of earthly possessions—even joyfully—because they *knew* what awaited them in Heaven. If we are sacrificing little for the cause of Christ, it may be because we have put our hope on temporal treasures instead of heavenly ones.

Hear C. S. Lewis' thoughts on the matter:

> Indeed, if we consider the unblushing promises of reward and the staggering nature of the rewards promised in the Gospels, it would seem that Our Lord finds our desires not too strong, but too weak. We are half-hearted creatures, fooling about with drink and sex and ambition when infinite joy is offered us, like an ignorant child who wants to go on making mud pies in a slum because he cannot imagine what is meant by the offer of a holiday at the sea. We are far too easily pleased.[70]

Don't you agree that our desires for God's rewards are too weak? Are we far too easily pleased with the stuff of this world? We often think Christianity is about loss... but it's really about gain!

(◉) Read *Matt. 20:20–28* **and record what you learn concerning the criteria of heavenly greatness.**

On more than one occasion, the issue of who would be the greatest in the Kingdom came up for discussion among the disciples. Jesus did not rebuke them for desiring greatness! But He did teach them that the least, the servant, and the humble would be the greatest (Luke 9:48; Mark 9:35; Matt. 18:4). In one instance, He donned a towel and washed their feet, giving them an example of the path to greatness (John 13:4–17). In God's economy, the way up is down!

The two sons of Zebedee, James and John, did "drink the cup" of suffering for the sake of Christ. James was the first apostle martyred (Acts 12:2). John lived a long life, yet as a "companion in the suffering" of Jesus (Rev. 1:9). The highest honors in Heaven are not without cost. Consider Jesus. He left the wonders of Heaven and became man, making Himself nothing for our sake, humbling Himself even unto death on a cross. Therefore God highly exalted Him (Phil. 2:6–11). Our sacrifice could in no measure match Jesus,' but we *are* called to lay down our lives for others (John 15:12–13). Let's not back off from seeking the fullest prize of Heaven! But let's do it by humbling ourselves under God's mighty hand—serving anyone, anywhere, anytime, in any way He asks. Then He will exalt us at the proper time (1 Peter 5:6).

Printed below is a selection of scriptures that reveal the secret to heavenly reward. Pay particular attention to the *attitudes* God desires for us to have. Some of these scriptures we have studied before, but I think you will enjoy seeing them together as we complete this segment on the Judgment Seat. Besides, we will need to read them often! Like the Hebrew Christians, we have need of endurance!

(‽) **Underline or write in the margin what *earthly action or attitude* results in reward.**

1 Sam. 26:23 The LORD rewards every man for his righteousness and faithfulness.

Prov. 19:17 He who is kind to the poor lends to the LORD, and he will reward him for what he has done.

Matt. 5:11–12 Blessed are you when people insult you, persecute you and falsely say all kinds of evil against you because of me. Rejoice and be glad, because great is your reward in heaven…

Matt. 5:19 …whoever practices and teaches these commands will be called great in the kingdom of heaven.

Matt. 6:6 But when you pray, go into your room, close the door and pray to your Father, who is unseen. Then your Father, who sees what is done in secret, will reward you.

Matt. 10:41–42 Anyone who receives a prophet because he is a prophet will receive a prophet's reward, and anyone who receives a righteous man because he is a righteous man will receive a righteous man's reward. And if anyone gives even a cup of cold water to one of these little ones because he is my disciple, I tell you the truth, he will certainly not lose his reward.

Matt. 19:29 And everyone who has left houses or brothers or sisters or father or mother or children or fields for my sake will receive a hundred times as much and will inherit eternal life.

Luke 6:35 But love your enemies, do good to them, and lend to them without expecting to get anything back. Then your reward will be great, and you will be sons of the Most High…

Luke 14:13–14 But when you give a banquet, invite the poor, the crippled, the lame, the blind, and you will be blessed. Although they cannot repay you, you will be repaid at the resurrection of the righteous.

1 Tim. 6:18–19 Command them to do good, to be rich in good deeds, and to be generous and willing to share. In this way they will lay up treasure for themselves as a firm foundation for the coming age, so that they may take hold of the life that is truly life.

James 1:12 Blessed is the man who perseveres under trial, because when he has stood the test, he will receive the crown of life that God has promised to those who love him.

1 Pet. 5:2–4 Be shepherds of God's flock that is under your care, serving as overseers—not because you must, but because you are willing, as God wants you to be; not greedy for money, but eager to serve; not lording it over those entrusted to you, but being examples to the flock. And when the Chief Shepherd appears, you will receive the crown of glory that will never fade away.

2 Tim. 4:7–8 I have fought the good fight, I have finished the race, I have kept the faith. Now there is in store for me the crown of righteousness, which the Lord, the righteous Judge, will award to me on that day—and not only to me, but also to all who have longed for his appearing.

Rev. 2:10b Be faithful, even to the point of death, and I will give you the crown of life.

🙂 Wow! What a way to live! What earthly good does heavenly-mindedness produce?

🙂 What do you think would happen to your relationship with Jesus Christ if you were fervently believing and acting upon these scriptures?

Now we know why pursuing God's rewards is a *good* thing! Anyone who begins living out these scriptures will also begin to live like Jesus! Every reward is a means to experience Jesus—His love, His sufferings, His servant's heart, and His outreach. Every reward puts self-centered living to death and gives rise to abundant, joyful living. Every reward has the power to sustain, strengthen, and reassure us in times of stress and sacrifice.

John Wesley wrote these words to encourage his friend Ann Bolton in her time of need:

> When the Son of Man shall come in His glory and assign every man his own reward, that reward will undoubtedly be proportioned (1) to our inward holiness, our likeness to God; (2) to our works; and (3) to our sufferings. Therefore whatever you suffer in time you will be an unspeakable gainer in eternity... your joy is to come! Look up, my dear friend, look up! and see your crown before you! A little longer, and you shall drink of the rivers of pleasure that flow at God's right hand for evermore.[71]

Oh that we would simply *look up!* All of life—the ordinary, the sorrowful, the plentiful—all provide opportunities to bless God by believing in what He has promised. The type of life God rewards not only honors Him on Earth, but it will also honor Him in Heaven.

⟨♫⟩ Read *Revelation 4:9–11*. **How will we express our love for God in Heaven?**

This will be our true crowning moment, when our gold, silver, and precious jewels—our very best, our lavish devotion—is laid before the Throne of God. No greater gift can we give.

But no greater gift can we receive! Genesis 15:1 is a precious declaration from God to Abram. I've taken the liberty to delete Abram's name from the scripture in order that you may insert yours. (I don't think he'll mind.) In the original language, the word "I" is separately expressed, and therefore, emphatic.[72] So read it with the emphasis on the "I":

"Do not be afraid, _____, *I* am your
(your name)

shield, your very great reward."

God is not only our Rewarder, He is our Reward! In King James style, He is our Exceedingly Great Reward! Jesus is our Ultimate Treasure in Heaven. *And the way we love Him today will enhance our relationship with Him forever.* We may cast our crowns before Him, but His rewards are eternal, for He is eternal.

> *In that day the LORD Almighty will be a glorious crown,*
> *a beautiful wreath for the remnant of his people.*
>
> (Isa. 28:5)

Therefore, "Look up, my dear friend, look up! and see your crown before you!"

WEEK 8
The Profound Mystery

*O*ften in Bible studies, the author will conclude with regret that the journey is about to end. Not me! I am absolutely thrilled to be at this point! I have dreamed of the day when all that God has poured into my heart will make its way into another person's heart. At last I am privileged to extend the invitation to this glorious place called Heaven. How awesome it will be to stand side-by-side in God's Banquet Hall with you! I long for it to be bursting with people—people I may not know now, but people I will have the incredible pleasure of spending eternity with. I can hardly wait to have so many friends!

A long, long, long time ago, after my heart heard God's command to "Write!" this message on Heaven, I could hardly wait to get started! But before I wrote much more than an outline, my sweet daughter became engaged. I proudly took up the job of M.O.B. (Mother of the Bride) and got to work! My husband opened a bank account and my daughter and I had a blast spending every nickel allotted to the cause! We planned and shopped and doted over every detail for six fast-paced months. One of my favorite jobs was taste-testing wedding cake. (Which required visiting several bakeries!) Needless to say, the Bible study was put on hold. Her wedding was one of the greatest joys of my life.

But I often wondered, "Why the interlude?" Why didn't the Lord just wait until after the wedding to announce my new assignment? Now, two years later, I marvel at the gift He gave me—not only of precious time with my daughter, but also of precious insight into His Heaven. How perfect that the Lord began my research into Heaven not with a textbook, but with a field trip! For no event better pictures Heaven than a wedding. That is what we will study this week—from the proposal, to the engagement, to the ceremony. But I give you fair warning! We won't be attending this Wedding as the M.O.B. or F.O.B.—for all who belong to Christ, whether male or female, young or old, will attend as the Bride!

> "For this reason a man will leave his father and mother and be united to his wife, and the two will become one flesh." This is a profound mystery—but I am talking about Christ and the church.
>
> (EPHESIANS 5:31–32)

A profound mystery indeed! Yet the union between Christ and humankind is the essence of Heaven. So grab your Wedding Planner and come along. Let's learn what our Heavenly F.O.B. has in store for us! It's the grandest, most lavish affair ever planned for the greatest, most lavish love ever offered.

DAY 1 *a match made in heaven*

THE GOSPEL OF JOHN RECORDS Jesus' very first miracle. Can you guess where it took place? At a *wedding,* of course! I think it is so appropriate for Jesus' glory to *first* be revealed at a wedding, for we will discover this week that the *culmination* of His glory will be at a wedding as well. At the wedding in Cana, Jesus took ordinary water and transformed it into extraordinary wine. Although this first miracle demonstrated the power and kindness of God in a small matter, it astounded His disciples and caused them to put their faith in Jesus (John 2:1–11).

In a much more amazing feat, Jesus takes us—ordinary as we may be—and transforms us into extraordinary, eternal beings—reflecting His very own image. He fills our empty vessels with the wine of the Holy Spirit. This far greater miracle is accomplished by the same means—entirely by God's power and His kindness.

For the rest of the week, we are going to study Jewish wedding customs typical of Jesus' day. Doing so will awaken us to a new understanding of God's love and a deeper revelation of His saving grace. As with the disciples, I hope it will astound us and cause us to put our faith lavishly in Him. Scripture is many things, but more than anything it is a *Love Story.* From cover to cover, it proclaims God's desire for our hearts and His pursuit of our affections. Hear God's love language in these excerpts:

Isa. 54:5, 10 For your Maker is your husband... Though the mountains be shaken and the hills be removed, yet my unfailing love for you will not be shaken...

Hosea 2:16, 19–20 "In that day," declares the LORD, "you will call me 'my husband'; you will no longer call me 'my master.' I will betroth you to me forever; I will betroth you in righteousness and justice, in love and compassion. I will betroth you in faithfulness, and you will acknowledge the LORD."

Jer. 3:14 "Return, faithless people," declares the LORD, "for I am your husband. I will choose you... and bring you to Zion."

Isa. 62:5... as a bridegroom rejoices over his bride, so will your God rejoice over you.

(☺) **How does God describe His relationship to us?**

(☺) Read *Matthew 9:14–15.* **Who is the Bridegroom?**

(☺) **Who are the guests, or the attendants, of the Bridegroom?**

As the curtain rises on Heaven's Great Love Story, we see God in the role of a Husband to Israel. In the acts that follow, God casts His Son as the Bridegroom to the Church. Such language is used to communicate the deepest level of intimacy, faithfulness, and devotion. In today's world of broken marriages, we may not appreciate the extent of what God is saying, but the Jewish people did. The Jewish marriage consisted of three parts: the arrangement (shiddukhin); the betrothal (erusin); and the wedding ceremony (nisuin). We'll begin today with *Act I: The Arrangement.* I'll provide the wedding trivia (marked with 🕊); you make the parallels from Scripture. Let's get started!

🕊 According to ancient Jewish tradition, marriage was initiated by the father of the potential groom. This was perhaps in imitation of the Heavenly

Father who provided Adam with a wife.[73] Although the father chose the bride, the prospective groom's wishes were most always honored.

Read *2 Thessalonians 2:13–14.*

(?) **As the Bride for God's Son, were you chosen? By whom?**

(?) **What were you chosen for?**

(?) **How is salvation accomplished?**

(?) The Groom had His eye on you as well. **Make note of Jesus' words:**

"You did not _____ me, but I _____ you . . ."

(JOHN 15:16)

Ours was not a blind date! Jesus long ago declared His love for you and for me. In the Song of Songs, the romance between Solomon and his bride is symbolic of the love between Christ and the Church:

All beautiful you are, my darling; there is no flaw in you. You have stolen my heart, my sister, my bride; you have stolen my heart with one glance of your eyes...

(SONGS 4:7, 9)

Do you believe Jesus has such affection for you? Or that God deliberately makes Himself vulnerable to the power of love? It's *true*! He has chosen *you* for the sole purpose of sharing His glory with you! He seeks *you* out. And so did the Jewish father and groom:

❧ When a possible match was made by the father of the groom, the groom-to-be would leave his home and travel to the home of the bride-to-be. Often his father, a representative of his father, or a friend would accompany him.

Read *John 6:38–40*. **Where did our Groom come from and at whose initiative?**

Read *John 3:27–30*. **How does John the Baptist describe his relationship to Jesus?**

Interestingly, John the Baptist plays the role of the friend of the Bridegroom, the one who was sent before Jesus to prepare the heart of the Bride-to-be. Jesus referred to His disciples as "attendants" or "children of the bridechamber" (Matt. 9:15, kjv). These were friends who "had the charge of providing what was necessary for the nuptials."[74] These two insights will mean more to us when we arrive at the Wedding Feast, so file them away for later.

Sometimes the father of the groom enlisted help in finding a bride for his son. A matchmaker (shadkhan) might be hired, who would seek out the perfect mate. Abraham's servant, Eliezar, served as a matchmaker of sorts. When Abraham desired a wife for his son Issac, he sent Eliezar to his relatives in his former country. God led Eliezar to Rebekah at a gathering around the local well. After Eliezar made the proper negotiations with the family, Rebekah agreed to be wed to Issac. Eliezer then escorted her safely back to her new home and life, to a man she had never met (Gen. 24).

Read Jesus' words in *John 15:26*. **Who does the Father send to woo our hearts to the love of His Son?**

We have a Matchmaker! Amazingly, the name *Eliezar* and the Holy Spirit both mean "the Helper." Upon the initiative of the Father, the Holy Spirit convicts us of our need of Jesus. And because of His ministry to us, like Rebekah:

> Though you have not seen him, you love him; and even though you do not see him now, you believe in him and are filled with an inexpressible and glorious joy…
>
> (1 Pet. 1:8)

Without our Matchmaker, we inevitably choose the wrong objects to love. The human race isn't so good at knowing what will lead to happiness and satisfaction in life.

🖊 **Read the scriptures that follow and circle what we often seek in life that fails to satisfy our souls.**

Eccl. 2:10–11 My heart took delight in all my work, and this was the reward for all my labor. Yet when I surveyed all that my hands had done and what I had toiled to achieve, everything was meaningless, a chasing after the wind; nothing was gained under the sun.

Eccl. 5:10 Whoever loves money never has money enough; whoever loves wealth is never satisfied with his income. This too is meaningless.

🖊 **Now let's read and underline the secrets to being *satisfied*.**

Ps. 63:3, 5 Because your love is better than life, my lips will glorify you…My soul will be satisfied as with the richest of foods; with singing lips my mouth will praise you.

Isa. 58:10–11 …if you spend yourselves in behalf of the hungry and satisfy the needs of the oppressed, then your light will rise in the darkness, and your night will become like the noonday. The LORD will guide you always; he will satisfy your needs in a sun-scorched land…

Matt. 5:6 (NAS) Blessed are those who hunger and thirst for righteousness, for they shall be satisfied.

Ps. 42:5 Why are your downcast, O my soul? Why so disturbed within me? Put your hope in God…

Matt. 11:29 Take my yoke upon you and learn from me, for I (Jesus) am gentle and humble in heart, and you will find rest for your souls.

God alone can fill the void in the human soul and satisfy the longings of the human heart. Although mankind often ignores God's advances, the pages of human history reveal our acute inability to be satisfied apart from a relationship with Him. I'm so thankful that we have a Helper—a Matchmaker—to help lead us to the Perfect Lover of our Souls. I have made so many wrong choices in an attempt to satisfy my need for love and significance. Have you done the same? If you have, you know that the things the world claims will satisfy are unable to do so. Our souls are shaped *by God* and *for God.* So we can never be happy apart from Him! It is God's greatest pleasure to *fill us up*…with Himself!

Remember the Parable of the Wedding Feast? (See *Day Four/Week Six;* Matthew 22:1–14.) Jesus tells the story of a king who sent out his servants with invitations to his son's wedding. Many paid no attention or refused to come, so he sent out a second and third set of invitations. *He wanted the wedding hall full of guests!* Thankfully, our matchmaking Holy Spirit makes repeated visits to issue the Father's invitation to the heavenly feast. Have you read your invitation?

It is found in *Isaiah 55:1–9.*

(?) **Who is invited to come?** (v. 1)

(?) **How does God's offer contrast to what we can buy from the world?** (vs. 1–2)

(?) **List what God promises us if we come to Him.**

(?) Listed below are the "richest of fare" that God offers those who respond to His invitation to come to Him. **Which one(s) are you presently in need of?**

- ❑ A nourished and satisfied soul
- ❑ A delight in God's Word
- ❑ Security of eternal life
- ❑ His personal love
- ❑ Freedom from evil ways and thoughts
- ❑ A splendor that attracts others to God
- ❑ His nearness
- ❑ His mercy and full pardon over my sin

(?) Look back over verses 1–7. What actions are required of us to experience all of the above?

(?) Overall, what is your impression of God's desire for you?

Do you believe God desires your company? That He yearns for you to join Him in Heaven? He *pursues you* with His love. He offers it *freely and lavishly.* He unabashedly promises you "the moon" if you will simply *come* to Him! Hear His promises! He has sent out His Matchmaker to knock at the door of your heart. He has the perfect match for you, the Lord Jesus Christ. He is your Soul Mate, *your match made in Heaven.* Don't labor for what does not satisfy! Look to Him to meet every need of your soul. *He loves you so!*

Here I am! I stand at the door and knock. If anyone
hears my voice and opens the door, I will come in and
eat with him, and he with me.

(REV. 3:20)

DAY 2 *the proposal*

MY HUSBAND, DON, LEFT FOR work one morning not suspecting that by lunch he would have to face one of his worst fears—losing his daughter to "another man." When our daughter's boyfriend Andy called him from the road and asked him to lunch that day, Don innocently responded that he would give me a call and see where we could all meet. Andy then told him he'd prefer it be just *the two* of them. Uh-oh. All Don could get out of his mouth was "Oh! Can I call you right back?" Then he hung up! Head in his hands—heart in his throat—he struggled to pull himself together. He knew what *this* meant. This was the moment he had been dreading all of his daughter's life. And it was here.

Don't misunderstand—*Don really liked Andy!* That's what made it so hard, I suppose. Andy did ask for Don's permission to marry Taylor at lunch that day. And Don managed to say "Yes." But then he followed with some inane advice (something about paying your bills every month...). The conversation *did* improve and even had its tender moments, with both men shedding a few tears. But Don remembers little else that was said. The man was in shock and remained in shock for the *entire* engagement. There was the moment he first saw Taylor in her wedding dress... the moment with Andy in the Groom's Room... the moment when he choked out "Her mother and I do" at the altar. Whew! Weddings are hard on daddies! They don't step out of first place in their daughters' hearts easily.

But Andy earned kudos with Don by respecting him enough to *ask* for Taylor's hand. Not many young men ask permission of the fathers these days! But in first century Israel, the fathers of both the bride and groom played a *major* role. As we learned yesterday, the father of the groom initiated the search for a bride for his son. When a potential match was made, the son journeyed to the bride's home. A Jewish marriage was not a matter to be determined over lunch, however. Much haggling went on among the men involved. I'm trying to picture Don and Andy negotiating over Taylor, and I'm *so* thankful some traditions have changed!

Today we'll continue with the same format as yesterday. I'll provide the background material of the Jewish wedding (), and you will make the Scriptural parallels to our heavenly Wedding. Keep in mind that, just as the purpose of earthly marriage is for two lives to become one, the same is true of our match made in Heaven. God's purpose in His proposal is to *share His life* with you in a loving, fulfilling, and intimate relationship.

When the fullness of time arrived, God sent His Son into the world, born of a woman, born under the Law (Galatians 4:4). The Son left Heaven to propose His love in a way that would draw all people to Himself (John 12:32).

With that in mind, let's pick back up with our potential Jewish bride and groom:

When the groom left for the bride's home, he brought with him four items: the bride price, the marriage contract, a skin of wine, and gifts. We'll study the gifts tomorrow. The bride price (mohar) was required by law. It usually was a sizeable sum of money, often an entire year's wages or more. It reflected not only the wealth of the groom's family, but also the value of the bride to the groom.

The marriage covenant (ketubah) stated the rights of the bride and the ability of the groom to give the bride a better life. The groom-to-be and the father of the bride would haggle over these two terms of marriage and the negotiations could take weeks. Only when the father of the bride was totally satisfied with both the bride price and the marriage contract could the young man approach the prospective bride. In the ceremony that followed, he would read the marriage contract out loud, proclaiming her value to him and his promises to her. The groom would pour a cup of wine, take a sip, and set the cup before the prospective bride. If the bride accepted his proposal of marriage, the groom would sign the marriage contract along with two witnesses.

Now let's consider the parallels to our heavenly Groom and His Bride, the Church. In our case, the Father of the Groom is also the Father of the Bride!

Read each scripture below and find the matching parallel to the Jewish wedding customs listed on the next page.

1. The Law required that without the shedding of blood there is no forgiveness (Hebrews 9:22); all have sinned and fall short of the glory of God (Rom. 3:23).

2. For you know that it was not with perishable things such as silver or gold that you were redeemed from the empty way of life handed down to you from your forefathers, but with the precious blood of Christ, a lamb without blemish or defect (1 Pet. 1:18–19).

3. "Father, if you are willing, take this cup from me; yet not my will, but yours be done." An angel from heaven appeared to him and strengthened him. And being in anguish, he prayed more earnestly, and his sweat was like drops of blood falling to the ground (Luke 22:42–44).

4. On him (Jesus) God the Father has placed his seal of approval (John 6:27). Jesus humbled himself and became obedient to death—even

death on a cross! Therefore God exalted him to the highest place (Phil. 2:8–10).

5. Christ is the mediator of a new covenant, that those who are called may receive the promised eternal inheritance (Hebrews 9:15).

6. Then he (Jesus) took the cup, gave thanks and offered it to them (the disciples), saying, "Drink from it, all of you. This is my blood of the covenant, which is poured out for many for the forgiveness of sins" (Matt. 26:27–28).

Now match the scriptures to the custom. (I'll get you started.)

_ The Bride Price reflected the value of the Bride to the Groom and to the Father.

_ The Groom wrestled with the terms of the Bride Price with the Father of the Bride.

1 God's Holy Law demanded a Bride Price be paid for the sins of the world.

_ The Father of the Bride was satisfied with the Groom's provision for the Bride.

_ The Groom offered the cup of wine to His Bride.

_ The Groom offered a Marriage Covenant that declared His promises the Bride.

Aren't you awed at the deliberate and lavish steps of love that God took to bring you into a permanent relationship with Himself? (Answers: 2, 3, 1, 4, 6, 5.) *Everything* necessary for you to be the Bride of Christ has been done. The Bride Price has been paid. The Law has been fulfilled. The Marriage Proposal has been written. It was signed in red by the Groom on the cross and witnessed by the Father and the Spirit. Assurances of love and promises of eternal bliss have been spoken over you through God's Covenant Word. The Cup is set before you. The next move is up to you.

Let's learn what to do from our Jewish bride-to-be:

The prospective bride had the right to refuse to marry, although she most always deferred to her father's wishes. To accept the cup was to say "Yes" to a proposal of marriage. She would drink the wine to the dregs, symbolic of the bitter and sweet of marriage. The marriage covenant was then *sealed*.

Read *John 6:53–54*.

As the potential Bride, what "cup of wine" does our Groom offer us?

When we drink His cup, what do we receive?

Just as the Jewish bride-to-be declared her desire to be wed by drinking the cup of wine, so we declare our desire to be wed to Jesus Christ by drinking the cup of wine He has set before us. But our cup is not filled with ordinary wine. It is filled with the blood of Jesus, the sacrifice of His life for ours. To accept His proposal, we must accept His blood poured out on our behalf.

We might at first respond like the disciples when they first heard these words of Jesus, "This is a hard teaching. Who can accept it?" (John 6:60). But we *must* accept it; it is our provision for eternal life! So let's take a closer look at the way of salvation. We don't want a shred of confusion or doubt regarding our salvation—Heaven is at stake! Tomorrow we will pick right back up with our couple as they enter into their time of betrothal.

To better understand Jesus' words concerning drinking His "blood," let's read more of John 6, looking for Jesus' explanations as to how to receive eternal life. It may be repetitive to you, but if *anything* bears repeating, it would be this!

Read *John 6:26–58*, noting each time Jesus teaches how to enter into eternal life.

(☺) Let's read a few other scriptures concerning how to enter the Kingdom of Heaven. **Underline what they reveal about the way of salvation:**

John 1:12–13 Yet to all who received him, to those who believed in his name, he gave the right to become children of God—children born not of natural descent, nor of human decision or a husband's will, but born of God.

John 10:9 I am the gate; whoever enters through me will be saved.

John 3:5–7 Jesus answered, "I tell you the truth, no one can enter the kingdom of God unless he is born of water and the Spirit. Flesh gives birth to flesh, but the Spirit gives birth to spirit. You should not be surprised at my saying, 'You must be born again.'"

Rom. 10:9–11… if you confess with your mouth, "Jesus is Lord," and believe in your heart that God raised him from the dead, you will be saved. For it is with your heart that you believe and are justified, and it is with your mouth that you confess and are saved. As the Scripture says, "Anyone who trusts in him will never be put to shame."

Matt. 7:21–23 Not everyone who says to me, "Lord, Lord," will enter the kingdom of heaven, but only he who does the will of my Father who is in heaven. Many will say to me on that day, "Lord, Lord, did we not prophesy in your name, and in your name drive out demons and perform many miracles?" Then I will tell them plainly, "I never knew you. Away from me, you evildoers!"

(☺) **In the passage above, what did the "evildoers" *not* do?**

What is the will of the Father, but to believe upon His Son? Those saying "Lord, Lord" to Jesus were not in a relationship with Him; He did not *know* them! Salvation is all about a relationship with Jesus Christ. Eternal life comes from accepting Jesus as the Son of God. Just as we must eat and drink for physical life, so we must partake of Jesus for spiritual life. To eat and drink of Him implies we depend upon Him to sustain our life.

Many things accompany salvation—repentance, confession, baptism—but salvation is first and foremost a matter of *receiving Christ as your Lord and Savior.* There is only *one* plan, *one* way, *one* Name by which we may be saved—HIS! (Acts 4:12). There is *no* one else who has the words of life. There is *no* other way to the Father (John 14:6). Just Jesus.

And although salvation is simple and direct, it is also deeply personal and serious. One cannot partially or casually eat Jesus' flesh or drink His blood. Jesus isn't a *way* of life—Jesus *is* life. He gave Himself completely to us. We respond by giving ourselves completely to Him.

For years, I struggled with a "partial relationship" with God. I always wanted Heaven, but not enough to let go of Earth. I wanted assurance of eternal life while retaining control of my present life. I made God many vain promises, I foolishly tried to bargain with Him, and I "started over" more times than I'd like to remember. Then, during a Bible study in my church, God used the truth of Matthew 5:3 to show me what in my relationship with Him was lacking: "Blessed are the poor in spirit, for theirs is the king-dom of heaven."

As I learned what "poor in spirit" meant, I saw very clearly how "des-titute" I was without Him. My desire for control over my life was shat-tered by this one verse from His Word. I finally "gave up" and willingly and thankfully surrendered my life to Him. Then the miracle happened—God entered into my life for keeps! Although I had not considered the "rest of the scripture" when I relinquished my life, God had a precious point to make. He graciously gave me the "bonus"—assurance that the Kingdom of Heaven was mine!

When we "die" to self and yield ourselves to the love of God, we are "born" from above. The Spirit of Christ takes up residence in our hearts and begins the miracle of forming Christ in us. It is a work of God, "from the first dawning of grace in the soul, till it is consummated in glory."[75] It begins with the one step: *faith in Jesus.*

One day, out of the clear blue, a friend's five-year-old son asked her, "When you accept Jesus into your heart, He keeps you from going to Hell and gets you into Heaven, right?" She affirmed him and he followed with a deeper question, "Then why doesn't everybody just accept Him?"

Don't you wonder that as well? God makes it so simple, so compelling, and so profound. His offer of salvation is *not* to fix your problems or to make you obey certain rules. God is not after your money or your service. He is after your *heart. He loves you.* Salvation is a proposal of *marriage,* of *union*—God to man, the Creator to His created. It is an invitation to join Him *in* life, *for* life! He wants you with Him now and forever.

Let's not miss the opportunity to respond to Him in faith. Consider the cup He offers you…the Bride Price he paid for you…His Marriage

Covenant to care for you now and forever. Believe the permanence of His commitment to you! He sought *you* out!

The following is a prayer that we will build upon this week as we learn more about God's marriage covenant. Pray it to accept His proposal to you, or pray it as a renewal of your vows.

Dear Heavenly Father,

*Thank You for sending Jesus. Thank You for inviting me into union with You through Your Son. Thank You, Jesus, for choosing me to be Yours. I believe that You, Jesus, are the Son of God! I believe You alone are the source of eternal life. I believe that You left Your Home in Heaven to come to my home to proclaim Your love for me. Although I feel unworthy of Your love for me, I gratefully receive it. You love me as I am—a sinner, who needs a Savior. You proved Your love to me when You paid for my sin. You paid my Bride Price with Your own life. Thank You for accepting the cup of suffering for my sake. Thank You!!! I accept Your forgiveness and the cup You offer. I **accept!** I drink the cup to the dregs, Lord—the bitter with the sweet. I want a relationship with You at any cost, above anything and all things. I receive Your life and lay down mine. I give You my sins, my fears, my doubts, my rebellious ways. Free me to love You with all my heart, mind, soul, and strength. Keep me close to Your side and safe in Your love. Thank You that You will forever be faithful to me. I promise, by Your grace and power, to be faithful to You, until death we do meet. Amen!*

DAY 3 *starry eyed*

HOW I PRAY THAT YOUR love for Jesus is being stirred as we begin to think of Him as our Bridegroom. If you accepted His proposal of love for the first time yesterday, please know there is a *party* going on in *your* honor in Heaven! (And I'm throwing a shindig over you too!) If you have been engaged to Christ for some time now, I hope that you are falling in love with Him all over again! Our Triune God is a romantic at heart. In Genesis 15, God took Abraham outside and said, "Now look toward the heavens, and count the stars, if you are able to count them." Picture Abraham standing alone with God under a *brilliant* desert sky—counting... counting... counting…and counting. After what must have been a very long time, God whispered in his ear, "So shall your descendants be." *Oh!* The greatest desire of his heart—*granted!* The deepest hurt in his life—*healed!* In one earth-shattering, life-changing, heart-rending moment, Abraham *believed* God and God proclaimed Him righteous!

You are going to love *Galatians 3:6–9*. **Who is a descendant of Abraham?**

Just think—as a fellow believer and a descendant of Abraham, there is a star in the sky representing you! *You* were a star in the sky Abraham counted so long ago—a star hand-placed in an infinite sky at Creation. *Wow!* What a brilliant promise of your faith in God and His in you! Perhaps that is why God calls each of the stars by name (Ps. 147:4)—each one is a child of His! Next time you look up at a night sky, *find your star,* and enjoy a magical moment with your God.

> You were a star in the sky Abraham counted so long ago—a star hand-placed in an infinite sky at Creation.

Yesterday we concluded with the prospective bride accepting the cup of wine that her groom-to-be set before her. Let's rejoin them at that very moment in *Act II: The Betrothal.*

When the young lady gave her consent to marry and took a drink from the cup, she was officially a bride. The couple was *legally* bound and entered into the betrothal period. They were treated as if they were married, yet they could not live together or consummate the marriage. A divorce was required to dissolve the betrothal and could only be sought by the groom. The groom would give her a ring, or a coin, and declare: "With this ring, you are consecrated to me, according to the tradition of Moses and Israel." The bride was literally referred to as "one bought with a price."

Read *Jude 1:1*. (You'll find Jude right before Revelation.)

When we say "Yes" to Jesus' offer of salvation, what is our new status?

Now turn to *1 Corinthians 6:9–11, 19–20.*

(image) **How does God describe you after your salvation?** (vs. 11, 19)

(image) **How are you to regard yourself?** (vs. 19–20)

I love the idea of being "kept" by Jesus. The Greek word *tereo* denotes "to watch over, preserve, keep, watch." It is used to describe the "keeping" power Christ exercised over His people.[76] He is the Keeper of our hearts.

Our betrothal to Jesus Christ is *legally* binding. "Justification" is a legal term meaning "to justify; to acquit; to declare righteous." Upon your declaration of faith in Jesus Christ, God deems you are "right" with Himself. This means that *regardless* of your former sins, *regardless* how you "feel" and *regardless* of your imperfection, *God* says YOU ARE HOLY. You are washed clean by the blood of Jesus.

"Sanctification" means "to set apart." It carries with it the sense of consecration, of being *made* holy. The Holy Spirit is the agent of sanctification. When He takes up residence in your heart, you become the Temple of God. An inward transformation begins to take place that leads to purity and godliness.

At justification, righteousness is *imputed* to your account. During sanctification, righteousness is *imparted* into your life. At glorification, righteousness *is* your life!

When Paul told the Corinthians they had been "bought with a price," they understood the marriage language. Corinth was an immoral, sinful city. In fact, the saying "to act the Corinthian" meant "to practice fornication." Yet now, as the betrothed to Christ, God had *pronounced* them holy. Therefore, they were to *treat themselves* as holy. They were to honor God with their bodies.

(⟳) What impact does it make upon you that you are "not your own; you were bought at a price" by Christ?

The Jewish betrothal wonderfully illustrates *our* sanctification process:

➤ The Betrothal period was called the *kiddushin*, which actually means "sanctification." Purity was a priority for the bride. She would visit a *mikveh*, a ritual bath where she would be totally submersed in a pool of water.[77] It was symbolic of a radical change of heart and a total commitment to a new way of life.[78] The bride would wear a veil whenever she left her home as a sign that she was spoken for. She spent this time learning how to be a wife.

Read *Acts 22:16* and *Ephesians 5:25–27.*

(⟳) How are we washed and prepared for a new way of life?

Read *2 Corinthians 11:2.*

(⟳) How will we be presented to our Husband?

Baptism powerfully symbolizes the washing of our sins and the rising to newness of life. We are washed clean with God's Living Water—sanctified *by truth* and *by faith.* The essence of *true* salvation is *transformation* (2 Cor. 5:17). We become a new creation, guided by a radical change of heart to a new allegiance!

Our time of betrothal is lived *loving* and *believing* God. Like the young bride, we are learners. The word "disciple" literally means "learner." We learn to be one with our Groom—learning to live like Him and love like Him and think like Him. We are "spoken for" and must not give our hearts to another.

We have a copy of the promises from our Groom in our Marriage Contract. Like precious love letters, read them often! Nothing can soothe an aching heart, boost a doubting heart, or disarm an angry heart like reading God's Word. During our engagement period, we will be tempted to forget our heavenly Groom and flirt with the things of the world. Regularly opening our ears to our Bridegroom's voice will keep us in love with our One and Only.

Often the young couple would not see each other until the wedding ceremony. Therefore, the groom would give his bride gifts (mattan) to remind her of his love and his promise to marry her. The father of the bride would also give his daughter a dowry (shiluhim) as part of her inheritance to help prepare her for her new life. Maidservants and land might be part of her dowry.

Read *John 14:26.*

What gift does your Heavenly Father and Heavenly Groom give you upon your betrothal?

What will this Gift remind you of?

Also turn to *Matthew 5:5.* **What land will we one day inherit?**

The Holy Spirit is our bridal gift from our Father and pledge of love from our Groom. He will keep us in contact with Jesus and remind us of His unfailing love. Jesus may be out of our sight for a season, but thanks to the work of the Holy Spirit, He will never be out of heart or mind! In the scripture below, I've emphasized two specific works of the Holy Spirit in the life of the new believer:

> In Him (Christ), you also, after listening to the message of truth, the gospel of your salvation—having also believed, you were *sealed* in Him with the Holy Spirit of promise, who is given as a *pledge* of our inheritance, with a view to the redemption of God's own possession, to the praise of His glory.
>
> (EPHESIANS 1:13–14 NAS, EMPHASIS MINE)

The Holy Spirit "seals" us at the first moment of salvation. The Greek word *sphragizo* was a stamp, a signet, or private mark for preservation. It was used to indicate security and permanency. The presence of the Holy Spirit in your life is *your* guarantee of salvation! You have been *claimed* and *marked* with the love and power of God!

The Greek word for "pledge" or "deposit" (NIV) is *arrhabon*. Originally, *arrhabon* meant "earnest-money that was deposited by the purchaser and forfeited if the purchase was not completed." In the era of the New Covenant, the Holy Spirit is "given as the divine pledge of a believer's future blessedness, particularly of their eternal inheritance."[79] And guess what? In modern Greek, *arrabona* is an engagement ring!

Don't you love God's Word? When you say "Yes" to Christ, He puts a ring on your finger—the Holy Spirit of God! Now that's what I call a Rock!

If you are unsure of God's marvelous love for you, just ask the Holy Spirit to convince you! It is His pleasure to bear witness with your spirit that you belong to God (Romans 8:16) and fully assure you of eternal life (1 John 5:13).

The church of Jesus Christ is His *Bride*. Above all things, a bride is desperately and wildly in love with her groom…and that is how we are to be. The Holy Spirit's greatest joy is to make Jesus known to you! He truly *pours* the love of God into your heart (Rom. 5:5). Don't be shy in asking God for more ability to love His Son. Scripture directs us to ask to be *filled* with the Spirit—and keep on being filled! (Eph. 5:18) His is the gift that keeps on giving and keeps on pouring! Just *ask* and then *trust*. The Father only gives good gifts (Luke 11:11–13).

And He has given us many! **Read the scriptures and circle the gifts you discover:**

John 14:27 Peace I leave with you; my peace I give you. I do not give to you as the world gives. Do not let your hearts be troubled and do not be afraid.

John 15:11 I have told you this so that my joy may be in you and that your joy may be complete.

Rom. 5:17 …how much more will those who receive God's abundant provision of grace and of the gift of righteousness reign in life through the one man, Jesus Christ.

1 John 1:9 If we confess our sins, he is faithful and just and will forgive us our sins and purify us from all unrighteousness.

Rom. 6:23 ...the gift of God is eternal life in Christ Jesus our Lord.

John 14:14 You may ask me for anything in my name, and I will do it.

What a Bridal Shower we have been given! (And truly, the list of all God has given us would be endless, wouldn't it?)

(?) **What would you consider the greatest gift your Heavenly Father has given you?**

After my daughter was married, there was not enough room in their one-bedroom apartment for all of the wedding gifts. So she stored the excess at my house. Just recently, she and Andy purchased their first home. They had such fun re-opening the stored gifts and finding the perfect place for them. In a similar way, if any of God's gifts have been "hidden away" from you for a time, re-open them! Peace, joy, grace, righteousness, forgiveness, and love—just to mention a few—are ours to unwrap each day. They are new *every* morning. Don't forget you have them!

🐦 After the giving of gifts at the Betrothal ceremony, the groom would return to his father's house. His departing words to his bride would be: "I'm going back to my father's house to prepare a place for you. When my father says it's ready, I will return and take you there to be with me forever."

Those words have a familiar ring! Remember Jesus' words in *John 14:2–3?*

In my Father's house are many rooms; if it were not so, I would have told you. I am going there to prepare a place for you. And if I go and prepare a place for you, I will come back and take you to be with me that you also may be where I am.

When Jesus spoke these words to His disciples, He was intentionally speaking like a Groom to His Bride. In Jesus' day, extended families often lived together. When a young man became engaged to be married, he would often return to his father's land and build an addition to his father's house for he and his bride. The complex (insula) had a central open courtyard and the family wings were built around it. The father's house could become quite large as sons, grandsons, and even great-grandsons added living quarters.

Jesus' disciples knew the wedding traditions of the day. Undoubtedly they formed a much more realistic picture of the place Jesus was preparing for them than we might. We shouldn't visualize ourselves *isolated* in a gigantic mansion in Heaven! Heaven *will* be spacious, but it will be more like a big insula—a family-oriented, close-knit community. How heavenly to have a courtyard adjacent to our rooms where the entire clan will gather with the Father!

However, there was a drawback to the Jewish tradition of building on to the father's house:

> The father of the groom would supervise his son's addition to the family insula, and it was *his* decision when the project was finished. Only with the father's permission could the groom return for his bride. Therefore, the bride knew the *season* of her wedding, but not the day or hour.

Another Father has the ultimate say-so concerning the timing of His Son's Wedding. Read *Matthew 24:36–44*.

What did Jesus say concerning when He will return for His Bride? (v. 36)

Therefore, how should we live? (vs. 42, 44)

I always wondered why Jesus did not know the exact day of His return! But in light of the Jewish wedding, it makes sense. The bonds of love between Father and Son are seen in the intricacies of their relationship. I like the thought of the Two of Them in different roles concerning me!

It's easy for me to trust my Heavenly Father with the timing of Jesus' return. But I cannot fathom how the mother of the Jewish bride kept from nagging the father of the groom for an exact wedding date! At least not having to tend to the many details of a wedding allowed the Jewish bride and her mother to be occupied with personal preparations. They did have one important task to complete for the wedding, however.

🖋 During the engagement, the bride would prepare her wedding dress with the help of the women in the community. She would also select the finest jewels to wear at the wedding.

Read *Isaiah 61:10*.

🎶 **Who will help us with our wedding attire and what will it consist of?**

🎶 Thinking back to last week's lessons concerning "gold, silver and costly stones" (1 Cor. 3:12), **what jewels might we wear on our Wedding Day?**

On our Wedding Day, we will be clothed in His righteousness; the work of God's hands for the display of His splendor (Isa. 60:21). Our wedding dress will be the bright, fine linen of righteous deeds woven on Earth (Rev. 19:8). Our ornaments may be the gold, silver and precious jewels of eternal works strung by His hand.

I'll never forget the day Taylor tried on wedding gowns. It's one of those days in which you remember even the smallest details. Elegant dressing rooms welcomed us. Platforms stationed before an array of mirrors allowed the brides-to-be to twirl about and scrutinize themselves from every angle. And that's just what they did... for hours! Moms and grandmothers, aunts, sisters, and friends crowded in to see. "Oohs" and "aahs" and an occasional gasp communicated what words could not. Taylor had an idea of the type of dress she wanted. Since her reception was going to be outdoors, she was hoping to find a mid-length, less formal dress that would be easy to get around in. But once we started shopping, a few of the full-length formal gowns caught her eye. One in particular was *so* beautiful on her…it was as if it was made just for her! I had to exert all my M.O.B. willpower and keep silent while she tried to decide.

There will be no moment like that first moment, when we see our Bridegroom's face.

At one point she walked out of the dressing room into an adjoining one. When she returned, she had made up her mind. Seeing herself in a mirror from a long way off, she realized Andy's first sight of her would be at the end of a *very* long church aisle. So she decided upon the full-length wedding dress because it had the most "wow power" from a distance. She wanted to look as beautiful as possible at his *first sight* of her on their wedding day! She chose her dress for that *one* moment—for *one* pair of eyes.

God spoke such a spiritual truth to my heart that day. There will be *no* moment like that *first* moment, when we see our Bridegroom's face. No moment—from all our earthly days to Heaven's eternity beyond—will compare to *that* moment. Oh may we live our lives and make our choices for that one moment; for one pair of eyes.

Dear Heavenly Father,

*Thank You Father for loving me so! I confess I cannot fathom what that moment will be like when my eyes meet Your Son's. All I know is that I want to be **ready** to see You and Your Son on that Glorious Day. Help me to consider myself Your Bride, Jesus! Wash me clean of all impurity—of all wrong thoughts, words, motives, and deeds. Immerse my mind in Your Truth just as the Jewish bride was immersed in water. Sanctify me entirely—spirit and soul and body. Clothe me in Your righteousness, Jesus. Adorn me with forgiveness, kindness, and grace. Cause me, Holy Spirit, to be madly in love with Jesus, just as a Bride should be! Remind me constantly of my Marriage Covenant, of the ring on my finger, of Jesus' present work of preparing a place for me. **Keep me**, Lord Jesus, keep me close to Your heart. May my star in the sky shine as a sparkling diamond, a symbol of your love and commitment to me! In Jesus' name I pray. Amen.*

DAY 4 *sounds of joy*

YESTERDAY WE LEFT OUR COUPLE in a state of preparation. One was sewing a gown and the other was swinging a hammer. (Aren't you glad our Groom is a skilled Carpenter?) I'm still floored at the thought of the father of the groom deciding the time of the wedding. It seems like the groom would have had a pretty good idea however, since he knew how much progress was being made on the living quarters. Surely word got back to the bride that the time was nearing. Although the wait must have been difficult and intense at times, I think it would also be exciting and romantic. To live in expectancy of your dreams coming true is a good way to live!

Because the bride did not know the exact day of her wedding, she had to be ready at all times. Think of what it takes for a bride to be ready! Manicures, pedicures, hair-dos, make-up... it takes a lot of work to look perfect! And she had to look that way every day, all day—and even all night! (I know it may be hard for the men to relate to all this wedding talk, but hang in there! Just keep in mind that the Bride is the *Church*... and we *all* need to be ready!)

🖐 According to Jewish tradition, the groom would often come for his bride in the night in order to surprise her. So as the time drew nearer, the bride would have an oil lamp lit and ready. She was even known to sleep in her wedding dress! Sisters and bridesmaids would wait at her house every night, hoping to be present when the groom's party arrived.

If you are familiar with Jesus' parables, I'm sure you're thinking what I'm thinking. Please read *Matthew 25:1–13.*

(❓) **What is Jesus' main point? How are we to live as the Bride of Christ?**

(❓) **At what hour did the bridegroom come? (v. 6)**

(?) **What spiritual truth can we draw from the foolish virgins' inability to borrow or purchase oil in time for the wedding banquet?**

Jesus really knows how to make a point, doesn't He? It is *crucial* for us to be occupied with our relationship with Him. Like a bride in love, we should look forward each day to the possibility of His coming, supplied with faith and lit by the Holy Spirit! We can't be dependent upon another person for our relationship to Jesus. Faith cannot be borrowed or purchased quickly. It is not put on one day and left behind another. It's not to be taken for granted. What we need to do to be ready, we need to do *today,* for we do not know the day or the hour of His coming.

Read *Colossians 3:4–14.*

(?) **What are we to take off, or rid ourselves of?** (vs. 5, 8–9)

(?) **What are we to put on?** (vs. 10, 12–14)

How terrible for Jesus to return to fetch us for the Wedding and find us clothed in greed, anger, slander, or filthy language. Like the Jewish bride, we must *deliberately* put on our wedding clothes *every day*—and sleep in them— that we might be found ready! Picture each of the virtues in Colossians 3 as pieces of fine linen, sewn together with threads of love for our wedding garment. It requires work, but "godliness has value for all things, holding promise for both the present life *and* the life to come" (1 Tim. 4:8, emphasis mine). Our godliness *now* will impact our eternity.

Let's catch up with our groom:

🕊 The groom, at the go-ahead from his father, would put on festive attire, which included a garland on his head (Song of Songs 3:11), and travel with his companions to the home of the bride. Part of the wedding tradition was to "steal away" the bride, which is why he might choose to go at night. But as the wedding party neared the bride's house, they were required to give the bride a warning! A friend would shout the arrival of the groom, sometimes calling out the name of the bride. Then they would sound the trumpet (shofar). As the groom waited outside, the groomsmen would enter the house and "abduct" the bride and her companions. The father of the bride and any brothers would make a half-hearted effort to fight them off. Once together, they would make their way back to the groom's home in a torch-lit processional, singing and dancing along the way. By this time, the townspeople would have awakened and lined the streets in celebration.

It is at this point that we begin *Act III: The Wedding Ceremony* (Nisuin). Unger's Dictionary states: "The essence of the ceremony consisted in the removal of the bride from her father's house to that of the bridegroom or his father. There seems, indeed, to be a literal truth in the Hebrew expression 'to take' a wife, for the ceremony appears to have mainly consisted in the taking."[80] *Nisuin* actually means "taking."

Let's look once more at a rather wild Scripture passage in light of this rather wild wedding tradition: *1 Thessalonians 4:13–5:2.*

🕊 **Who does our Bridegroom bring with Him, and where does He come from?** (vs. 14, 16)

🕊 **In what ways will Jesus announce His arrival for His Bride?** (v. 16)

(&) **In what manner will He come? (5:2)**

(&) **What is your reaction to Jesus' coming for His Bride in such a manner?**

- ❑ I think it's exciting.
- ❑ I'm afraid I won't be ready.
- ❑ I wish He'd give me a week's notice.
- ❑ I'll never sleep again.
- ❑ It makes me feel loved.
- ❑ I'm not sure I believe it.

Regardless of your opinion concerning the Rapture of the Church, one thing is clear: Paul was talking wedding talk again, this time to the Thessalonians! In doing so he communicated the passionate love of God and His romantic plan to snatch us away from this world to take us to the place of our dreams. This is the moment of our glorification, our Act III, when we are given our new, eternal bodies in a "twinkling of an eye."

My thoughts go to the believers in the Present Heaven. Since they do not know the day or hour of Jesus' return (Rev. 6:10), I'm confident Jesus will steal them away in an equally dramatic way. They will have the great joy of being the companions who travel with Jesus to the Earth and surprise the Bride who remains! Perhaps John the Baptist is the friend who gives the "loud command" of arrival. It would only be fitting for him to once again have the honor of announcing the arrival of the Groom! The angel Gabriel might out-shout him, though—Gabriel was heralding Jesus' coming when John was just a gleam in his daddy's eye! (See Luke 1.) I can just imagine Peter, James and John in their role as groomsmen—tagging along with Jesus and sharing His excitement! What wondrous joy we will have as we see the entire body of believers gathered together. Perhaps the torches that light our way to the Father's House will be the night stars!

This phenomenal parade is described at the end of our Wedding invitation, almost like instructions to the Church!

Turn to *Isaiah 55:12.*

(?) Who (or what) will point the way to our heavenly Altar—singing, applauding, and rejoicing with us on the way?

As if our Groom's coming for us wasn't dramatic enough, He enlists all of creation to herald us Home. (Can it get any better?) And we're not even to the Wedding yet…

(?) Once the Jewish bride and groom arrived at his father's house, a *seven-day* wedding feast would begin. A crowd of friends and family would greet them and a great marriage supper would ensue. The bridegroom was treated as king for a week; the bride as a queen. It was an all-out celebration. Weddings were not even permitted on days of fasting, mourning, or holidays that required introspection. There was singing, dancing and games; speeches were made in the couple's honor and blessings were pronounced. The bride and groom would again drink of the fruit of the vine, as they did at the Betrothal Ceremony.

(?) Since the Bride is the *Church*, who might be assembled at the Father's House as wedding guests? (Matthew 8:11)

It sounds like Abraham, Isaac, and Jacob started the feast without us, doesn't it? Try and visualize the crowd that will await us:

> But you have come to Mount Zion, to the heavenly Jerusalem, the city of the living God. You have come to thousands upon thousands of angels in joyful assembly, to the church of the firstborn, whose names are written in heaven. You have come to God, the judge of all men, to the spirits of righteous men made perfect, to Jesus the mediator of a new covenant…
>
> (HEBREWS 12:22–24)

Can you hardly wait? Read with new eyes *Revelation 19:6–9*.

(?) What event is about to take place? (v. 7)

(?) **What is the atmosphere?** (vs. 6–7)

At the Wedding Feast of Jesus Christ there will be an *explosion* of joy! The sounds of joy will be like the roar of rushing waters and loud peals of thunder! Hallelujahs will reverberate throughout the universe! Singing, dancing, leaping, skipping… twirling about in ecstatic delight are just a few of the ways Scripture defines such gladness. And talk about a Feast! The Father will spare no expense at this Wedding Banquet!

(?) Our Wedding menu is revealed in *Isaiah 25:6–9*, printed out below. **Circle why those at the Marriage Supper at the Heavenly Zion will be so joyful:**

On this mountain the LORD Almighty will prepare a feast of rich food for all peoples, a banquet of aged wine—the best of meats and the finest of wines. On this mountain he will destroy the shroud that enfolds all peoples, the sheet that covers all nations; he will swallow up death forever. The Sovereign LORD will wipe away the tears from all faces; he will remove the disgrace of his people from all the earth. The LORD has spoken. In that day they will say, "Surely this is our God; we trusted in him, and he saved us. This is the LORD, we trusted in him; let us rejoice and be glad in his salvation."

I can barely stand it! Can't you feel their joy? They are *so* glad, *so* thankful they had *trusted in Him!* And we sometimes wonder if trusting in God is worth it…

Let's end our time today with a toast and a blessing. Read *Luke 22:17–20*.

(?) **When did Jesus say He would drink the fruit of the vine again?** (v. 18)

(?) **Why are we to drink of the cup?** (vs. 19-20)

While He is away, Jesus wanted you to have a meaningful way to remember His love. Communion is the perfect opportunity to reflect upon not only His past work for you, but also upon His present work for you. As you drink of the cup during this time of Betrothal, remember Him as your *Bridegroom*. Visualize the Day when you will drink of the fruit of the vine *with* Him. He's not taking a sip until *you* arrive! Practice saying your vows to Him. As Jesus and the Father prepare for you, allow the Holy Spirit to prepare you for Them.

Today's Jewish brides will often have Song of Songs 6:3 inscribed on the inside of their engagement ring: *"I am my beloved's, and my beloved is mine."* May we inscribe it upon the inside of our hearts, until that Day when we will say it to our Groom, face-to-face.

Our closing prayer today is one of the seven blessings (Sheva Brachot) recited at a Jewish wedding. Declare it out loud if you can, with great joy and thankfulness. *This is our God; we trusted in Him, and He saved us!*

> *You are blessed, Lord our God, the sovereign of the world, who created joy and celebration, bridegroom and bride, rejoicing, jubilation, pleasure and delight, love and brotherhood, peace and friendship. May there soon be heard, Lord our God, in the cities of Judea and in the streets of Jerusalem, the sound of joy and the sound of celebration, the voice of a bridegroom and the voice of a bride, the happy shouting of bridegrooms from their weddings and of young men from their feasts of song. You are blessed, Lord, who makes the bridegroom and the bride rejoice together.*

DAY 5 *come, Lord Jesus*

EIGHT WEEKS AGO, WE DETERMINED to read the *endings* to our earthly stories. I congratulate you on completing the course! Let's take a moment to reflect upon our journey to Heaven. We began with a prayer that God would make Himself and His Heaven known to us. We prayed for hope-filled, faith-filled, power-filled, and joy-filled lives:

*God of my Lord Jesus Christ, the glorious Father, I ask
You to give me the Spirit of wisdom and revelation,
so that I may know You better. I pray also that the
eyes of my heart may be enlightened in order that I
may know the hope to which You have called me, the
riches of Your glorious inheritance in the saints, and
Your incomparably great power for us who believe. To
the praise of Your glory!*

How has the Lord answered your prayer?

Are you thoroughly convinced of God's desire to share His Home and His Self with you? At times I have to pinch myself to believe it is true. Father, Son, and Spirit love *me*... and love *you*... entirely and eternally. Our Matchmaker has placed engagement rings around our hearts as a *guarantee* that our Groom is personally coming back for us! He will sweep us off our feet and escort us through the heavens to His Father's House. We will be led forth by mountains, serenaded by a myriad of angels, and embraced by a host of saints. Thank goodness we will be clothed in our new, glorified bodies, because these old models might literally split open in pure joy!

With cups raised, we ended our time yesterday with one of the seven blessings that would be pronounced over the bride and groom while they stood under the huppah at a traditional Jewish wedding. Today we'll begin with the eight blessings pronounced over us by our Groom on a hillside overlooking the Sea of Galilee. You'll find them in *Matthew 5:3–12*. Let's just drink them in as refreshment for our souls. Take your time and reflect on what you've learned about Heaven. Be fortified in your resolve to live for and by the love of your Groom. Allow His blessing to wash over your heart and guide you closer to His Kingdom.

Fill in the benefits of living this life for His life: (Matthew 5:3–12)

1. Blessed are the poor in spirit, for theirs is_____

    _____.

2. Blessed are those who mourn, for they will be_____.

3. Blessed are the meek, for they will_____

    _____.

4. Blessed are those who hunger and thirst for righteousness, for they

    will be_____.

5. Blessed are the merciful, for they will_____.

6. Blessed are the pure in heart, for they will_____.

7. Blessed are the peacemakers, for they will be_____

    _____.

8. Blessed are those who are persecuted because of righteousness, for

    theirs is_____.

    Blessed are you when people insult you, persecute you and falsely say

    all kinds of evil against you because of me. Rejoice and be glad, be-

    cause great is your_____, for

    in the same way they persecuted the prophets who were before you.

Now that you and I are *eternally* blessed, let's move on to the Ceremony! *Psalm 45* was written for the wedding of the King of Israel, yet it beautifully foreshadows the future Wedding of the King of Kings (Hebrews 1:8–9). Let's read verses *10–15*. It will help us capture the moment of being wed to our King.

How does the king feel towards his bride? (v. 11)

What is the atmosphere of the wedding and where is it held? (v. 15)

Did you notice that we will be presented to our King? Let's return to our Jewish traditions for more insight:

> In a Jewish wedding, a *special friend* of the bride would escort her in a processional to the groom. The bride would choose a devoted friend who had helped her prepare throughout the engagement period.

If you were allowed to select someone to present you to Christ, who would you choose?

I wish I could see your choice and hear how he or she aided in deepening your relationship with Jesus Christ! I am so thankful for the special people in my life who show me what it means to love God. Aren't you glad we don't have to go it alone?

If I were to choose my attendant from Scripture, I think I'd pick the Apostle Paul. I'm tempted to choose Peter because we started our journey with his epistle. (Remember his exhortations in *Week One* and *Week Two*?) But he's so impulsive, he might do something crazy at the Wedding—like tying bells to my get-away horse! Paul seems like the safer choice. Recall with me Paul's affection for the Bride:

> For what is our hope, our joy, or the crown in which we will glory in the presence of our Lord Jesus when he comes? Is it not you? Indeed, you are our glory and joy.
>
> (1 THES. 2:19–20)

> I am jealous for you with a godly jealousy. I promised you to one husband, to Christ, so that I might present you as a pure virgin to him.
>
> (2 COR. 11:2)

My daughter chose her brother to be the "Bride's Best Man" at her wedding. It was really special for Don and me to see our son standing by our daughter's side at the altar. But he was also an usher, a groomsman, and the worship leader! Don and I were more afraid of him collapsing during the ceremony than the bride or the groom! The poor guy had his hands full *and* his heart full.

The Apostle Paul may have to pace himself at the Lord's Wedding if he actually *presents* all of his spiritual children to Jesus as the previous scriptures suggest! Can you imagine the "glory and joy" if we have the awesome privilege of presenting to Jesus those with whom we shared the gospel? Talk about a special moment! Oh to have our hands and hearts full at Jesus' Wedding because we had led so many people to Christ!

🖋 Another word used for the wedding ceremony is *huppah*, which means "canopy." Later in Jewish history, when couples no longer went to an actual room prepared by the groom, they were married under the *huppah*—a tent-like structure symbolic of the home that was being established.

Sources differ as to when the bride and groom entered the bridal chamber to consummate the marriage. Some placed it at the beginning of the seven-day celebration and others place it at the end. Most likely in Jesus' day, the bride and groom entered the bridal chamber upon arriving at the father's house. The bride remained veiled until that time.

One strange custom was for a friend of the groom to stand outside the chamber door, waiting on word from the groom that the marriage had been consummated. When he heard his voice, he would announce it to the wedding guests and more rejoicing would take place!

Perhaps it is in the bridal chamber that Christ will judge our earthly works. It would be a fitting time of "unveiling," when all is laid bare before Him and our unworthy works are removed. We will be perfected by His judgments and adorned with His accolades. Then, in the profoundest of mysteries, Christ and the Church become one. We are pronounced Husband and Wife, in perfect union for eternity (Rev. 21:9).

Amazingly, John the Baptist long ago claimed the role of announcing the consummation of the marriage! Marvel over his words as recorded in John 3:29 (emphasis mine):

> The friend who attends the bridegroom *waits and listens* for him, and is full of joy when he *hears the bridegroom's voice*. That joy is mine, and it is now complete.

Perhaps it is then, with "inexpressible and glorious joy," we lay our crowns at His Throne.

On a much lighter note...I'm wondering when we get to cut the cake! None of my resources seemed to be concerned with such matters, so I'm adding my own tradition to our heavenly Wedding. I told you in the introduction about my fondness for cake. I can never leave a reception until I've had at *least* one slice! I may be pushing the imagery a bit, but I think I found a Wedding Cake.

Read *Revelation 2:17.* **What two things we will receive when we join Jesus in Heaven?**

I'm quite sure this hidden manna is the Bride's Cake! Manna is called "angel's food" (Psalm 78:25 KJV) and that sounds like cake to me! If you aren't familiar with manna, it was food that came down from Heaven to sustain the Hebrew people while they made their way through the wilderness to the Promised Land. (See Exodus 16.) Manna was white, flake-like, and tasted like wafers and honey. An omer of manna was placed in the Ark of the Covenant in Moses' day as a testimony to future generations of the faithfulness of God. Jesus has promised a mouthful for every believer entering the Gates of Heaven! Can you imagine how wonderfully sweet the faithfulness of God will taste when we stand in Heaven with Him?

I also love the thought of receiving a new name. We will bear God's Name as His Wife (Rev. 3:12), but *this* name is a *secret name* for our ears only. It is one more promise of the individual attention we will receive in Heaven. Although the entire body of Christ is His Bride, *we are special to Him*, created to fill a place in His heart no one else can. We are never one of many to God!

Believers were often renamed by God to reflect His purpose for their lives. Abram became Abraham, Jacob became Israel, Simon became Peter, and Saul became Paul.

What would you like your new name to mean?

Your new name will be written on a *white stone*. In ancient courtrooms, white stones were used to vote for the acquittal of an accused person. They were also given as tokens of favor and worn around the neck. Could this engraved white stone be a Wedding gift from our Groom? Just as the Jewish bride was adorned with jewels, perhaps our stone will be placed as a gem around our neck, engraved with our new name, as a precious reminder of our Savior's love and sacrifice.

Now that we've gotten our new name and slice of cake, let's get back to the first century wedding traditions:

🕊 At the conclusion of the seven-day celebration, the wedded couple would depart from the groom's house and return to the bride's hometown to present themselves as husband and wife.

❓ Let's pick back up in *Revelation 19:9–16*. **Describe what happens after the Marriage Supper.**

What a way to begin our Honeymoon! Are you picturing yourself on a horse, flying through the stratosphere towards Planet Earth? Whoa! Surely my fear of horses *and* my fear of heights will miraculously vanish at the sight of my Fearless Leader, the King of Kings and Lord of Lords! Some believe the seven-day duration of the wedding feast of the Jewish tradition indicates that the Bride is in Heaven during the seven year Tribulation upon the Earth. Perhaps, but regardless of the order of events, we *will* exit the Wedding with Jesus and accompany Him on His way back to Earth, this time to stay for good!

Isaiah 62 beautifully pictures Jerusalem receiving her King. Read *verses 1–5 and 11–12.*

❓ **How is the land described?**

(⊙) **How are the people described?**

Even the land is declared "married!" God will delight in and rejoice over His people—redeeming, renaming, restoring, and rewarding each and every one. *Plan "R."*

The full and ultimate consummation of Christ and His Bride is pictured in the descent of the Heavenly Jerusalem to Earth in *Revelation 21:9-10*.

(⊙) **Turn to it and write out the declaration of the angel:**

Heaven and Earth kiss—and we live happily ever after in the Eternal Heaven with our God and with one another!

Wow! How do we respond to such Good News? What can we possibly say in light of so great a salvation? God graciously gives us the words, recorded at the conclusion of His Word (Rev. 22:17, 20). Let's make this declaration together with fully devoted hearts:

> The Spirit and the bride say, "Come!"
> And let him who hears say, "Come!"
> Whoever is thirsty, let him come; and whoever
> wishes, let him take the free gift of the water of life.
> He who testifies to these things says, "Yes, I am
> coming soon."
> Amen. Come, Lord Jesus.

As we implore Jesus to *"Come!"* to Earth, may we simultaneously invite the world to *"Come!"* to Heaven. *You* are His mailman; *you* are the postage stamp God needs to deliver His Good News to a thirsty soul.

So be it! Thank you for being my traveling companion on our trek through God's Word. May your heavenly-minded spirit make your earthly journey rich and full and wonderfully *good*.

QUESTIONS
for Group Discussion

Session One: A Happy Ending

1.1 How did Paul describe Paradise?

1.2 If you were to visit Heaven like Paul, how might it impact your life?

1.3 What are some popular images of Heaven?

1.4 Do you have any ideas about Heaven that are not "better by far" than Earth?

1.5 According to 1 Corinthians 2:9-10, is it possible to visualize Heaven? How?

2.1 How does Peter describe Heaven in 1 Peter 1:3-9?

2.2 Why were the apostles willing to die for their faith in Jesus?

2.3 Do you believe that faith in Jesus Christ results in everlasting life? Why or why not?

3.1 What does it mean to "prepare your mind for action"? Any examples?

3.2 In light of Heaven, why are we to live self-controlled lives?

3.3 When are you most likely to drift away from seeking God?

4.1 Are you eager for the return of Jesus? Why or why not?

4.2 What are believers to set their hearts upon? How is that possible?

4.3 Do you think Paul attained the goals he set for his life? Why or why not?

4.4 What was Abraham looking for and how did he regard his earthly life?

5.1 Is the goal of your life to win the prize of Heaven? If not, what is?

5.2 What does Paul pray for the Ephesians? (Eph. 1:17-19) Will you commit to pray this for yourself?

(Small group question) How could knowing "the end of the story" change your present life experience?

Session Two: Things Worth Bothering About

1.1 How is life apart from God described in 1 Peter 1:18?
1.2 How do we participate in God's nature and escape the corruption of the world?
1.3 What does the hope of Jesus' appearing make us eager to do? (Titus 2:14)
1.4 Why would a crown of "righteousness" be given to those who have longed for Jesus' appearing?

2.1 What does it mean to fear God?
2.2 Have you ever felt like a stranger? When and why?
2.3 What "motivational material" does Peter give in order to "live as strangers here in reverent fear"?
2.4 Why do you suppose God paid the highest possible price to make you His own?

3.1 What two things are "worth bothering about" according to 1 John 3:23?
3.2 Have you ever determined to love someone better? How did you do it?
3.3 Why would hope for Heaven result in greater love and faith?

4.1 How does Jesus describe the life of one who takes the message of His Kingdom to heart? (Matt. 13:22-23)
4.2 How do you attempt to "save your life"?
4.3 What does Jesus promise in light of His exhortation to "lose your life" for His sake?
4.4 How does this promise encourage you to live whole-heartedly and sacrificially for Christ?

5.1 How did Moses choose Christ over the treasures of Egypt?
5.2 Have you ever set your sights upon an earthly goal and then found it lacking? What did you learn?

5.3 Knowing the rest of Moses' story, did God bless his earthly life? How?

5.4 What follows us to Heaven?

❧ How should the truth that you will live forever impact your daily living and decisions?

Session Three: Lost and Found

1.1 What was God's original intent for mankind?

1.2 Describe how you visualize the Garden of Eden.

1.3 How did the consequences of Adam and Eve's sin affect the Earth?

1.4 What will happen to creation when Jesus returns to Earth?

1.5 What is the Plan "R" God has set in motion?

2.1 How is Plan "R" greater than Plan "A"?

2.2 What do the mirror images in Genesis and Revelation tell you about God's plan for the ages?

2.3 What do you most desire for God to make new in your life?

3.1 What is Jesus' claim concerning Heaven in John 3:13?

3.2 What happened in the Temple on Earth and the Temple in Heaven when Jesus died on the cross?

3.3 Who do we have in Heaven and what does that allow us to do and have on Earth?

3.4 Where are the Old Testament believers today?

4.1 Do you believe that Stephen immediately went to be with Jesus upon his death? Why or why not?

4.2 What is going to happen on the Resurrection Day?

4.3 How is it going to happen according to 1 Thessalonians 4:13-18?

4.4 How are those who believe in Jesus to live in light of His surprise return?

5.1 What will God accomplish during the Tribulation?

5.2 What will life be like during the Millennium?

5.3 What sounds the best to you about the New Heaven and New Earth?

❧ What was your favorite discovery on our road trip across God's plan for the ages?

Session Four: Blueprints of Heaven

1.1 What makes you homesick for something beyond this world? Why?

1.2 What does Jesus teach about Heaven in His description of His Father's House?

1.3 How do we find our way to the Father's House?

2.1 What is Jesus' main message in the story of Lazarus and the rich man?

2.2 What do you learn about the after-life from His description of Abraham's Side and Hell?

2.3 What impact does the rich man's plight make upon the way you live?

3.1 What is your impression of the descriptions of Heaven by Isaiah, Ezekiel, Daniel, and John?

3.2 From reading the elders' declarations and songs, what filled their hearts?

4.1 How will the Earth be made new? (2 Peter 3:10-13)

4.2 Where does the Holy City come from?

4.3 What will not be in the Eternal Heaven?

4.4 What additional "no mores" would you add to Heaven's list?

5.1 If you could live anywhere on the Earth, where would it be?

5.2 What is your impression of the New Jerusalem?

5.3 Do you think the description of the Holy City is symbolic, literal, or both?

Did you identify a "real want for Heaven" in your heart as you examined Scripture's blueprints?

Session Five: A Change of Clothing

1.1 What would you like your eternal body to be able to do?

1.2 How does Paul feel about the prospect of being without a body in the Present Heaven? How do you feel about it?

1.3 How are the occupants of the Present Heaven described in Revelation 7:9-17?

2.1 How would you answer Paul's questions: "How are the dead raised?" and "With what kind of body do they come?"

2.2 According to Phil. 3:20-21, what will our new bodies be like, and how is resurrection accomplished?

2.3 How should we live in light of our ultimate victory over death? (1 Cor. 15:58)

3.1 From Scripture's eyewitness accounts, how would you describe Jesus' resurrected body?

3.2 What did Jesus want His followers to understand about His resurrected body?

3.3 How does Jesus' physical state impact your expectation of Heaven?

4.1 What can we learn about our heavenly bodies from Jesus' appearance on the island of Patmos?

4.2 What will our "insides" be like in Heaven? Which quality excites you the most?

5.1 How does our present knowledge compare to the knowledge promised in Heaven?

5.2 What parts of God's Word are you most anxious to understand?

5.3 What will it be like to be fully known by others?

5.4 What did you learn about marriage in Heaven?

5.5 Who in Heaven would you most like to sit down with and enjoy a good long chat?

⚮ Did you identify a "real want for Heaven" through the study of your eternal "change of clothing"?

Session Six: Hell Week

1.1 In what ways do people try to cope with the idea of Hell?

1.2 What are the four words used in Scripture for "Hell"?

1.3 Who stands at the Great White Throne and why are they judged?

2.1 What atrocities occurred at Gehenna?

2.2 What is Jesus' warning about Hell in Mark 9:42-49?

2.3 What things lead to sin and need to be cut out of our lives?

3.1 How does Hell contrast with Heaven in Matthew 8:10-12?

3.2 Who was Hell prepared for?

3.3 What is destroyed in Hell? Does that mean the person in Hell ceases to exist?

3.4 From Jesus' descriptions of Hell, how do you visualize it?

4.1 Look at your chart on Hell Prevention. What does God do to get people into Heaven?

4.2 Look at your chart on Hell Promotion. How do some people respond to God's invitation to Heaven?

4.3 From what you have read in Scripture, why is there a Hell?

5.1 Does every person have an opportunity to know God?

5.2 What did you learn about God in Psalm 145?

5.3 Are there degrees of punishment in Hell? If so, on what are they based?

5.4 Review the truths concerning God and His salvation at the end of Day Five. What do you learn about God's role versus our role in salvation?

☜ What had the most impact upon you during Hell Week? How has Hell's reality challenged you to live?

Session Seven: The Crowning Moment

1.1 What were Jesus' final recorded words? Why do you suppose He chose that message?

1.2 How would you summarize the relationship between faith and works?

1.3 Why might Jesus wait to judge earthly works until all believers are in Heaven?

2.1 What is a "bema"?

2.2 How would you describe Paul's attitude toward life in light of the Judgment Seat of Christ?

2.3 What about our works will be judged?

2.4 What does an athlete do to win a prize that we should do to win an eternal prize?

3.1 What will be the result of our works being tested by fire? (1 Cor. 3)

3.2 Will some receive greater reward in Heaven than others? If so, how does that make you feel?

3.3 What does 1 Cor. 3 teach you about how to live your life?

3.4 What do we learn from Mary and Martha and the church in Ephesus about our pursuit of works?

4.1 According to the parables of the talents and minas, what "earns" Jesus' praise and Heaven's reward?

4.2 Sometimes we may feel like a one-talent servant when we compare ourselves to others. What is Jesus' message to us at those times?

4.3 What is your reaction to being placed in a position of rule and authority in Heaven?

5.1 Has the promise of reward, or loss of reward, ever positively motivated you? Explain.

5.2 How can we have confidence at the Judgment Seat and not fear punishment?

5.3 What do you learn from Matt. 20:20-28 about the criteria for heavenly greatness?

What would happen to your relationship with Jesus Christ if you were fervently believing and acting upon the promise of heavenly reward? What earthly good would result?

Session Eight: The Profound Mystery

1.1 Who is the Bridegroom and who is the Bride?

1.2 Who does the Father send to woo our hearts to the love of His Son?

1.3 Based upon Isaiah 55, how would you rate God's desire for you?

2.1 Discuss the parallels between God's offer of salvation and the ancient Jewish wedding customs.

2.2 When we drink the cup of our Heavenly Groom, what do we agree to and what do we receive?

2.3 Summarize Jesus' instructions regarding the way to eternal life in John 6.

3.1 According to 1 Cor. 6:9-11 and 19-20, how does God describe us once we say "Yes" to Jesus' offer of salvation? How are we to regard ourselves?

3.2 What do the Groom and His Father give as wedding gifts?

3.3 What would you consider the greatest gift God has given you?

3.4 Who knows the date of our Wedding?

4.1 What spiritual truths can we draw from the foolish virgins' inability to borrow or purchase oil in time for the wedding banquet?

4.2 In order to be ready for our Groom's surprise coming, what are we to take off and put on, according to Colossians 3:4-14?

4.3 In what ways will Jesus announce His arrival for His Bride?

5.1 If you were allowed to select someone to present you to Christ in Heaven, who would you choose?

5.2 What would you like your new heavenly name to mean?

5.3 Describe what follows the Marriage Supper in Heaven.

5.4 What is the desire of the Spirit and the Bride? (Rev. 22:17) Do you desire the same?

How has God answered your heavenly-minded prayer over the last eight weeks? What "incomparably great power" is yours as you live on Earth with your eyes on Heaven?

For further information or teaching materials, visit:
www.karenchaffin.com

ENDNOTES

Introduction

1   C .S. Lewis, *Mere Christianity*, (HarperCollins Edition 2001), 136.

Week One

2   C. S. Lewis, *The Last Battle*, (New York: Collier Books, Macmillan Publishing Company, 1970), 184.

3   Peter Kreeft, *Everything You Ever Wanted to Know about Heaven* (San Francisco: Ignatius Press, 1990), 19.

4   Ibid, 196.

5   Spiros Zodhiates, *The Complete Word Study New Testament* (AMG Publishers 1991), 918.

6   *Vine's Expository Dictionary of New Testament Words* (Oliphants Ltd. 1940, 1952), 220.

7   *Matthew Henry's Commentary* (Marshall, Morgan & Scott, Ltd., 1960), 1913.

8   Spiros Zodhiates, *The Complete Word Study New Testament* (AMG Publishers 1991), 961.

9   John Wesley, *Sermons on Several Occasions*, as quoted in *The Spiritual Formation Bible* (Grand Rapids, Michigan, Zondervan Publishing House, 1999), 1567.

Week Two

10   C. S. Lewis, *Mere Christianity*, (HarperCollins Edition 2001), 74.

11   John Piper, *Future Grace*, (Sisters, Oregon: Questar Publishers, Inc.1995), concept taught 332–333.

12   *Vine's Expository Dictionary of New Testament Words* (Oliphants Ltd. 1940, 1952), 84.

13   Ibid, 84.

14   Concept from Ancrene Riwle, written in 1215.

15   John Wesley, *The Sermons of John Wesley* 1872 Edition, Sermon 109 (Thomas Jackson, editor).

16   C. S. Lewis, *Mere Christianity*, (HarperCollins Edition 2001), 131.

17   Ibid, 134.

18   C. S. Lewis, concept from *The Screwtape Letters*, as quoted in *A Year with C. S. Lewis*, (HarperSanFrancisco, 2003), 61.

Week Three

19   *Vine's Expository Dictionary of New Testament Words* (Oliphants Ltd. 1940, 1952), 267.

Week Four

20   C. S. Lewis, *Mere Christianity,* (HarperCollins Edition 2001), 135.

21   Augustine, *Confessions I.i,* quoted in Peter Kreeft, *Heaven: The Heart's Deepest Longing* (San Francisco: Ignatius Press, 1989), 49.

22   Mark Stewart, Barry Blair, Will McGinnis, & Bob Hendman, *Big House,* (Up In the Air Music, 1993).

23   C. S. Lewis, *Weight of Glory* as quoted in *A Mind Awake, An Anthology of C. S. Lewis,* edited by Clyde S. Kilby (San Diego: Harcourt Brace & Company),182–183.

24   *Matthew Henry's Commentary* (Marshall, Morgan & Scott, Ltd., 1960), 1589.

25   Don Piper, with Cecil Murphey, *90 Minutes in Heaven: A True Story of Death and Life* (Grand Rapids, Michigan, Revell, 2004), 29, 32.

26   C. S. Lewis, *Letters to Malcolm,* ch. 22, as quoted in *A Mind Awake, An Anthology of C. S. Lewis,* edited by Clyde S. Kilby (San Diego: Harcourt Brace & Company), 187.

27   Randy Alcorn, *Heaven,* (Wheaton, Illinois: Tyndale House Publishers, Inc. 2004), 55

28   George G. Ritchie, M.D. with Elizabeth Sherrill, *Return From Tomorrow,* (Grand Rapids, MI: Fleming H. Revell/Baker Book House Co. 1978), 73–74.

Week Five

29   Merrill F. Unger, *The New Unger's Bible Dictionary,* (Chicago: Moody Press, 1957), 420

30   Joni Eareckson Tada, *Heaven, Your Real Home,* (Nashville, Tenn., LifeWay Press, 1996), 32.

31   Grant R. Jeffrey, *Armageddon, Appointment with Destiny,* (New York: Bantom Books, 1988), 83.

32   Joseph Thayer, *Thayer's Greek Definitions,* 1 Thes. 4:11, (Electronic edition; as found in the *e-Sword* electronic Bible Study program; http://www.e-sword.net.html, (Copyright 2005 by Rick Meyers), August 11, 2006.

33   *Vine's Expository Dictionary of New Testament Words* (Oliphants Ltd. 1940, 1952), 311.

34   *Thayer's Greek Definitions,* John 20:17, (Electronic edition; as found in the *e-Sword* electronic Bible Study program; http://www.e-sword.net.html, (Copyright 2005 by Rick Meyers), August 11, 2006.

35   C. S. Lewis, *Weight of Glory and Other Addresses* (Grand Rapids: Eerdmans, 1949), 13.

36   C. S. Lewis, *Letters to Malcolm,* ch. 20, as quoted in *A Mind Awake, An Anthology of C. S. Lewis,* edited by Clyde S. Kilby (San Diego: Harcourt Brace & Company), 183.

37   Spiros Zodhiates, *The Complete Word Study New Testament,* (AMG Publishers, 1991), 64.

38   Ibid, 878.

39   Ibid, 948.

40   Charles Spurgeon, *A Sermon (No. 39–40),* delivered Tuesday evening, Sept. 4, 1855, in a field, King Edward's Road, Hackney.

41   Peter Kreeft, *Everything You Ever Wanted to Know about Heaven... But Never Dreamed of Asking* (San Francisco, Ignatius Press, 1990), 106.

Week Six

42   *Vine's Expository Dictionary of New Testament Words* (Oliphants Ltd. 1940, 1952), 188.

43   Edward Snyder, *BL 425–Parables of Jesus* (December 13, 2000).

44   Merrill F. Unger, *The New Unger's Bible Dictionary* (Chicago: Moody Press, 1957), 462.

45   Ibid, 571, 1296.

46   Barnes, Albert, *Albert Barnes' Notes on the Bible*, Matthew 5:22 (Electronic edition; as found in the *e-Sword* electronic Bible Study program; http://www.e-sword.net.html, (Copyright 2005 by Rick Meyers), January 25, 2006.

47   C. S. Lewis, *A Year with C. S. Lewis, Daily Readings from His Classic Works*, ed. by Patricia S. Klein (New York: HarperSanFrancsico, 2003), 105.

48   C. S. Lewis, *The Problem With Pain* (HarperCollins Edition 2001), 131.

49   *Vine's Expository Dictionary of New Testament Words* (Oliphants Ltd. 1940, 1952), 302.

50   Ibid, 276.

51   C. S. Lewis, *The Problem With Pain* (HarperCollins Edition 2001), 127.

52   C. S. Lewis, *The Great Divorce*, (New York: Collier Books; MacMillian Publishing Co, 1946), 123.

53   *Albert Barnes Notes on the Bible*, Matthew 25:46, (Electronic edition; as found in the *e-Sword* electronic Bible Study program; http://www.e-sword.net.html, (Copyright 2005 by Rick Meyers), February 1, 2006.

54   *John Wesley's Explanatory Notes*, Matthew 25:46 (Electronic edition; as found in the *e-Sword* electronic Bible Study program; http://www.e-sword.net.html, (Copyright 2005 by Rick Meyers), February 1, 2006.

55   Dante Alighieri, *Inferno*, canto 3, line 9.

56   From the hymn *"Oh for a Thousand Songs to Sing"* (words by Charles Wesley, 1739)

57   C. S. Lewis, *The Problem With Pain* (HarperCollins Edition 2001), 130, 121.

58   Ron Mehl, "Right on Time" as told in *Stories for the Heart*, compiled by Alice Gray (Sisters, Oregan: Multmnah Books, 1996 by Questar Publishing), 265–267.

59   Beth Moore and friends, *Voices of the Faithful*, (Brentwood, TN. Integrity Publishers, 2005), 45.

60   Tony Evans, *The Best Is Yet To Come*, (Chicago: Moody Press, 2000), 305.

61   *Schindler's List*. Dir. Stephen Spielberg. Perf. Liam Neeson, Ben Kingsley, Ralph Fiennes. 1993. Universal Studios; based on the novel *Schindler's List* by Thomas Keneally. Quote as found at http://www.auschwitz.dk/listen.html

Week Seven

62   *Vine's Expository Dictionary of New Testament Words* (Oliphants Ltd. 1940, 1952), 282.

63   *Jamieson, Fausset and Brown Commentary*, Colossians 1:22, (Electronic edition; as found in the *e-Sword* electronic Bible Study program; http://www.e-sword.net.html, (Copyright 2005 by Rick Meyers), March 2, 2006.

64   Spiros Zodhiates, Th.D., *The Complete Word Study New Testament*, (AMG Publishers, 1991), 34.

65   *Webster's New World Dictionary*, Second Concise Edition, David B. Guralnik, General Editor (New York: Simon and Schuster, 1982), as found in *Student Handbook* (Nashville, Tennessee: the Southwestern Co., 1988) 252.

66   *Vine's Expository Dictionary of New Testament Words* (Oliphants Ltd. 1940, 1952), 163.

67   Ibid, 72.

68   Ibid, 94.

69   *John Wesley's Explanatory Notes*, Revelation 7:9 (Electronic edition; as found in the *e-Sword* electronic Bible Study program; http://www.e-sword.net.html, (Copyright 2005 by Rick Meyers), May 2, 2006.

70   C. S. Lewis, *Weight of Glory and Other Addresses* (Grand Rapids: Eerdmans, 1949), 2.

71   Wesley Center Online, Wesley Center for Applied Theology, Northwest Nazarene Center (©1993–2005) http://wesley.nnu.edu/john_wesley/letters/1790b.htm, May 22, 2006.

72   *Albert Barnes' Notes on the Bible*, Genesis 15:1 (Electronic edition; as found in the *e-Sword* electronic Bible Study program; http://www.e-sword.net.html, (Copyright 2005 by Rick Meyers), May 18, 2006.

Week Eight

73   Merrill F. Unger, *The New Unger's Bible Dictionary* (Chicago: Moody Press, 1957), 818.

74   *Vine's Expository Dictionary of New Testament Words* (Oliphants Ltd. 1940, 1952), 149.

75   John Wesley, *The Scripture Way to Salvation*, Sermon 43 (text from the 1872 edition) http://gbgm-umc.org/umhistory/wesley/sermons/serm-043.stm, June 6, 2006.

76   *Vine's Expository Dictionary of New Testament Words* (Oliphants Ltd. 1940, 1952), 287.

77   Rabbi Yisroel and Rebbetzen Judy Finman, *Jewish Key West, Overview of a Jewish Wedding*, http://www.jewishkeywest.com/Traditions.html, June 22, 2006.

78   My Jewish Learning.com, *Mikveh; Immersing in the Ritual Pool*, Rabbi Maurice Lammhttp://www.myjewishlearning.com/lifecycle/Conversion/IdeatoRealization/RabbinicRequirements /Mikveh.htm, June 7, 2006.

79   *Vine's Expository Dictionary of New Testament Words* (Oliphants Ltd. 1940, 1952), 11.

80   Merrill F. Unger, *The New Unger's Bible Dictionary* (Chicago: Moody Press, 1957), 818.

listen|imagine|view|experience

AUDIO BOOK DOWNLOAD INCLUDED WITH THIS BOOK!

In your hands you hold a complete digital entertainment package. Besides purchasing the paper version of this book, this book includes a free download of the audio version of this book. Simply use the code listed below when visiting our website. Once downloaded to your computer, you can listen to the book through your computer's speakers, burn it to an audio CD or save the file to your portable music device (such as Apple's popular iPod) and listen on the go!

How to get your free audio book digital download:

1. Visit www.tatepublishing.com and click on the e|LIVE logo on the home page.
2. Enter the following coupon code:
   e0e4-4d2f-65f9-2327-7f93-a5c2-6e30-c290
3. Download the audio book from your e|LIVE digital locker and begin enjoying your new digital entertainment package today!